D1327865

FRONT PAGE
HISTORY
HAROLD
EVANS

EVENTs OF OUR cENTURy

FRONT
HISTO

Quiller Press
Published in association with
The Photo Source

THAT SHOOK THE WORLD

PAGE

RY

HAROLD EVANS

With event summaries
and picture research by
Hugh Barty King

The Harold Evans Selection of
FRONT PAGE STORIES
1900-1984

ACKNOWLEDGEMENTS

The Publishers would especially like to thank the following:
The John Frost Historical Newspaper Service for its efficient help in obtaining the original newspaper front-pages from its magnificent collection.
Mr Gerry Conrad at the Photo Source for his cheerful assistance in picture research.

The Publishers also acknowledge the following:
For the picture on pp. 26–7 – Mr Nicolas Ekstrom for *Diaghilev and the Ballets Russes* by Boris Kochno.
For the other pictures on pp. 26–7 – Harper & Row Inc for *Nijinsky Dancing* by Lincoln Kirkstein.
For three Low cartoons – Victor Gollancz for *The Years of Wrath*, by David Low, 1949.
For the drawings of famous faces in the text – Dennis Dobson Ltd for *Faces Behind the News* by Richard Zeigler, 1946.
For the cartoon on page 7 – Tom Stacey Ltd for the 'Poy' cartoon in *The Cartoon History of the World* by Michael Wynn-Jones, 1971.
For the photos: 1975 – Fall of Saigon, 1978 – Jonestown Massacre, 1981 – Sadat Assassination, 1983 – Korean Airliner – all U.P.I.

Hugh Barty King acknowledges the following sources for his resumés and captions:
An Historical Introduction to the Twentieth Century, R. W. Harris, Blandford Press, 1966.
A Dictionary of Modern History 1789–1945, A. W. Palmer, Penguin, 1969.
The Modern World since 1870, L. J. Snelgrove, Longman, 1968.
Hutchinson's History of the World, Hutchinson, 1976.
World History in the Twentieth Century, R. D. Cornwell, Longman, 1963.
History of the Twentieth Century, Chief editor A. J. P. Taylor, Phoebus, 1973.

Designed by Tim McPhee. Design and Production in association with Book Production Consultants, Cambridge.
Typeset by Cambridge Photosetting Services.
Printed in Yugoslavia.

Mr Evelyn Waugh, the chronicler of the *Daily Beast*, has told us in his book *Scoop* that when the *Beast*'s owner Lord Copper asked his underlings to confirm that black was white they tempered honesty with prudence. 'Up to a point, Lord Copper,' they murmured. Lord Macaulay, the majesty of his writings notwithstanding, provokes the same response with his remark that the only true history of a country is to be found in its newspapers.

It depends which newspapers in which country and over what period. When our century opens the deadly rivals William Randolph Hearst and Joseph Pulitzer are still fresh from having taken the U.S. into the Spanish-American war by 'ruthless, truthless, newspaper jingoism'. In London *The Times* is still reeling from lending its authority to the publication of letters forged by a blackmailer to compromise Charles Parnell. Alfred Northcliffe's new *Daily Mail* in London soon goes to town in the Boxer rebellion with a massacre that never happened (ALL WHITE, MEN, WOMEN, AND CHILDREN PUT TO THE SWORD): *The Times* runs a glowing obituary of its correspondent who is alive. And very soon the *New York Herald* joins the fun with a big banner headline in three decks (2 Sept 1909): THE NORTH POLE IS DISCOVERED BY DR. FREDERICK A. COOK, WHO CABLES TO THE HERALD AN EXCLUSIVE ACCOUNT OF HOW HE SET THE AMERICAN FLAG ON THE WORLD'S TOP. Only he didn't and he hadn't.

The lies were bolder than ever before because newspaper editors had become technically able to write banner headlines across the full width of the front page. All the British papers were slow with this, and with using the front page at all, except the new *Daily Express* which was founded

---

Daily Express

NO. 23.   LONDON, SATURDAY, MAY 19, 1900.   ONE HALFPENNY.

WHEN SHALL THEIR GLORY FADE?

HISTORY'S MOST HEROIC DEFENCE ENDS IN TRIUMPH.

THE BOERS' LAST GRIP LOOSENED.

MAFEKING AND BADEN-POWELL'S GALLANT BAND SET FREE.

---

in September 1909 in time to announce the relief of Mafeking with a bugle of a banner (page 12). And that one was true.

The history of journalism is one of courage and vision, it has to be said, as well as propaganda and chirpy ignorance. Newspapers are constantly accused of being preoccupied with tragedy. The truth is they exult in whatever they can recognise is exceptional. They can usually recognise firsts and lasts, achievement as well as disaster. They were as eager to headline the four-minute mile as the fall of Dien Bien Phu. They are thirsty for celebrities, so thirsty that in our time there are people who are famous for being famous. They have taken on board Chesterton's sally that journalism consists in saying 'LORD JONES DEAD' to people who never knew Lord Jones was alive. Newspapers have become manufacturers of popular mythology and slaves to it. There is a certain mysterious point after which men and women become newsgods, their doings always destined for ink. The Beatles and Mahomet Ali passed it; it is hard to remember they were cast as ill-mannered bad boys before they became romantic heroes. Newspapers will not for long withold their columns from crowd-pullers. So far as the true history of a country consists, then, in what the masses do and delight in, one can say Definitely, Lord Macaulay. Valentino and Charlie Chaplin and the Beatles are here with Roger Bannister, Len Hutton, Captain Knud Carlsen and Hillary and Tensing.

Certain other, more significant, truths of our century come to us because of the bravery and resource of a single reporter. I will name a few, and there are others in this book. But, before we plunge in, it is as well to remind ourselves and Lord Macaulay that newspapers have a very hard time focussing on history in the making. Karl Marx, scribbling away in the British Museum, was never front page news, though his ideas, and corruptions of them, convulsed the world's front pages. Reporters in the twenties and thirties did not beat a path to the door of John Maynard Keynes, though the conventional wisdom he debunked wrought great misery throughout the West and destroyed democracy in Germany. The messages an obscure mullah exiled in Paris spoke into a tape recorder produced a whirlwind in Iran and trauma in the United States, but no newspaper would have paid loose coins for the Ayatollah's cassettes on Muslim values. A true history may be the history of the Idea. For the newspaper headline, Idea has to become Event if it is to qualify as front page news.

It is a thought to carry through the apparently random sequence of photographs and news-

KAISER: "And as for 'German Atrocities,' will not the world say they are nothing but the malicious inventions of my perjured enemies?"
CAMERA: "The answer's in the negative!"
(The camera is accumulating a terrible and unanswerable indictment against the Modern Huns.)

paper front pages in this book. Our century comes at us in capsules, an anthology of icons. Smoke over the rubble of San Francisco. The Union Jack at Mafeking, the Stars and Stripes at the South Pole. Horsemen in spiked helmets ride into Belgium. Suitcases full of paper Deutsche-marks are exchanged for a sausage. Two men with little black moustaches, one funny, the other insane. Red Shirts in Rome, Black Shirts in Bermondsey. GI's and Russians, who have fought west and east across a continent to meet, grin and shake hands at the Elbe, then a wall is driven through the heart of Berlin. War is the midwife of a new nation in the Middle East. A helicopter lurches from a roof in Saigon with refugees clinging to the skids, another purrs on the lawn of the White House as the band plays and the disgraced President waves goodbye.

It is all big news, interesting in itself for its immediate human drama, but still more intriguing for the connections we can vaguely discern between what can be headlined and photographed and what cannot – the ideas of national-ism, of justice, the processes increasing the domination of the state or driving individuals to defiance, adventure and exploration, the eddies in the eternal conflicts between equality and order. We may all debate the intellectual origins of the events, some of us lived through them, but none of us knows the endings of the most signifi-cant. Editors – to a man – assumed they had wrapped up the story of women's equality when the Suffragettes won the vote. The idea of non violence as a potent political force in modern times must have seemed to have died with Mahatma Gandhi and the bloody separation of the Indian subcontinent, Fascism with the char-red body outside the Berlin bunker. But the

Journalists rush out of No 10 Downing St after receiving the statement from Mr Chamberlain that he intends flying to Germany to see Herr Hitler.

newspaper front pages which recorded these apparently climatic events might well have carried the slug line which reporters and editors write on a hot running story: *mf*, telling the printer that more follows. What followed was a black seamstress in Montgomery, Alabama, refusing to give up her seat on a city bus to a white passenger, Martin Luther King subpoenaing the conscience of the nation, and the great civil rights march on Washington. What followed was General Idi Amin's grisly impersonation of Hitler. And Lech Walesa and Solidarity.

And civil disobedience as the principal weapon of the anti nuclear movement. And General Galtieri seizing his Rhineland in the South Atlantic. Watch this space. The threads of tomorrow's news are here today. But we will all be taken by surprise.

Science and invention are more natural front page history than the *isms* which refuse to be *wasms*. Man in space. Heart Man Speaks. Man Walks on the Moon. Test Tube Baby. Not merely do the sensations of one decade become the commonplaces of the next, but the language of the popular newspaper headline, urgently invented to fit within the confines of a few columns, survives the sniffs of the experts and passes into the vernacular. The birth in 1978 of the first child from an egg fertilised outside the womb is the birth, we all say, of a test tube baby, though she was incubated in her mother's womb. The oral contraceptive is The Pill. And the atomic device exploded over Hiroshima is The

Bomb. A remarkable confidence is manifest in the British popular newspaper treatment of these stories. The *Daily Express* front page on Hiroshima on 7 August 1945 was not content merely to say (as was the *New York Times*) FIRST ATOMIC BOMB DROPPED ON JAPAN. It looked to the future warned us in two huge banners: THE BOMB THAT HAS CHANGED THE WORLD. When the Soviet Union launched its successful sputnik satellite in 1957 the banner was SPACE AGE IS HERE. In the early part of the century scientific thought was ignored by the newspapers, like political thought, but the inclination to prophecy has seemed to come more easily with science. Even as early as 1922, when a few cranky husbands drove their wives wild by forever tinkering with crystal sets, the *Evening News* in London (page 44) subordinated all the world's news to an eight column banner headline WIRELESS IN EVERY HOME. This unqualified statement was based on no more than an interview only a year after Marconi engineers had managed to broadcast from Chelmsford but the headline writer was unflagging in his enthusiasm. It would be AS CHEAP AS THE TELEPHONE. There would be CONCERT GOING AT THE FIRESIDE.

It would be idle to pretend the front pages have reverberated with every scientific discovery. The proof of Jonathan Salk's polio vaccine was front page news everywhere in 1955, announced in a University of Michigan press conference to 150 reporters and TV cameras. But there was no instant recognition or even development following the discovery of penicillin in 1928 nor of the unravelling of the DNA double helix in 1953, and the computer has crept upon us almost by stealth. The *New York Times* derided Proessor Robert Hutchings of Clark University, Worcester, Mass., for talking in 1929 of the day man would reach the moon with a new breed of multistage rockets propelled by liquid fuel. He had fired a 9ft rocket a quarter of a mile into the sky but *The Times* said he ought to realise that a rocket had to have 'something better than a vacuum against which to react.' More surprisingly, it was not world wide front page news when on 17 December 1903, Orville and Wilbur Wright contrived the first powered, controllable heavier-than-air craft for fifty nine seconds at Kitty Hawk on the North Carolina coast. Editors had become soured by all the wild talk about controlled flight. Only one newspaper gave it full treatment, the aptly but coincidentally named Virginian Pilot (Norfolk, West Virginia). Two lines of thin sans italic capitals letters fluttered across the full width of the page:

FLYING MACHINE SOARS 3 MILES IN TEETH OF HIGH WIND OVER SAND HILLS AND WAVES AT KITTY HAWK ON THE CAROLINA COAST.

That was technically noteworthy as an early banner headline and there was poetry in the wording. There was an inspired editor in Norfolk, West Virginia, that day. But the scepticism persisted. The Wrights did not seek publicity. And, crucially, there was no photograph to prove the flight. Even looking at that front page today we are vaguely dissatisfied. It is not just a question of corroboration, as in the My Lai massacre, the death of Che Guevara and so on. We know they did it. It is that the event is incomplete. The Coronation Day front page of the ascent of Everest aches for pictures of the men on top. Compare the wholeness of the Chicago Daily Times on the day the Hindenburg crashed (page 80) with picture and headline reinforcing each other to dominate our imagination, or the

photograph of Kim Philby, master spy, standing affably in Red Square, Moscow, on the day in 1967 that *The Sunday Times* revealed how stupendous had been his betrayal. The reporter Arthur Ruhl well expressed our longing for an image, and the role of the newspaperman, when he went with Jimmy Hare the photographer to try and pin down the 'Wright myth'. It was a full five years after that first flight; people had remained sceptical and the Wrights secretive. Ruhl and Hare trekked for days through forest and across sanddunes and inlets to reach the remote outer banks where the Wrights were thought to be experimenting. They hid in scrub timber and gazed across a mile of level beach to where two black dots, which were men, moved about something set on the sand. 'This white streak and the skeleton lines beneath it,' Ruhl wrote later, 'was, in a way, the center of the world. It was the center of the world because it was the touchable embodiment of an Idea, which presently is to make the world something different than it has ever been before. . . . The bedraggled men crouching behind the trees were the first uninvited, as it were, official jury of the world at large to see the thing in action and judge its success. Really it was not newspaper reporters, it was the world's curiosity which was peering across the intervening sands.'

Well, the white streak tilted and rose and the hazy rectangle with two dots amidships bore down across the field and flew for two minutes and fifty seconds, and in that time Jimmy Hare had his picture. The Wrights could fly and he could prove it.

The world's curiosity makes large claims on the lives of newspapermen. I think first always of

Nick Tomalin of *The Sunday Times* whose dispatches guided the readers with great acuity in the first week of the Yom Kippur war in October 1973. He was killed on 17 October on the Golan front when his car was hit by a Syrian missile. Vietnam claimed scores of reporters and photographers. Jon Swain of *The Sunday Times* and Sydney Schanberg of the *New York Times* risked their lives by staying in Pnomh Penh when the Khymer Rouge won the war in Cambodia. Swain filed the first story of Pol Pot's mass evacuation to the countryside. It is made, as well, by what Nick specified as a necessary requirement of journalism, 'rat-like cunning'.

The Reuters man at Mafeking sent London news of the relief by smuggling his bulletin out of Pretoria in a sandwich and bribing a railwayman at the frontier. Carr Van Anda, the managing editor of the *New York Times*, scooped everyone on the sinking of the Titanic, first by taking a chance on the mass of confused and contradictory dispatches, and then by persuading Signor Marconi to take his 'business manager' aboard the rescue ship Carpathia – *Times* reporter Jim Speers.

Front page history sometimes walks in off the street. It happened to me with two of the biggest stories at *The Sunday Times*. In 1977 Mr Henry Kyemba dropped in. He maintained a calm air though he knew an agent of General Amin had been sent to kill him. Kyemba was Amin's Minister of Health. He had quietly dismissed himself as head of the Ugandan delegation to the World Health Organisation in Geneva and made his way secretly to London. 'It was only a question of time before I was due to be killed. I'd like you to help me make sure that what I know about Amin will not die with me.' We hid Henry in a cottage I had in Essex and there over days he told Russell Miller how Amin had murdered Archbishop Jonan Luwuum and two Cabinet Ministers and also Mrs Dora Block, the British-Israeli grandmother who vanished from hospital in Kampala after the Entebbe hijacking.

Kyemba's story probably helped to shorten Amin's reign. I have no doubt that what Anthony Mascarenhas did saved untold lives and more. He, too, walked into our office in London, a soldierly man in his early forties. He had just come back, he told us, from an official press visit to East Pakistan. As the assistant editor of the *Morning News* in Karachi he had been invited with seven others to report on how normal the country was after a Bengali rebellion. The seven had written that story. He had come to London because he had to tell the truth – that the army was systematically massacring thousands of civilians. Famine was close and there were at least five million refugees.

Mascarenhas was *The Sunday Times* correspondent in Karachi, but we had little experience of him. We talked to him and we believed him. 'If I do not write the full story of what I have seen,' he told us, 'I will have to stop writing. I would never again be able to act with any integrity.' His decision to tell meant he had to give up his home and his job in Karachi. We agreed he should return to evacuate his family before the paper published. Ten days after he left the office the cable came 'Export formalities completed. Shipments begin Monday.'

The front page story by Mascarenhas, with the banner *Genocide*, created an international sensation. It was cited by India as a principal justification for her invasion of East Pakistan. All that Mascarenhas had reported, and worse, was found to be true when Indian troops entered Dacca, not long afterwards the capital of the new state of Bangladesh

> 'Declare among the nations and proclaim,
> set up a banner and proclaim,
> conceal it not, and say:
> Babylon is taken,
> Mer'odach is dismayed
> Her images are put to shame
> her idols are dismayed'
> *Jeremiah 50*

Front page history, an old business.

HOLD THE FRONT PAGE

by George Freston

'Hold the Front Page' refers to space or even the whole front page left by the news/picture editor of a newspaper until the last possible moment for 'putting the paper to bed' – awaiting the latest and most newsworthy or sensational picture. It is always hoped that this picture will be a 'scoop', something the rival papers have not got.

Today we see live news on our TV screens, often with a crowd of press photographers to record the occasion. However when national newspapers were first distributed at the beginning of this century, they only had engravings to illustrate their articles. The camera may have been invented some fifty years earlier, but the equipment was far too heavy and the exposures were far too long for any sort of news story. In 1907 the journalist was carrying a heavy camera with glass plates – no light meter, no synchronized flash – and perhaps achieved some sort of picture to accompany his piece.

At this point the cameraman became a separate unit, still with cumbersome equipment, but recognised as having the time, patience and skill to create a better picture to accompany the journalist's story. They were always depicted in films up to the 1930s in shabby raincoats with a trilby hat with PRESS written on it!

Times have certainly changed although not the excitement of the newspaper world itself. Today's motorised cameras are sophisticated, taking up to 36 frames in less than a minute and time is also cut with the invention of the telewire printer which can get the shots straight to the various papers and agencies from the far corners of the earth.

The gifted and experienced press photographer may have to wait days in adverse conditions for his picture. He will not be satisfied with anything but the best, nor will his editor! The whole story in one picture. The photographer is a perfectionist and his picture may be there and gone in a split second, so he must look beyond what is actually happening to what is going to happen – in war, riots, for sport or royalty. Each editor wants something different for the front page: a 'scoop' that is exclusive to them.

The equipment for the front page, the technical knowledge and ease of travel may have speeded up the process, but it is still the dedication of the press photographer himself which counts at the end. He does not seek, or get, personal fame. Perhaps his agency's name or a by-line is all he can expect. More important is total satisfaction with his product. It is far removed from the glamorous life depicted by fashion photographers, who have all the time to take the picture they need.

All newspapers have their own photographic staff, but they still rely heavily on press agencies, on freelance photographers with an eye for something just a little bit better – against all the others – plus perhaps a little luck sometimes at being in the right place at the right time to achieve the picture that will hold our attention when we pick up our daily paper.

In this book you will see many examples of this; pictures that have been worthy of the editors cry 'Hold the Front Page'.

Pressmen using long and short focus cameras in the 1930s.

George Freston

At the age of 15, George joined a small studio in East London as general dogsbody. Later in the same year, 1950, he transferred to Fox Photos as darkroom assistant.

By 1959 he was a fully fledged photographer, specialising in colour, and for three decades has been actively engaged in the UK and overseas in all aspects of press photography. In 1975, he won the Royal Photographer of the Year Award.

In 1983 Fox Photos was acquired by Keystone Press Agency, part of the Photo Source and George Freston is now Photographic Director for Keystone, Fox Photos, Central Press and Colour Library International.

His time and energy is now engaged on co-ordinating all photographic work and passing on his vast knowledge to a young team.

1900

Daily Express

NO. 23.   LONDON, SATURDAY, MAY 19, 1900.   ONE HALFPENNY.

WHEN SHALL THEIR GLORY FADE?

HISTORY'S MOST HEROIC DEFENCE ENDS IN TRIUMPH.

THE BOERS' LAST GRIP LOOSENED.

MAFEKING AND BADEN-POWELL'S GALLANT BAND SET FREE.

"LET ME TELL MOTHER."

HOW THE "EXPRESS" FIRST GAVE THE NEWS

TO BADEN-POWELL'S HOME.

The British arrived unprepared for both the terrain and the field craft of their enemy

'Boers' were Dutch farmers. The Dutch first colonised the Cape of Good Hope, the southern tip of Africa, but when in 1814 'Cape Colony' became British, settlers poured in from Britain bringing their own laws and lifestyle, reducing the privileges of the Boers and applying humanitarian attitudes to 'the natives' alien to Dutch thinking. So in 1835 the Boers moved out on a Great Trek north. In the two British South African colonies certain Africans could vote but in the two Boer republics of the Orange Free State and the Transvaal they could not. The discovery of gold and diamonds, acquisition of other areas by other European powers and the entry of imperialistic adventurers and arrogant financiers, increased the tension between British and Boer republics until Paul Kruger, President of Transvaal, could take no more. In October 1899 he issued an ultimatum of war, which found the British forces in South Africa wholly inadequate to defend the colony. But after initial disasters the capitals of the Boer republics were captured, the besieged Ladysmith was relieved (16 February 1900) and then, after eight months, Mafeking. The *Daily Mail* announced that when the news came through 'London went simply wild with delight, Fleet Street was as if by magic transformed into a thoroughfare crowded and jammed with an excited throng of cheering, shouting, gesticulating, happy people.' They were 'mafficking'.

On 31 May 1900 Lord Roberts, C-in-C, entered Johannesburg, and five days later Pretoria. Kruger fled. But the Boer War was by no means over; bitter guerilla warfare continued until the spring of 1902. It was the climax of Britain's imperialism. With the signing of the Peace of Vereeniging the imperialists were deflated. Sadly the Boer War did not solve the Boer Problem. Inevitably the Dutch-Africans (the Afrikaans), retained their own life-style and un-British attitude towards 'the natives'.

At the end of the 19th century China was dying as an integral empire, and the 'living nations', Britain, France, Germany, Russia, Japan and the United States, were vying with each other to share her partition. In 1898 they competed to lend China money and exercise influence by acquiring concessions to establish ports, railways, telegraphs, banks, mining rights. In that year Russia occupied Port Arthur, Germany Kiaochow, Britain Wei-hai-wei and more of Kowloon. China was in danger of disintegrating; and at a time of drought and plague in the north the Chinese decided they had had enough. In June 1900 they mounted an uprising in Peking to oust the 'foreign devils', spear-headed by a secret society which the English called The Boxers, who attacked foreign legations and killed the Japanese and German ministers. The remainder of the diplomatic corps sought refuge in the British Legation to which the insurgents then laid seige.

An international naval force captured the Taku forts on the seafront to the east of Tientsin, and sent a force to get into Peking. But this was ambushed and had to retreat. The Chinese then disrupted rail and telegraph links to Peking. For weeks the area was cut off from all communication with the outside world. Rumours reached London that the British Legation had been stormed and everyone in it slaughtered. Arrangements were being made for a memorial service in St Paul's Cathedral when a message got through that the report was unfounded.

The foreigners were finally relieved by an Allied Expeditionary Force which managed to seize Peking as the Chinese Empress and her court fled. Order was restored, and next year China agreed to punish those involved in the Boxer Rising and pay a large indemnity.

Right *No mercy was shown to the Boxers – a summary execution*

Below *German cavalry arrive in Peking*

1901

'F., who had just come from Fleet Street, said to me yesterday that from a journalist's point of view the Queen died as she had lived, with absolute correctitude and punctuality. She was ill just long enough to make the public appetite keen for every available scrap of information which could be thrown to them: – not long enough to let the daily bulletins flag in their interest. Her "demise" at 6.30 p.m. gave ample time for obituary notices to be trimmed, polished and enriched for the morning papers, which ought always to have the first chance of big news. Whatever her personal faults, Victoria has been a very great Queen, who took her calling very seriously, and in whose small hands – with their grip of steel on all and everything – England has advanced and spread almost incredibly. It is surely right that as a person in supreme charge of anything receives all the blame if matters go wrong, so full credit should not be grudged to them when matters go right. If our country had deteriorated in the last sixty years, posterity would have held the Sovereign largely responsible; as England has prospered immeasurably, to the sovereign posterity must pay a large tribute of gratitude. I always like to remember that when she was driving in Paris with the Empress, who was then in the full flush of her beauty, someone in the crowd said, "Une belle femme avec une reine à côté." The Queen was always Her Majesty in life, and was never more majestic than when in death. I wonder if she recognised the Kaiser? If so, I hope she signified her royal pardon for all his misdoings which his rather theatrical, and not altogether convenient, journey to her bedside, will do little to cover up.'

24 January 1901

from *Some Letters From A Man of No Importance, 1895–1914* (Cape, 1928)

Right *The Queen at Osborne House in 1897 with her grandson, the future King Edward VIII*

Below *The Duke of Connaught, Kaiser Wilhelm II of Germany and King Edward VII in the funeral procession*

DAILY MAIL

DEATH OF THE QUEEN.

HER MAJESTY PASSED AWAY IN PEACE.

SURROUNDED BY HER CHILDREN AND GRANDCHILDREN.

MESSAGE FROM THE KING.

With deep regret we record the sorrowful news that our beloved Queen is no more

The official bulletin announcing her Majesty's death was made known shortly after seven o'clock at Osborne yesterday. It ran:—

Osborne, Jan. 22, 1901. 6.45 p.m.

Her Majesty the Queen breathed her last at 6.30 p.m. surrounded by her children and grandchildren.

(Signed)   JAMES REID, M.D.
R. DOUGLAS POWELL, M.D.
THOMAS BARLOW, M.D.

The Lord Mayor of London received from the Prince of Wales the following telegram, which was at once exhibited at the Mansion House:—

Osborne, 6.45 p.m.

My beloved mother, the Queen, has passed away surrounded by her children and grandchildren.

(Signed)   ALBERT EDWARD.

There were two Wright brothers – Americans. Wilbur was the older, born in 1867 and dying in 1912. Orville, his younger brother, was born in 1871 and lived until 1948. They had little formal education, but early on became fascinated by the new science of aeronautics and built un-powered gliders at Kitty Hawk in North Carolina. But these were toys beside the 'aeroplane' which they built in 1903 which they named 'The Flyer'. This was powered by a 12-horse power petrol engine which turned a wooden propeller. On 17 December 1903, 32 year old Orville drove this machine as fast as it would go along the ground, tilted the wings and got it to lift off and fly under its own power for 40 yards. It was the world's first flight in a powered aircraft and lasted for 12 seconds.

Orville and Wilbur Wright spent the next two years improving 'The Flyer' so that by the end of 1905 they got it to fly 24 miles. They obtained their first patent in 1906. Two years later they brought their aircraft to Europe and pioneered powered flight in Britain, France and Italy.

The means of transport were taking great strides. It was in 1903 too that one Henry Ford started making cheap 'Tin Lizzy' motor cars, and four years later was setting up a production line for his famous 'Model T'.

1903

Orville Wright lifts off to make the world's first powered flight

Far left *American brothers Orville and Wilbur Wright (with sister Katharine)*

Left *Wilbur Wright in* The Flyer *which he and his brother Orville built in 1903*

1906

One of the greatest natural disasters ever to affect a city in the Western world struck San Francisco at 5.13 on the morning of Wednesday, April 18, 1906. The disjointed rocks of the San Andreas Fault in California, the greatest fracture anywhere on the earth's crust, flexed themselves violently and the glamorous city, developed in the Gold Rush days of the previous century, began to crumble. The first building to fall was the skyscraper belonging to the Postal Telegraph company, but within seconds, as the first wave of the earthquake was followed by others, 'tall skyscrapers began to tumble every which way' – as one newspaper report put it that very day. Hundreds of people died as the buildings collapsed and innumerable fires broke out. The water supply was cut off, thus hampering the fire department in its efforts to douse the flames. The shock waves were recorded on the far side of the vast country, in Washington, but it was in San Francisco that all the damage occurred: about 700 people died, 250,000 were left homeless and 28,000 buildings – valued at more than £200 million even in those days – were destroyed in the business district built on the site of the Gold Rush city.

Incredibly, some buildings in the centre were left standing and one reporter from Washington composed this verse to celebrate the survival of the local distillery:

'If, as they say, God struck the town
For being over-frisky,
Why did He burn the churches down
But spare Hotaling's whisky?'

The people of San Francisco were spurred by the disaster and rebuilt their city with remarkable speed. Within ten years, every trace of the earthquake had disappeared. The city grew in size and importance with its strategic position in the First World War, when 500,000 war workers settled temporarily in the area. By the 1980s the city was dominated by huge, new skyscrapers. But the fear of earthquake remained. The most important work in trying to measure and forecast the scale of earthquakes was carried out in Southern California and the experts – and some engineers – warned that the new towers of San Francisco would be vulnerable to the next great heaving of the San Andreas Fault.

In two minutes and 18 seconds the 'Pearl of the West' looked like this

For three days following the quake a non-stop fire destroyed any building still standing

Opposite *The Chinese quarter of San Francisco devastated by the earthquake*

EXTRA

THE MARION CHRONICLE.

News of the World Covered by Scripps-McRae Press Association and Other Special Service

VOL. 21. NO. 44. MARION, INDIANA, WEDNESDAY, APRIL 18, 1906. PRICE 2 CENTS.

TERRIBLE EARTH-QUAKE IN SAN FRAN-CISCO, MANY KILLED

Meagre Reports Have Been Received Over One Line of Telegraph---Indications are That 1,000 Buildings are Wrecked and 1,000 People are Killed.

SUFFRAGETTES

Women who mounted a militant campaign to gain female suffrage in Britain – votes for women in parliamentary elections – were accused of taking the law into their own hands. Their action coincided with the constitutional crisis provoked by Lloyd George's 'People's Budget', considered by some to be a direct attack on landed property. The die-hard resistance of the House of Lords to this 1909 Finance Bill not only seemed out of touch with the spirit of the times but unconstitutional. But were the 'suffragettes', as the newspapers called them, trying to force political change equally illegally?

Mrs Emmeline Pankhurst founded the Women's Social and Political Union in October 1903 and from then until 1914 her fight for women's rights, with the aid of her daughters Christabel and Sylvia, took many forms of extra-Parliamentary agitation, to which she turned however with some reluctance. 'We did not begin the fight', she said, 'until we had given the new (Liberal) government every chance to give us the pledge we wanted.' At a meeting in the Albert Hall in 1905 held by the Prime Minister, Sir Henry Campbell-Bannerman, attended by most of his Cabinet, suffragettes unfurled banners demanding 'Votes for Women'.

'In the midst of the uproar and conflicting shouts the women were seized and flung out of the hall. This was the beginning of a campaign the like of which was never known in England or for that matter in any other country.'

In June 1909 an imprisoned suffragette went on hunger stike, and others followed her example. The protest of Emily Davison took the form of suicide by throwing herself in front of the runners in the Derby on Epsom Downs; that of another campaigner the slashing of the famous 'Rokeby Venus' in the National Gallery.

Women over 30 in Britain were enfranchised in 1918; between 21 and 30 (the 'flapper vote') in 1928.

Below *Mrs Emmeline Pankhurst is arrested outside Buckingham Palace*

Below right *Women suffragettes demonstrate at Enfield*

Daily Herald
THE LABOUR DAILY NEWSPAPER.

APRIL 15, 1912.

PRESIDENT TAFT'S DANGER

Fierce Struggle with an Armed Man.

"FORCIBLE FEEDING."

Miss Sylvia Pankhurst's Plea for Imprisoned Suffragists.

AN M.P. SHOUTED DOWN.

POISON SUSPECTED.

Mysterious Death of a Child near Preston.

IDEALS FOR WORKERS.

Mr. James Parker, M.P., on National Prosperity.

MOTOR ACCIDENT IN PORTUGAL.

COLOUR BLINDNESS.

*Riots outside
Buckingham Palace lead
to firm action by the
police*

Below left *Mrs Pankhurst
who fought for Votes For
Women from 1903 to
1914.*

Below *Mr Herbert
Asquith, the prime
minister, smiles as
suffragettes are ejected
from a meeting in the
Albert Hall*

DEATH OF KING EDWARD VII

The Edwardian Era came to an end in Britain on 6 May 1910. The death of King Edward VII on that Friday evening came to the nation as a 'painful surprise'. Parliament had adjourned a week earlier and Herbert Asquith the prime minister had gone off on a cruise in the Mediterranean with the First Lord of the Admiralty. He had the ship turned back when he heard of the King's illness and learnt of his death on the return voyage. 'I went up on deck', he wrote, 'and I remember well that the first sight that met my eyes in the twilight before dawn was Halley's comet blazing in the sky. It was the only time, I believe, that any of us saw it during the voyage. I felt bewildered, and indeed stunned.'

King Edward was carrying out formal duties up to within 36 hours of his death, giving audience to Lord Islington, the new Governor of New Zealand. On the last day of his life he reminded his secretary he had an appointment for 12 noon. He was 69. His successor, King George V, was without political experience at a time when the country, in Asquith's words, was 'nearing the verge of a crisis almost without example in our constitutional history [the blocking of Lloyd George's Finance Bill by the House of Lords].'

As constitutional monarch Edward VII had no 'policy' of his own, but after 1904 he never concealed his opinion of the 'dangerous antics' of his nephew Kaiser Wilhelm of Germany, and Edward's refusal to visit or meet him in 1905 gave a new dimension to the policy of Entente Cordiale with France stimulated by his government. A genial, convivial character who liked the company of beautiful women and horse-racing, card-playing male companions, he brought colour and gaiety to court life and high society which contrasted strongly with the last sombre years of his mother's long reign.

Caesar, Edward VII's favourite dog, takes its place in the late king's funeral procession

Right *King Edward VII on his deathbed*

The Daily Mirror
THE MORNING JOURNAL WITH THE SECOND LARGEST NET SALE

No. 2,037. Registered at the G. P. O. as a Newspaper SATURDAY, MAY 7, 1910 One Halfpenny.

THE WORLD IN MOURNING: DEATH OF EDWARD THE PEACEMAKER, KING AND EMPEROR.

The King died during the night from an attack of bronchitis which had confined his Majesty to his room for three days. His Majesty, who was born on November 9, 1841, and was thus in his sixty-ninth year, had reigned since the death of Queen Victoria on January 22, 1901.

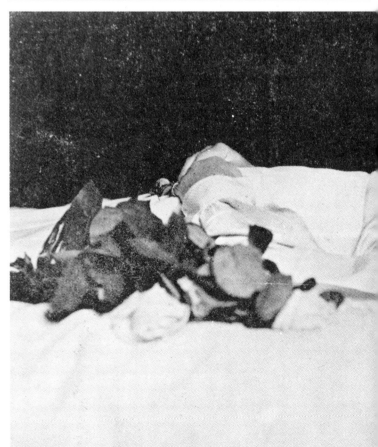

1910

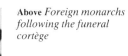

Above *Foreign monarchs following the funeral cortège*

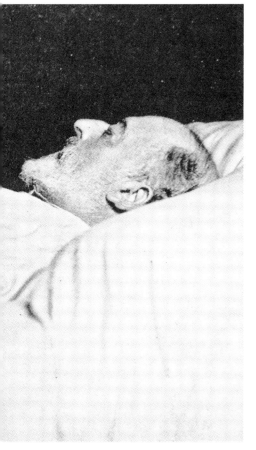

George V, who succeeded Edward VII, seen here with his mother Queen Alexandra

1910

Two hours after the couple who had registered as Mr John Robinson and son had boarded the SS *Montrose* at Antwerp that July evening in 1910 bound for Quebec, the ship's captain H G Kendall, suspected the elder man might be the American Dr Hawley Crippen, wanted in London for the suspected murder by poison of his wife, the actress Belle Elmore who had 'disappeared' in January, and the boy the typist Ethel Le Neve who was his mistress. Two days out he sent wireless signals to another ship the *Montreal Star* and to Reuters news agency describing how he had seen the boy, whose trousers he noted were attached to his waist by safety pins, treating his father 'with extraordinary signs of endearment'; how Mr Robinson carried a revolver but had no baggage, and had told him he was taking his son to California for his health. But throughout the voyage, in which newspaper readers throughout the world were being told of their adventurous

crossing, which they believed would enable them to evade the consequences of their crime, Dr Crippen and Ethel Le Neve had no idea they had been detected. It was with some surprise therefore that they were arrested in the Gulf of St Lawrence by the pilot who came on board from Father Point who turned out to be Inspector Dew of Scotland Yard in disguise. A few years before they might have got away with it. As the *News of the World* reported, 'a scientific interest attaches to the arrests. The long arm of the law had been lengthened by the Marconigram – the capture now effected will long be remembered in connection with the development of wireless telegraphy.'

A search of Crippen's house in Hilldrop Crescent in North London revealed the poisoned woman's remains; the doctor, a US citizen, who had settled in England in 1900, was convicted of murder and hanged.

The news that the 39-year-old Captain Roald Amundsen and his four companions, comprising the Norwegian Antarctic Expedition, had reached the south pole – the first people in the world to stand on those frozen wastes – took three and a half months to travel to England. It was on 20 October 1911 that they set out with 52 dogs and sledges loaded with food and equipment from their winter quarters. Walking 25 kilometres a day they came to the south pole of the earth's rotation (as opposed to the magnetic south pole on Adélie Land) after a freezing march of 53 days on 14 December. The first report of the great achievement was not received in Fleet Street until 8 March 1912. The *Daily Chronicle* scooped all its competitors with an exclusive personal narrative of the perilous journey written by the great man himself.

It was only when Amundsen learnt that Robert Peary had discovered the north pole (in 1909), which he had set his heart on reaching first, that he sailed from Norway in June 1910 – heading south. On one day in mid-August the temperature for the five explorers dropped to minus 59 degrees Centigrade. But 'by far the most unpleasant part of our march' was across the hollow, frozen sea which Amundsen called the Devil's Dancing Room. They could not use skins on their feet, and their marching 'sounded like walking on upturned barrels'. One man and two dogs fell through the ice. By 7 December they were 10,000 ft up in what Amundsen called the Queen Maud Mountains; and on the following day he got to the place where the English explorer Ernest Shackleton had abandoned his attempt to reach the south pole in 1909. The actual 'discovery' was undramatic. 'The day went on without incident, and at 3 pm we made a halt. According to our reckoning we had reached our destination. All of us gathered round the colours; all hands took hold of it and planted it on the spot, and gave the vast plateau on which the pole is situated the name "King Haakon VII Plateau".'

The British Antarctic 'Terra Nova' Expedition led by Captain Robert Falcon Scott was seeking the same goal. But Amundsen's base was 60 miles closer to the pole than Scott's, and this enabled him to beat the British explorer to the post by a month. Captain Scott's expedition reached the pole on 17 January 1912 – to find to their great disappointment that the Norwegians had got there first. But there was worse to come. Amundsen's party of skiers and dog teams, using the Axel Heiberg Glacier route, managed to get back to Framheim Station at the Bay of Whales without mishap. Scott's man-hauling polar party however – Scott, E A Wilson, H R Bowers, L E G Oates and Edgar Evans – using the Beardmore Glacier route for their return to base, got caught in a blizzard on the Ross Ice Shelf – and perished to a man.

Inset *Norwegian explorer Roald Amundsen, who was destined to die in 1928 in a flying accident at the north pole*

REVOLUTION IN CHINA

The Manchu family were proclaimed the Imperial Dynasty of China in 1644 and remained in power until the beginning of the 20th century. Secret revolutionary groups aiming at the overthrow of the Manchu emperors began operating in 1905, but the revolution can be said to have come out into the open with the discovery of their headquarters in Hankow in 1911: Widespread disturbances broke out which the government were powerless to control. Matters came to a head with the establishment of two rival regimes both opposing imperial rule. A 'national assembly' appointed a General Yuan Shih-Kai prime minister with his seat at Peking; a 'revolutionary assembly' in Nanking elected peasant's son Sun Yat-sen president of the United Provinces of China. Educated in Honolulu and a Christian convert, Sun Yat-sen was for some years an American citizen. He trained as a doctor in Hong Kong and in 1894 formed the Save China League. While in London in 1897 he was held prisoner by consular officials in their Portland Place embassy but released after intervention by the Foreign Office.

By 1913 he had the support of Canton businessmen and soldiers in the south of China but patriotically resigned as president of the United Provinces in the interests of national unity, and handed over authority to Yuan Shih-kai, who became provisional President of the Chinese Republic. In 1915 Yuan took a constitutional step backward by having himself proclaimed Emperor.

The 1911 revolution in China ended a period in which the ideals of Confucius had held the nation together for 2000 years, dominating Chinese culture and society.

Dr Sun Yat-sen with his wife and staff officers

The Daily Mirror

THE MORNING JOURNAL WITH THE SECOND LARGEST NET SALE

No. 2,487.   Registered at the G.P.O. as a Newspaper   SATURDAY, OCTOBER 14, 1911   One Halfpenny.

PU YI, CHINA'S FIVE-YEAR-OLD EMPEROR, WHOM THE REVOLUTIONARIES ARE SEEKING TO DEPOSE.

Dr. Sun Yat Sen   The Regent and his second son   The Emperor

China is in the throes of a revolution, the aim of which is nothing less than the overthrow of the Manchu dynasty and the establishment of a Republic. Pu Yi, the present Emperor, who is now five and a half, came to the throne when only three years old. Ruler over 300,000,000 souls, he lives a life secluded from the world, even his mother only being allowed to pay him occasional visits. In the palace he is addressed as Waa-Sui-Yeh (Lord of Ten Thousand Years). Prince Chun, the Regent, is the little Emperor's father. Dr Sun Yat Sen is named as the President of the first Republic—if it is established.

The New York Times.

THE WEATHER.
Unsettled Tuesday; Wednesday, fair, cooler; moderate southerly winds, becoming variable.

VOL. LXI...NO. 19,906. NEW YORK, TUESDAY, APRIL 16, 1912—TWENTY-FOUR PAGES. ONE CENT In Greater New York, Jersey City and Newark. TWO CENTS Elsewhere

TITANIC SINKS FOUR HOURS AFTER HITTING ICEBERG; 866 RESCUED BY CARPATHIA, PROBABLY 1250 PERISH; ISMAY SAFE, MRS. ASTOR MAYBE, NOTED NAMES MISSING

Col. Astor and Bride, Isidor Straus and Wife, and Maj. Butt Aboard.

"RULE OF SEA" FOLLOWED

Women and Children Put Over in Lifeboats and Are Supposed to be Safe on Carpathia.

PICKED UP AFTER 8 HOURS

Vincent Astor Calls at White Star Office for News of His Father and Leaves Weeping.

FRANKLIN HOPEFUL ALL DAY

Manager of the Line Insisted Titanic Was Unsinkable Even After She Had Gone Down.

HEAD OF THE LINE ABOARD

J. Bruce Ismay Making First Trip on Gigantic Ship That Was to Surpass All Others.

The admission that the Titanic, the biggest steamship in the world, had been sunk by an iceberg and had gone to the bottom of the Atlantic, probably carrying more than 1,400 of her passengers and crew with her, was made at the White Star Line offices, 9 Broadway, at 8.30 o'clock last night. Then P. A. S. Franklin, Vice President and General Manager of the International Mercantile Marine, conceded that probably only those passengers who were picked up by the Cunarder Carpathia had been saved. Advices received early this morning tended to increase the number of survivors by 200.

The admission followed a day in

The Lost Titanic Being Towed Out of Belfast Harbor.

PARTIAL LIST OF THE SAVED.

Includes Bruce Ismay, Mrs. Widener, Mrs. H. B. Harris, and an Incomplete name, suggesting Mrs. Astor's.

Special to The New York Times.

CAPE RACE, N. F., Tuesday, April 16.—Following is a partial list of survivors among the first-class passengers of the Titanic, received by the Marconi wireless station this morning from the Carpa-

Biggest Liner Plunges to the Bottom at 2:20 A. M.

RESCUERS THERE TOO LATE

Except to Pick Up the Few Hundreds Who Took to the Lifeboats.

WOMEN AND CHILDREN FIRST

Cunarder Carpathia Rushing to New York with the Survivors.

SEA SEARCH FOR OTHERS

The California Stands By on Chance of Picking Up Other Boats or Rafts.

OLYMPIC SENDS THE NEWS

Only Ship to Flash Wireless Messages to Shore After the Disaster.

LATER REPORT SAVES 866.

BOSTON, April 15.—A wireless message picked up late to-night, relayed from the Olympic, says that the Carpathia is on her way to New York with 866 passengers from the steamer Titanic aboard. They are mostly women and children, the message said, and it concluded: "Grave fears are felt for the safety of the balance of the passengers and crew."

Special to The New York Times.

CAPE RACE, N. F., April 15.—The White Star liner Olympic reports by wireless this evening

---

When the new British passenger liner *Titanic*, 'the biggest steamship afloat', hit an iceberg on her maiden voyage to the United States at 10.20 on the night of 14 April 1912, while the expensively dressed first-class passengers were happily dancing to the jazz band in the sumptous ballroom, she took four hours to sink. She was 95 miles south of the Grand Banks of Newfoundland. Some 866, mostly women and children, were able to clamber into the lifeboats and survive to tell the tale; but 1,513 passengers and crew were drowned. More should have been saved, but the 'luxury' liner only had 1,178 boat spaces for the 2,224 on board.

'Manager of the line insisted she was unsinkable even after she had gone down' ran the headline in the *New York Times*. His faith in its unsinkability derived from the fact that the ship's hull was divided into 16 watertight compartments, four of which could be flooded without the ship sinking. But the 300 ft gash made in her right side by the collision with the huge block of floating ice while steaming at 22 knots – much too fast for the conditions – ruptured *five* of her tanks. That meant serious trouble. First indication of this was the 'C.Q.D.' distress signal which the Marconi wireless station at Cape Race, Newfoundland, received from the ship at 10.25. The Leyland liner *Californian* was only 20 miles away and could have picked up the signals and been on her way to the rescue before the *Titanic* sank at 2.20 the following morning – if her wireless operator had been on duty! The Cunarder *Carpathia* received a message from the White Star liner *Olympic*, and was able to pick up survivors floating in the sea.

As a result of the sinking of the *Titanic* an International Convention for Safety of Life at Sea was called in London

in 1913. They agreed a document stipulating lifeboat drills had to be held during every voyage; ships had to maintain a 24-hour radio watch; and lifeboat space had to be provided for everyone embarked. In that year too an International Ice Patrol was set up to warn ships of icebergs in North Atlantic shipping lanes, run by the US Coast Guard.

E J Smith, captain of the Titanic, *with victims* Isadore Strauss *and* John Jacob Astor

1913

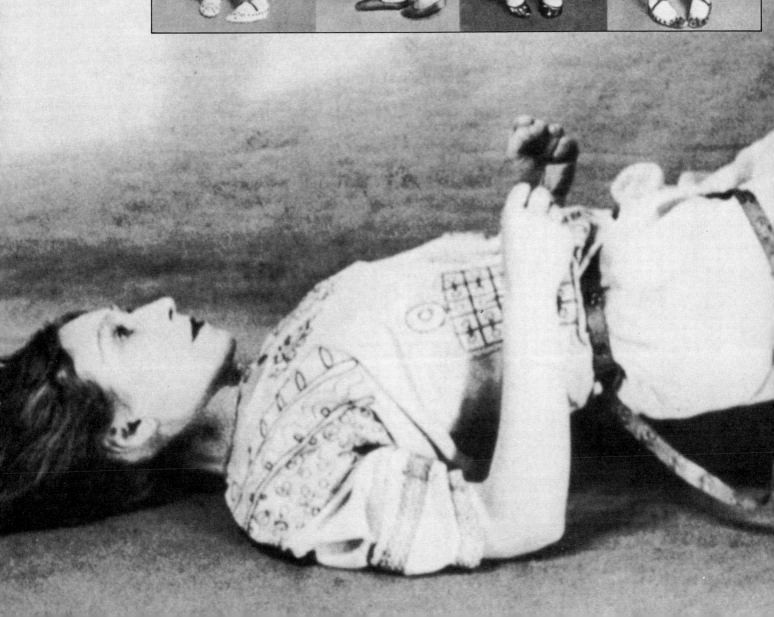

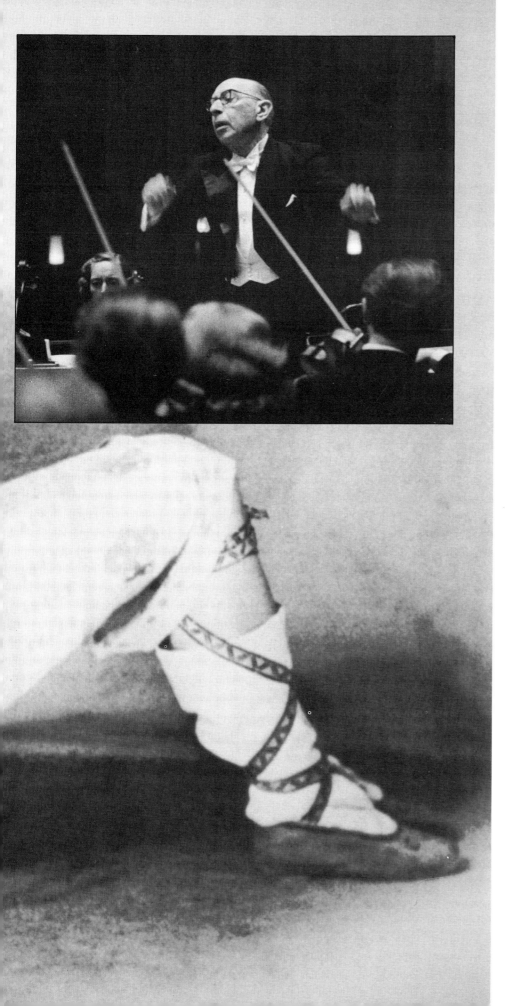

Boos and whistles, countered by applause, came from the audience minutes after the curtain rose in Paris on 29 May 1913 on the first performance by Les Ballets Russes De Serge Diaghilev's production of *Le Sacre du Printemps* (The Rite of Spring) choreographed by Vaslav Nijinsky to music of Igor Stravinsky. The riotous disapproval was aimed not only at the brutality of the subject and the violence of the music but at the ugly movements of the dancers which to many were ridiculous. Stravinsky had to hold tight to Nijinsky to stop him rushing on stage where the girls, unable to hear the music amid the uproar, were dancing the complicated steps as well as they could. 'Je vous en prie laisser achever le spectacle' shouted Diaghilev from his box, and had the house lights flashed on and off to stop the fighting in the fauteuils. But the protests grew, and when Maria Piltz got to the Sacrificial Dance there was pandemonium.

The 1913 audience were shocked at what they considered a negation of romantic taste and style. Based on ancient Russian pagan rituals, there was no plot, no mime, all dancing. Classical ballet was given a new lease of life as symphonic ballet. One critic said you submitted to the ballet with horror or pleasure according to your temperament – 'a kind of barbaric drunkenness seizes you'. The music, in which melody and harmony were subordinated 'by the chaotic onslaught of rhythms and sonority' was, however, later regarded as 'one of music's great single forward steps', a huge challenge suddenly flung at existing musical institutions.

Two more performances were given in Paris; and three more in London in July 1913. After that it was withdrawn. Diaghilev revived it in 1920 with new choreography by Leonide Massine.

Left *Sokolova in Massine's 1920 version of 'Le Sacre.'*
Inset left *Set ostensibly on a Central Asian steppe the first performance of Stravinsky's 'Le Sacre du Printemps' shocked Europe.*
Inset right *A later picture of Igor Stravinsky conducting at Copenhagen in 1959*

1914

World War One in the news
1 The outbreak of war

The photograph at the foot of this newspaper page is of Sarajevo, the city in the Austrian Empire where Archduke Franz Ferdinand and his wife were assassinated. People who read the dreadful story on that summer morning of 1914 did not imagine it would lead to war. Sarajevo and its troubles were a long, long way from England. Austria believed Serbia had been behind the assassination and the two countries went to war. Nobody in Europe wanted widespread war, but it was as though someone had thrown a pebble into a pond. The ripples of this local war spread out, and one by one all the European countries were drawn in by alliances and promises they had made. Before the end of this war that nobody wanted, the whole world had become involved and millions of men had died.

For 40 years a kind of balance had managed to keep the great powers of Europe in a fragile peace, but by 1914 the Hohenzollern emperors of Germany, the Hapsburgs of Austria-Hungary and the Romanovs of imperial Russia thought they would probably be able to gain more by a war, however risky, than by making the effort to maintain peace. Europe's stability was near to breaking point and many saw a period devoted to fighting for the fatherland as a relief from a creeping decadence. With the dismantling of the Ottoman Empire, the claims of Austria-Hungary and Russia for a 'sphere of influence' in South East Europe were intensified. Germany's Bismarck had been planning the isolation of France and the supremacy of Germany since 1870. Now the strongest military power in the world, for at least ten years Germany had threatened the naval supremacy of Britain. With Germany's seizure of Alsace and Lorraine, France drew towards Britain, and at King Edward VII's prompting welcomed an entente cordiale.

When Archduke Ferdinand, heir to the Austro-Hungarian empire was shot dead by a Bosnian terrorist at the Bosnian capital, Sarajevo, in June 1914, it was enough to set the states of Europe, and later the world, at each other's throats. Austria-Hungary declared war on her erstwhile ally Russia; according to the Schlieffen Plan modified by von Moltke, Germany attacked France through neutral Belgium, an event which, under obligations dating back to 1839, brought Britain to France's aid on 4 August 1914. Germany thereupon declared war against Russia.

The first really 'world war' had begun – Japan, Italy, Roumania and Greece ranging themselves with 'The Allies' (France, Britain and Russia), and the Ottoman Empire – the Turks – and Bulgaria with 'The Central Powers' (Germany and Austria-Hungary).

Top *This family group shows, in the back row, Archduke Ferdinand (3rd from left) and Kaiser Wilhelm II (5th from left)*

Above *Archduke Franz Ferdinand leaves Sarajevo town hall; minutes later he was shot dead*

Left *Franz Ferdinand's assassin, Gavrilo Princep, is arrested after being dragged from the river in which he had hoped to make his escape*

REVOLUTION IN MEXICO

A nyone who rules a country for 34 years could be excused for believing, like general Portfirio Diaz of Mexico, that the era of revolutionary uprising was over. Confidence in the stability of his dictatorship encouraged him to risk easing his grip on the nation by allowing the formation of an opposition party. But when Francisco Madero took him at his word and publicly, but peacefully, advocated the non-re-election of Diaz as president, he was arrested and imprisoned. On his release in October 1910, he turned to armed revolution, promising to restore to the Mexican villages the lands taken from them illegally by rich proprietors. To achieve this aim Emiliano Zapata pledged the support of his private army from Morelos in the south.

The resignation of Diaz in May 1911 and Madero's election as president in November so far from bringing democratic stability ushered in a six-year period of chaos in which upstart 'generals' fought each other with their bandit armies, issued their own currency and split Mexico asunder. Zapata was only concerned to secure the lost land of Morelos – his 'Plan of Ayala' – and started seizing the large states without paying heed to Madero's plea to disband his vicious horsemen. The private rebellion of another 'general', Francisco Villa, was suppressed by the federal army. In 1913 General Victoriano Huerta forced Madero to resign, whereupon Villa, Zapata, and a third – Venustiano Carranza – all declared themselves opposed to Huerta, though still no less opposed to each other. The US government also hated Huerta who in July 1914 felt obliged to resign. Of the three anti-Huertistas the respectable Carranza was alone capable of re-establishing order (in 1917) with a regime and a constitution for which he gained US recognition – a non-totalitarian, one party state which has lasted ever since. Land reform was never carried out to the extent Zapata would have liked, but the Mexican peasants got enough land to satisfy them, and they abandoned politics and revolution to till it in peace.

Right *Federal Mexican troops set off to rout 'General' Cedillo's guerillas*

Below *Detachments of the Mexican Army on the march against rebels at Monterey*

Is Stag-Hunting Cruel ? Remarkable Photographs on Page 16.

DAILY SKETCH.

No. 3,277.   Registered at the G.P.O. as a Newspaper   SATURDAY, APRIL 25, 1914.   One Halfpenny.

WILL THE UNITED STATES TROOPS HAVE TO FIGHT AGAINST WOMEN IN MEXICO?

Juana R. Uda de Flores.

Types of United States bluejackets who have been sent to Mexico.

Mexican soldiers marching into Torreon after the fall of the town.

United States infantry in a manœuvres battle.

News from Mexico yesterday was bad. The outstanding facts were that the United States Government are hurriedly preparing for a great naval and military movement, and that the Stars and Stripes has been trampled on in the streets of Mexico City.

There are a number of daring fighters among the Mexican women, and the question is will they take up arms against the United States? But none can beat the record of Juana Flores, who has taken part in no fewer than seventeen engagements.

The Daily Mirror

CERTIFIED CIRCULATION LARGER THAN ANY OTHER PICTURE PAPER IN THE WORLD

No. 3,641.   FRIDAY, JUNE 25, 1915.   One Halfpenny.

LORD KITCHENER THANKS SCOTTISH GIRLS WHO ARE MAKING SHELLS : VESTRY CONVERTED INTO A MUNITION FACTORY.

In the first modern war there was no place for camp followers. The Crimean War had been the last in which wives and daughters, and other admiring hangers-on, came to watch their fathers, husbands and brothers 'campaigning', and picnicked out on the slopes with Fortnum and Mason hampers to watch the brave fellows at war in their comic opera uniforms. In the Great War British women were required to stay in Britain, not only to keep the home fires burning but to take the place of their menfolk making shell cases in the munition factories, shovelling coke in the gasworks, as bus conductors, postwomen, railway ticket clerks. Those with the aptitude and the training had their traditional role as nurses and Women Auxiliaries and ambulance drivers, and women like Nurse Edith Cavell whom the Germans shot as a 'spy' became heroines. The Central Powers had their spies too of whom the best known is Mata Hari, the Dutch lady of easy virtue and double agent who was shot by the French. Her real name was Gertrud Zelle, the wife of an officer in the Dutch colonial service with the Scots name of MacLeod. They lived in Java until 1902, and when she left him she pretended to be a former temple dancer of Javanese birth. She went to Paris where she charmed members of both the French and German intelligence services into giving her their secrets, until the two-faced charade ended in front of a French firing squad in 1917. She was 41 – and a very second class spy. Edith Cavell was shot not for spying, but for organising an escape route to the Dutch frontier while matron of the Berkendael Medical Institute in Brussels. She helped some 200 English, French and Belgian soldiers to freedom. For this risky operation she was arrested in August 1915 and shot by the Germans on 12 October. Wanting her country to win was, for her, only part of what should be expected of anyone in her position. Most remember Nurse Cavell not only for her resolute bravery but her dictum 'Patriotism is not enough'.

Far left *Pseudo Javanese temple dancer and failed spy 'Mata Hari' (Gertrud Zelle)*

DAILY MAIL

ENGLISHWOMAN EXECUTED.

GERMAN SENTENCE AT BRUSSELS.

HOW NURSE CAVELL DIED.

GERMAN OFFICER'S PISTOL SHOT

PRESS BUREAU, Friday, Oct. 15.
The Foreign Office are informed by the United States Ambassador that Miss Edith Cavell, lately the head of a large training school for nurses at Brussels, who was arrested on August 5 last by the German authorities at that place, was executed on the 13th inst. (Wednesday), after sentence of death had been passed on her.

1916

Daily Express

'WHITE WEAPONS.'
British Infantry's Dash
and Daring.
By DR. T. MILLER MAGUIRE.
See Page FOUR.

Late War EDITION

"DAILY EXPRESS" FREE INSURANCE.
£1,000 at death
£1 10s. a week while disabled
£500 for loss of eye or limb
And other benefits
SEE PAGE 6.

NO. 5,428.   LONDON, WEDNESDAY, SEPTEMBER 13, 1916.   ONE HALFPENNY.

772ND DAY OF THE WAR.

Series of Great French Successes on the Somme Front.

GREAT ADVANCE BY THE FRENCH.

NEW LINE OF ENEMY TRENCHES CAPTURED IN 30 MINUTES.

MANY POSITIONS TAKEN.

DRAMATIC PUSH NEARER PERONNE.

Another dashing attack made yesterday by French troops north of the Somme resulted in splendid gains. It took place on a front of nearly four miles between Combles and the river, and at some points the advance was of considerable depth.

Hill 145, east of Le Forest, the Marrieres Wood, and the whole system of German trenches as far as the Bethune–Peronne road were taken, and the southern outskirts of the road are now held over a distance of a mile and a half. In addition, the French lines on Ridge 76, two miles north-west of Peronne, were pushed forward.

Up to last night 1,500 prisoners, including many officers, had been counted.

FIELD STREWN WITH DEAD.

TERRIBLE GERMAN LOSSES AT GINCHY.

BLINDED ARTILLERY

By PERCIVAL PHILLIPS.
"Daily Express" Special Correspondent.
WITH THE BRITISH ARMY IN THE FIELD, Sept 11.

The appearance of sixteen German balloons above the battle front beyond Ginchy to-day was in one respect a confession of defeat, for they signified that the enemy could no longer use the observation posts which overlooked our lines to the south and west.

They swung in the light breeze above the smoke-wreathed ruins of Ginchy and Guillemont, and the occupants attempted to direct a savage bombardment of the lost ground below, where British troops lay in new positions, with the German dead strewn about them, amid the wreckage of battle covering the fields and gullies over which they had advanced. Such counter-shelling was to be expected. The German guns, hastily concealed in new rear positions, searched the ground they once occupied with a variety of explosives.

ROUNDING UP CIVILIANS.

DONE TO PROVE THAT NONE ESCAPE THE NET!

The following remarkable explanation of the "rounding up" of men at railway stations, music-halls, picture palaces, and football matches was issued last night by the Secretary of the War Office:—

Allegations are constantly being received at the War Office and in the commands to the effect that large numbers of young men have escaped registration and are consequently unknown to the military authorities, evading service. These allegations have been received from practically all the large centres of population, and it has been urged on the War Office that so long as these young men are permitted, through the laxity of the Recruiting Department, to remain in civil life, it is grossly unfair to draw on the older groups and classes.

In order to test the accuracy of these allegations, an examination or certificates of exemption in possession of men of military age has recently been undertaken, and the so-called "rounds up" have been carried out in a number of districts. So far the result has been to demonstrate that in the sections of the country which have been tested these allegations are without foundation.

It has was the sole object of setting such ponderous machinery in motion it has been fully realised, for among the thousands of

NATIONAL TRIBUTE TO THE AIRMAN V.C.

GIFT OF ORNAMENTAL IRONWORK FOR THE MONUMENT.

HOW A PUBLIC DEBT MAY BE FULFILLED.

No one can tell how many lives and what amount of property were saved from destruction by Lieutenant W. L. Robinson's splendid deed in foiling the attempt of Zeppelin L 21 to raid London on Sunday, September 3. It is impossible to state where the bombs might have fallen, but every prudent and business firm of the metropolis and the surrounding suburbs is under a deep debt of gratitude to the heroic airman.

It is not only Londoners, however, who benefited by the bringing down of the airship. Had the Zeppelin escaped it is impossible to say what provincial towns it might not have attacked on its homeward journey or on some other occasion.

The public debt of gratitude to Lieutenant Robinson's V.C. can best be

DOUBLE DEFEAT FOR THE BULGARS.

FRENCH CAPTURE TWO MILES OF TRENCHES: BRITISH SUCCESS ON THE STRUMA.

GREEK CABINET CRISIS.

BALKAN FRONT.—The Allies' push on the Salonika front in the Balkans was extended and developed yesterday. Lieut.-General Milne, the British commander-in-chief, reports that the Bulgars suffered severely in the fighting which followed the crossing of the Struma by the British, and that our offensive has been extended to the Doiran front, where our guns are very active.

West of the Vardar the French have won an important success, capturing two miles of Bulgar trenches and taking some prisoners.

RUMANIAN FRONT.—The Rumanians report the conquest in twelve days of 7,500 square miles of Hungarian territory in Transylvania. On their southern front they are bombarding Rustchuk, the great Danube port.

GREECE.—The Greek Premier, M. Zaimis, has resigned. His action is said to be due to domestic difficulties.

Right French General Berdhoulat beside one of the German guns which had pulverised Verdun

Below The horror of poison gas – a later weapon

The first 18 months of the 'Great' War were terrible enough, but they were nothing compared with the horror of 1916 which began with the Germans trying to capture the French fortresses around Verdun. Their opening artillery barrage buried whole battalions. But the morale of the French, sustained by General Pétain's simple slogan 'Ils ne passeront pas' was never broken. Their determination to hold Verdun became unshakeable, in spite of the whole five-mile salient being battered into a terrifying No-Man's-Land. After five months of this hell and 700,000 casualties, the Germans had not passed and Verdun was still French. But if the Germans were to be defeated, it was time to go on the offensive.

For eight days shells from 2,000 British guns softened up the German positions around the river Somme just south of Amiens, and on 1 July 1916 the order was given for the British army to advance on their trenches which, contrary to expectation had suffered little damage from the bombardment because of their depth. Far from shell-shocked, the German machine-gunners fired with deadly accuracy and by the end of that first day 47,000 volunteer 'tommies' and their public school and university officers had been put out of action with very little to show for it – 'the choicest and best of our manhood' as Lloyd George put it. Casualties continued on that scale every day until November, in spite of the Allies' new secret weapon, the Tank, which merely got bogged down in the mud.

When a blizzard blotted out the landscape on 18 November the Battle of the Somme had killed or wounded 1,250,000 on both sides. The British had only captured 125 square miles of mud. At home the British public were horrified. What was it all in aid of? Poet/soldiers like Siegfried Sassoon lampooned 'The Staff', as 'incompetent swine'.

The General smiled as he passed them on their way to the line.

'He's a cheery old card,' grunted Harry to Jack
As they slogged up to Arras with rifle and pack,
But he did for them both by his plan of attack.

Soon afterwards the British Government introduced conscription and the following year the Americans came from Over There to help the Allies.

Top *Aircrew of the Royal Flying Corps*

Left *French troops who took part in the Battle of the Somme*

Above *Some of the American infantrymen who joined the fight in 1917 under shell fire in France.* **Right** *'Old Contemptibles' make the best of trench warfare in the mud of the Somme salient.* **Below** *French anti-aircraft gun at the Battle of the Somme*

A Bill to give the whole Emerald Isle home rule was passed by the British House of Commons, which had a Liberal majority, in 1912. But the Protestants who outnumbered the Catholics in Ireland's four north-eastern counties ('Ulster') feared they would suffer under a 'Catholic' government. So in 1913 Herbert Asquith, the Liberal prime minister, added a clause to the Bill to enable any county to vote itself out of a United Ireland, but only for six years. Sir Edward Carson, Protestant MP, denounced this as a meaningless gesture, but nonetheless in September 1914 the Irish Home Rule Bill became law. The triumph of the Irish Nationalists and their leader John Redmond was short-lived however, for the British Government felt unable to implement the Act until the war which had just been declared against Germany was over and won. For John Connolly, leader of the Irish working-class movement, this was tantamount to betrayal and he at once made plans for an armed uprising. Sir Roger Casement, a British civil servant, tried to recruit an Irish rebel army from prisoners-of-war in Germany, but was arrested on his return to Ireland and executed.

Though few followed Casement, Sinn Fein, the party founded by Arthur Griffiths, were determined to force the issue and on 24 April 1916 proclaimed an independent Irish Republic in Dublin – the Easter Rising.

On Easter Monday teacher Patrick Pearse led a squad of Irish Volunteers into Dublin. They seized the General Post Office, the Law Courts and a biscuit factory. They dug trenches in St Stephen's Green, firing on any soldier who approached; British armoured cars patrolled the streets; a British gunboat steamed up the river Liffey and bombarded the Law Courts.

By 1 May, after a week's bitter fighting, the would-be revolution had been suppressed. It had had little support from the people of Dublin who jeered the ringleaders as they were led off to prison. By shooting 14 of them

Edward Carson who helped raise a force of 80,000 men to resist Home Rule for Ireland

however the British Government turned Irish indifference to anger. Following guerilla warfare from 1919 to 1921 – 'the Troubles' – an Irish Free State of the 26 southern counties was created in 1922 as part of the British Empire and a separate parliament was created in Belfast for 'Ulster'.

Anglo-Irish politician Carson reviews his Ulster Volunteers

RUSSIAN REVOLUTION

1917

Mounting unrest in Russia erupted into revolution in 1917. A disastrous decade culminated in losses of a million men in the first two years of the Great War. Industry was weakened by further mobilisation and transport overloaded and this led to rapid inflation and food shortages. In the face of strikes, demonstrations and mutinies, Tsar Nicholas II abdicated on 15 March, thus ending the thousand-year-old Russian monarchy. But the Provisional Government which took over failed to quell the unrest. Peasants demanded land, workers control of their factories and an end to war. Their mood and fears of counter-revolution inspired leaders of the mushrooming Bolshevik party to act. When the Government tried to close party newspapers on 6 November, the Bolsheviks called out sympathetic troops and the workers' Red Guards and took over the capital city, Petrograd, with ease. Next evening Bolshevik forces stormed the Winter Palace and captured Cabinet members. The man who preached revolution, Lenin – who had returned from hiding only a fortnight before – took over the prime ministerial role. Communist Russia had been born.

Left inset *Nikolskiya Vorota, one of the Kremlin gates, guarded by mounted soldiers*

Right inset *Russian workers demonstrate in the streets of Petrograd (now Leningrad) in July 1917*

Below *Destruction in the streets of Moscow*

Throughout the spring of 1918 the Germans attacked the allied front unceasingly, but that autumn both they and Hapsburg forces were collapsing. The United States had entered the fight in April 1917 and been pouring troops and equipment into France from then on. Every day saw the surrender of more and more guns and the capture of thousands of prisoners. On 29 September the British 4th Army broke through the enemy line and Hindenburg and Ludendorff demanded peace. Bulgaria and Turkey capitulated in October; Austria-Hungary on 4 November. When the German fleet was called out for a final offensive, the sailors mutinied. The Kaiser and Crown Prince fled to Holland, and on 11 November 1918 an armistice was signed, suspending all hostilities.

'And now,' as Winston Churchill wrote in *The World Crisis*, 'it was all over. The unarmed and untrained island nation who with no defence but its navy had faced unquestionably the strongest manifestation of military power in human record, and completed its task. Our country had emerged from the ordeal alive and safe, its vast possessions intact, its war effort still waxing, its institutions unshaken, its people and empire united as never before.'

The Kaiser studies the latest troop dispositions with Field Marshal von Hindenburg and General Ludendorff

Above *Representatives of Red Russia negotiate an armistice with the Central Powers at Brest-Litovsk*

Above left *Marshal Foch, French army commander, receives German plenipotentiaries in a railway carriage to sign an armistice*

Left *German prisoners of war on the Western Front*

Daily Express LATE EDITION

BURROW'S MALVERN TABLE WATERS. *BRITISH TABLE WATERS of undoubted efficiency.* (STILL OR SPARKLING). SOLD EVERYWHERE.

Beer is the National Beverage **Mann Crossman's** retains the nutritive qualities of Malt

NO. 5,951.   LONDON, THURSDAY, MAY 8, 1919.   ONE PENNY.

FULL TERMS OF THE PEACE TREATY.

Ex-Kaiser to be tried by an international tribunal for his 'supreme offence' against morality.

Germany must pay for all war loss and damage both in money and in kind to her final limit.

Colonies, Alsace-Lorraine, other great territories and valuable concessions lost.

Army and navy reduced to skeletons. Air force and U boats absolutely prohibited.

Territory west of the Rhine to be occupied for 15 years by the Allies as a guarantee.

TOTAL LIABILITY TO BE FIXED IN 1921.

£1,000,000,000 IN 2 YEARS. TON FOR TON IN SHIPS. BONDS FOR £5,000,000,000. SAAR MINES FOR FRANCE. CIVILIAN COMPENSATION. MATERIAL for RESTORATION

PAYMENT SPREAD OVER 30 YEARS.

The draft Peace Treaty was presented yesterday to the Germans at Versailles, and we publish a complete official account of its fifteen clauses to-day. A copy of the official summary was delivered to the "Daily Express" soon after eleven o'clock on Tuesday night, but an agreement of honour bound all newspapers not to publish it before to-day.

The official summary will be found in full on Pages 6 and 7.

In the first instance, the Treaty is designed to set forth the conditions upon which alone the Allied and Associated Powers will make peace with Germany, and, in the second place, to establish those international arrangements which the Allies have devised for the prevention of wars in the future and the betterment of mankind. For this latter reason it includes the Covenant of the League of Nations and the International Labour Convention. The draft Treaty does not deal, except incidentally, with the problems arising out of the liquidation of the Austrian Empire, nor with the territories of Turkey and Bulgaria, except in so far as it binds Germany to accept whatever subsequent settlement may be decided on by the Allies in the case of these belligerents.

The main provisions are as follows:—

TRIAL OF THE EX-KAISER.

William of Hohenzollern is publicly arraigned for "a supreme offence against international morality and the sanctity of treaties." Holland will be asked to surrender him for trial before a tribunal consisting of one judge from each of the five Great Powers, which can fix any punishment.

Persons accused of violating the laws of war or of criminal acts are to be handed over by Germany and tried by military tribunals.

WHAT GERMANY MUST PAY.

Responsibility for all loss and damage must be accepted by Germany, but it is plainly stated that her resources are inadequate to meet the total bill. She undertakes to compensate civilians for damages under seven categories, including those caused by maltreatment of prisoners.

The map shows the new boundary lines as officially drawn in Paris.

must not exceed 15,000. All interned warships and certain additional warships will be finally surrendered.

AIR.—Germany is forbidden to possess any military or naval air forces. All military and naval aircraft, including dirigibles, are to be surrendered except 100 unarmed seaplanes to be used for mine-sweeping up to October 1. Aircraft manufacture of any kind is prohibited for six months.

FORTRESSES.—All fortifications and harbours in Heligoland and Dune are to be dismantled by the Germans themselves. The Kiel Canal is to be open to the war and merchant ships of all nations. Fortifications commanding maritime routes between the North Sea

THE HISTORIC SCENE AT VERSAILLES.

FRENCH FRIGIDITY AND GERMAN ARROGANCE.

Versailles, Wednesday, May 7

The meeting of the Allies and the German delegates for the presentation of the peace terms was declared open at one minute past three this afternoon by M. Clemenceau, whereupon the German plenipotentiaries were announced, and entered the room. M. Clemenceau spoke in French. His speech was translated as he proceeded into German and English at convenient intervals.

He said: Gentlemen plenipotentiaries of the German Empire, it is neither the time nor the place for superfluous words. You have before you the accredited plenipotentiaries of all the small and great Powers united to fight together in the war that was so cruelly imposed on them.

The time has come when we must settle our accounts. You have asked for peace. We are ready to give you peace. We shall present to you now a book which contains our conditions. You will be given every facility to examine those conditions and the time necessary for it.

Everything will be done with the courtesy that is the province of civilised nations. To give you my thought completely you will find no ready to give you every explanation you want, but we must say at the same time that this second Treaty of Versailles has cost us too much not to take on our side all the necessary precautions and guarantees that the peace shall be a lasting one.

While M. Clemenceau's speech was being translated into English M. Dutasta, secretary-General of the Peace Conference, stepped quietly across the floor between the tables and handed to Count von Brockdorff-Rantzau, who was opposite him, a bulky volume containing the text of the treaty.

GERMAN REPLY.

Count von Brockdorff-Rantzau, in his reply, which lasted about fifty minutes, accomplish the work without the technical and financial participation of the victorious peoples, and you cannot execute it without us.

"Gentlemen, the sublime thought to be derived from the most terrible sacrifices in the history of mankind is the League of Nations—the greatest progress in the development of mankind since the pronounced and will make the way. Only if the gates of the League of Nations are thrown open to all who are of good will can the aim be attained, and only then the ideal of that war will not have died in vain. The German people in their hearts are ready to take upon themselves their honest lot if the bases of peace which have been established, are not any more shaken.

We shall examine the document handed to us with good will, and in the hope that the final result of our interview may be subscribed to by all of us."

M. Clemenceau said:—Has anybody any more observations to offer? This no one wish to speak? If not, the meeting is closed. Thereupon, at 4.5 p.m., the meeting closed.—Reuter.

CHILLY RECEPTION.

SCENES AT THE ARRIVAL OF THE DELEGATES.

"Daily Express" Special Correspondent.
DANT EXPRESS" BUREAU.

Paris, Wednesday, May 7

Count von Brockdorff-Rantzau drove up and immediately before the Trianon Palace Hotel watched the arrival of the delegates. The first to arrive was M. Clemenceau, who drove up in a motor-car and had just two... He alighted briskly and was ushered by half a squadron of French cavalry looking spruck and spun on tips a bureau blue uniform.

SULTAN M'KWAWA'S SKULL.

RELICS THE GERMANS MUST RETURN.

The peace terms make special provision for three interesting restitutions, in which land about fifty must... and that Germans was also to return, within

---

David Lloyd George, prime minister, who signed for Britain

The Armed Truce of 11 November 1918 held good until a Peace Treaty was signed in the Palace of Versailles outside Paris the following June as the climax to the Peace Conference which had begun its sittings in January 1919.

The Treaty of Versailles was the punitive settlement imposed by the victorious Allies on the defeated Central Powers, making them formally responsible for starting the war. A major aim was so to burden Germany with economic reparations that another attack on France was inconceivable. Alsace and Lorraine were restored to France; new Balkan states had already been created in Czechoslovakia and Yugoslavia. The settlement followed the principles of self-determination. It was presented to the German delegation on 7 May and signed by them on 28 June. The peace conference was dominated by Georges Clemenceau for France, David Lloyd George for Britain; and President Woodrow Wilson for the USA. Russia had already surrendered and the Bolsheviks led by Lenin had replaced the imperial with a communist 'Soviet' regime. Many criticised the Treaty of Versailles, notably J M Keynes and A Hitler.

One of the arrangements of the Treaty was the Polish Corridor giving the Poles access to the sea through German territory to the free port of Danzig (since re-named Gdansk). 'If Germany and Poland are friendly it should

De G. A. Droite, President Wilson of the USA, President Clémenceau of France, Lord Balfour, and Prime Minister Orlando of Italy, at Versailles

work without friction or difficulty; if they are not it may easily be denounced as a ruthless and arbitrary sundering of German territory,' wrote J A Spender in 1936, adding, 'there is reason to hope that it will not prove to be the seed of mischief that in the early years it was expected to be.' Within three years that hope had been dashed.

Article 227 of the Treaty provided for the trial of Kaiser William II of Hohenzollern, to be publicly arraigned 'for a supreme offence against international morality and the sanctity of treaties'. A five-judge tribunal would be formed. Lloyd George was keen on a trial, but the Americans opposed the idea. In the event the Dutch Government refused to deny shelter to the former Emperor and handed him over.

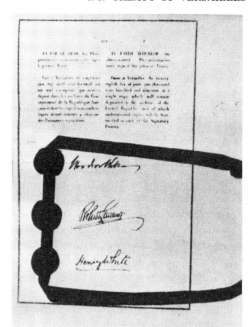

Right *The last page of the Treaty of Versailles with the signatures*

Delegates sign the Treaty of Versailles in the mirror hall of the Palace of Versailles – painting by Sir William Orpen

Daily Chronicle

No. 17,484. LONDON. MONDAY, JUNE 16. 1919. ONE PENNY.

"HOW I FLEW THE ATLANTIC."

CAPTAIN ALCOCK TELLS THE STORY OF HIS DARING FLIGHT.

"WE HAD A TERRIBLE JOURNEY."

1,900 MILES IN 16 HOURS; MACHINE LANDS IN AN IRISH BOG.

British airmen have made the first direct flight across the Atlantic.

Flying in a Vickers-Vimy machine, with two Rolls-Royce engines, Capt. Alcock (Pilot) and Lieut. Whitten Brown (Navigator) accomplished the 1,900 mile journey from St. John's, Newfoundland to Clifden, Ireland, in the amazingly short time of 16 hours 12 mins.

The news of the wonderful feat was conveyed in the following messages:—

THE VICTORIOUS AEROPLANE

The Vickers-Vimy aeroplane, which flew from St. John's, Newfoundland, to Clifden, Ireland, a distance of 1,900 miles, in 16 hours. On the left is the pilot, Capt. J. Alcock, D.S.C., and on the right the navigator, Lieut. A. W. Brown.

THE PILOT.

AIRMAN'S WAITING BRIDE.

THE NAVIGATOR.

TROOPS BURN CAMP.

20,000 AT WITLEY DURING RIOT.

NEW BLAZE LAST NIGHT.

Witley Camp, near Godalming, was the scene, on Saturday night, of a serious outbreak among the Canadian troops stationed there, telegraphs the "Daily Chronicle" representative.

Looping the loop and doing 'some very comic stunts' made it a hair-raising journey for Captain John Alcock, the British pilot of the Vickers-Vimy bomber, and his navigator Lieutenant Arthur Whitten Brown, when they made the first direct, non-stop fight by aeroplane across the North Atlantic in 1919. The young John Alcock – he was only 27 – was already a flying ace with many daring feats to his name as a pilot in the Royal Naval Air Service in the Great War, such as the bombing of Constantinople. In September 1917 he was forced down into the sea by enemy anti-aircraft fire near Suvla Bay, and spent the rest of the war as a prisoner of the Turks. On return to civilian life he became a test pilot for Vickers Aircraft who were making a plane to win the £10,000 prize offered by the *Daily Mail* for the first non-stop flight across the Atlantic.

He and Brown took off from St Johns Newfoundland at teatime on 14 June 1919, and flew doggedly on for 16 hours at an average speed of 100 miles an hour before coming down in a marshy bog in Clifden in County Galway, Ireland. The power for this pioneering flight was two Rolls-Royce 'Eagle' engines. Alcock was created a Knight Commander of the Order of the British Empire for his achievement, but sadly, a few months later, Sir John ran into bad weather while delivering an amphibian aircraft to Paris, crashed into a hillside and was killed.

With every exploit such as Alcock and Brown's, man's mastery of the air took one step nearer becoming the commonplace it is today. For the Americans and Europeans who flanked the Ocean, risky accomplishments of this order made the technique of aviation safer and the elimination of the lengthy ocean crossing more imminent.

For the Dutch the element they needed to tame was the sea; and when the British bomber was flying the Atlantic, they were starting to carry out a huge plan to reclaim land from the Zuyder Zee and elsewhere, by building a sophisticated network of dykes and sluices.

Below right Sluices and sea walls keep the sea at bay in the Netherlands

Below Dykes such as these enabled the Dutch to reclaim their low lands from the sea in 1919

The first session of the League Council, which came into existence when the Treaty of Versailles was signed in June 1919, took place in Paris in January 1920. The Assembly of the League of Nations met for the first time that year in Geneva. The United States, whose President Wilson had conceived the new international institution – it had been one of his 'Fourteen Points' – decided not to join, and communist Russia boycotted it from the outset. So the League was dominated by Britain and France. However 41 countries were represented at that first meeting, none of them 'ex-enemy' states – though Germany was admitted in 1926 and stayed a member till 1933. The league had no armed force to bring recalcitrant members to heel, relying on economic 'sanctions' to apply the necessary pressure. M Hymans, the delegate of the humiliated 'Little Belgium' was elected first president. It established a Permanent Court of International Justice at The Hague in Holland and spawned an International Labour Organisation. The League's permanent position as keeper of the peace between its members depended on disarmament and collective penalisation of any member who violated its Covenant.

Inside the League of Nations where 41 countries were represented at the first meeting of the Assembly in 1920

The League of Nations building at Geneva, Switzerland, from the air

FIRST WIRELESS BROADCAST

1922

Heinrich Hertz proved the existence of electro-magnetic waves in 1887, but when he died in 1894 no one had found a use for them. Detecting thunderstorms? suggested *The Electrician* editorial of that year. One or two people thought of applying them to telegraphy, notably 22-year old Guglielmo Marconi in Bologna who failed however to interest the Italian Government's Post and Telegraphs Dept in the idea. So he came to England where in June 1896 he was given the world's first patent for wireless telegraphy. That year the Secretary of the Post Office rejected his Chief Engineer's recommendation that the Government should acquire his patent rights for £10,000. They were not entirely sure that wireless *worked*.

So Marconi formed his own Wireless Telegraph & Signal Company. The application of the invention to telephony (transmission of speech) came much later and then only for point-to-point communication. But in 1921 a group of Marconi engineers led by Peter Eckersley began making regular *broadcasts* from Writtle near Chelmsford. In 1922 the manufacturers of wireless receiving sets called a Wireless Telephony Conference. This led to the formation by them of a commercial British Broadcasting Company which obtained a licence from the Post Office and appointed John Reith its general manager.

The world's first successful experiment in sound *recording* was made in 1857 by a French printer called Leon Scott de Martinville; but his 'Phonautograph' could not play back what its cylinder had recorded. It was not until 1877 that Thomas Edison's phonograph managed both to record and reproduce. He called his tin foil recording a 'phonogram', the word Emile Berliner transposed for his machine which recorded sound on disc – the gramophone. This arrived in England in 1897 and The Gramphone Company was formed to import and sell it in Britain. The 78 revolutions a minute became the official speed in 1910. Between 1919 and 1920 7½ million gramophone records were reproduced at Hayes, Middlesex, the HQ of the company known as 'His Master's Voice' after they had acquired the painting of that name by Francis Barraud.

The family listens to a nineteen-twenties gramophone which played solid, breakable records at 78 revolutions a minute

A chamber orchestra gives a 'wireless' concert from '2LO' at the British Broadcasting Company's Studios in Savoy Hill, London

A control room at Savoy Hill

EARLY SPECIAL

Evening Standard

THE "GAZEWAY" IS AN OLD HOUSE TRAN-FORMED

No. 30,657.   LONDON, MONDAY, OCTOBER 30, 1922.   ONE PENNY.

22,000 "BLACK SHIRTS" NEAR ROME

DIAZ SUPPORTS ROME REVOLUTION.

FAMOUS WAR VICTOR IN FASCIST CABINET.

HOMAGE TO THE KING.

FORCE OF 22,000 TO ENTER THE CAPITAL.

Twenty-two thousand Fascisti at the gates of Rome are to enter the city, following the almost bloodless revolution, and pay homage to the King.

Signor Mussolini, the Fascisti leader, who was called on by the King to form a Cabinet, has half accomplished his task. General Diaz, Italy's national war hero, is expected to become War Minister.

This and other information wired by Reuter from Rome indicates that Italy will quickly find her way back to peace.

There were sporadic conflicts yesterday in Rome itself, at Milan and in other provincial centres, but no serious fighting.

THE NEW CABINET.

FAMOUS WAR COMMANDER GOES TO WAR OFFICE.

The position in Rome is thus described in a Reuter telegram despatched last evening and received to-day:—

The "Giornale Di Roma" states that Signor Mussolini left Milan immediately for Rome after being summoned by the King to form a Cabinet. He will arrive in Rome this evening. Signor Mussolini will himself take over the portfolio of Foreign Affairs and Interior in addition to being Prime Minister. His Ministry is already in great part constituted.

General Diaz and Admiral Thaon di Revel will be Ministers of War and

ROME CONFLICT.

FASCISTI AND REDS IN FATAL FIGHT.

During the afternoon and evening bodies of Fascisti circulated continually in the streets of Rome yesterday (wires Reuter), and during the afternoon a conflict broke out between Communists and Fascisti as a result of which one person was killed and several injured, but order was soon restored again.

There were some disturbances at Bologna, where, as the result of a conflict between Fascisti and Government forces, one non-commissioned officer of the Royal Guards was killed and another wounded.

Other collisions occurred at San Ruffillo, near Bologna, where two Fascisti

SMALLPOX AT POPLAR.

TWENTY VICTIMS TAKEN TO HOSPITAL.

INSTITUTION ISOLATED.

An outbreak of smallpox is reported from Poplar.

Twenty victims from Poplar Institution have been taken to Dareuth Isolation Hospital, near Dartford, and there are two other cases. Two of the twenty are regarded as very serious.

A staff of a dozen doctors, including L.C.C. and Ministry of Health officials, spent a busy day in Poplar Institution yesterday, touring the wards till midnight.

All the inmates and the officials of the institution have now been examined, and the outbreak is said to be well in hand.

Doctor a Victim.

Though the origin of the outbreak has not yet been traced, it is thought to have been brought from Central Europe, where smallpox is common to the docks.

One of the victims is a doctor (not a permanent member of the institution staff), who contracted the disease while visiting the wards.

Poplar Institution has been isolated and a special committee of the Guardians appointed to deal with the matter.

Though two cases are certainly serious, the others are regarded as mild "as far as smallpox can be mild," said Mr. Edgar Lansbury, chairman of Poplar Guardians.

Importance of Vaccination.

Another case of smallpox has been reported from Bexley, Kent, and several from Dartford, near by.

There is no doubt that an epidemic of smallpox is overdue," an official of the Metropolitan Asylums Board stated.

"Only the special efforts of the Board to stamp out the disease have prevented a grave outbreak, following various cases reported in London during the last few months. The importance of vaccination and re-vaccination should be urged on the public.

LEADERS AND CO-OPERATION.

PROPOSAL BY MR. BONAR LAW?

WEEK-END TALK.

SIR GEORGE YOUNGER SAYS "NO PACT."

The position in regard to co-operation is made still more interesting by week-end developments.

Sir George Younger, the Conservative party organiser, declares that "no pact of any kind exists."

It is declared, however, that Lord Balfour took to Mr. Lloyd George in Scotland proposals made by Mr. Bonar Law.

These, it is said, were discussed by Mr. Lloyd George, Sir R. Horne, Lord Birkenhead, and Lord Balfour at Whittinghame during the week-end.

"NO PACT."

FAIR REPRESENTATION OF VIEWS.

Following is the text of the address by Sir George Younger, chairman of the Unionist party organisation, to the chairmen of Unionist Associations in every constituency in England and Wales:—

In consequence of statements appearing in the Press that an arrangement on something like the last Coalition lines has been made between the National Liberals and the Unionist Central Office with regard to seats at the coming election, it is necessary to state that no pact of any kind exists.

Perfect Freedom.

The situation was clearly explained by Mr. Bonar Law in his speech at Glasgow. The local Unionist executives are left in perfect freedom to select such candidates as they please, and where it is decided locally to run a Unionist candidate the Central Office will accept the local decision, and will officially support that candidate.

When, however, arrangements are

LIGHT-WEIGHTS AT THE N.S.C.

JOHNNY BROWN AND FRED ARCHER.

McTIGUE'S OFFER.

CONTESTS AT THE RING AND HOXTON.

It was the original intention of the N.S.C. to head the programme to-night with the match between George Cook, the Australian, and Dick Smith, the old cruiser-weight champion, but this had to be postponed until next week because of Cook's injury to his thumb.

There is every promise, however, of a good evening's sport at headquarters, and it is not easy to find the winner of the Johnny Brown and Fred Archer bout, which is popularly regarded as an eliminating bout to see who should be put up against Seaman Hall for the light-weight title.

Brown first came into notice down South, when, as Fleming, he won the amateur feather-weight championship. He showed much style and execution that his plunge into professional waters was easily anticipated. He has gone on improving, despite fine increasing weight, and to-day I think he is by far the best boxer we have in the light-weight division.

Archer should prove a worthy opponent to the shrewd combative Scot. He developed a native bent towards fisticuffs in a Spartan school, and as sparring assistant to Kid Lewis showed himself an enduring plucky fighter.

Brown should beat him on the science of the game, but the Aldgate man will give him an interesting trip over the course, I fancy.

Boxing at Hoxton.

We are to have an enlargement this week of our boxing considerations, as the inclusion entertainments will be resumed this afternoon at Hoxton. The district is keenly interested in the noble art, and amongst the boxers it has produced the name of the ever new Bombardier Billy Wells.

BARRACKS TRAGEDY.

THE INQUEST TO-DAY: BELIEF IN ACCIDENT THEORY.

I t was a socialist journalist Benito Mussolini who in 1919 formed the movement he called the Fascio di Combattimento with the bundle-of-rods (*fascio*) symbol of the lictors of ancient Rome. He and his supporters despised the inertia of the rulers of Italy who followed the excitement of the Risorgimento and the unification of the peninsula with bourgeois complacency and political ineptitude. His 'fascists' were out for power by *any* means. They trained gangs of thugs for violent attacks on 'socialists' and the working class. The uniform, the slogans, the street oratory, restored a sense of moving into the future with a purpose. The movement spread like wildfire through Italy's young population. In 1922 it achieved a certain success in Parliamentary elections and continued to terrorise 'communists'. The government was powerless against such naked violence. To avoid civil war the King, Vittorio Emanuele III, felt obliged to conciliate Mussolini when in October 1922 the 'Duce' demanded the formation of a Fascist Government. The king dismissed his prime minister and on 30 October invited Mussolini, who was in Milan, to come to Rome to assume power at the head of his own administration.

The events of the next few days have gone down in the party's mythology as 'The March on Rome', but in fact the corpulent dictator-to-be journeyed to the Eternal City by express train – the Italian form of transport which, the world remembered, he got at last to run on time.

Mussolini with four of his generals after the train journey/march 'on' Rome

Benito Mussolini at a Fascist Party meeting in Rome in 1921
Left *The Fascist leader enters the Palazzo Quirinale in Rome where King Vittorio Emmanuele III invites him to form a ministry*
Journalist Mussolini's passport issued 21 December 1921 – his last

1923

The Football Association was formed in Britain in 1863 when the game was already being played in other parts of the world – British navvies building railways in Argentina, for instance, introduced the game to that country in the 1860s and a Buenos Aires Football Club was formed in 1865. But the first FA Cup competition was not held until 1871 when 15 English clubs entered, and the final between Wanderers and Royal Engineers was played at Kennington Oval, later the Surrey club's cricket ground. Wanderers won 1–0. Subsequent Cup Finals were played again at The Oval and at Lillie Road, Crystal Palace and Stamford Bridge – until 1923. A stadium was part of the complex of buildings planned for the British Empire Exhibition of 1924. It was ready the year before, and its first use was for the FA Cup Final of 1923.

In 1913 128,028 people had watched the Cup Final at the Crystal Palace, and at the first held at Wembley 126,047 paid for entrance, but many more rushed the turnstiles and climbed over the walls. It was reckoned that more than 150,000 were inside the ground to see Bolton Wanderers beat West Ham United two nil, with goals by David Jack and J R Smith. A policeman on a white horse helped control the crowds who invaded the brand new stadium 'like some tidal wave carried along by its own momentum'. The match for that reason was from then on known as the White Horse Final. All the streets to Wembley were jammed tight with hooting, overheated cars and shouting fans 'up for the cup' whirling rattles and clanging handbells swathed in coloured scarves and cloth caps. Finally the police managed to restore order, but the kick off was forty minutes late. Among those kept waiting was that inveterate soccer fan His Majesty King George V. After that the FA limited attendance to 100,000 ticket holders.

Crowds invade the ground to watch the first football Cup Final to be played in Wembley Stadium

FINAL WEEKS OF £7,000 FILM CONTEST = See Page 5

SUNDAY · PICTORIAL

SALE MORE THAN DOUBLE THAT OF ANY OTHER SUNDAY PICTURE PAPER

No. 424. SUNDAY, APRIL 29, 1923 [24 PAGES] Twopence.

WEMBLEY STADIUM STORMED BY EXCITED CUP FINAL CROWDS

'The business of America is business,' declared Calvin Coolidge when he became Republican (right-wing) president of the USA on the death of Warren Harding, the most incompetent and most corrupt of all American presidents to date. Coolidge's hesitation to curb business excesses and profiteering was largely responsible for the Wall Street Crash of 1929 and the subsequent world economic depression but, in contrast to Harding, he was completely honest and based his policy on a return to 'normalcy'.

In Britain the coalition Government of Liberals and Tories under Liberal prime minister Lloyd George, which had won the war, continued in power until 1922 when some Conservatives led by Stanley Baldwin felt the time had come to fight an election as an independent party again. Lloyd George resigned, Bonar Law became prime minister and at once called an election at which the Tories won 347 seats to Labour's 142. Bonar Law retired in 1923 and was succeeded by the reliable, pipe-smoking Stanley Baldwin determined, not unlike Coolidge in the US, to keep his head and keep Britain on an even keel.

When he resigned in January 1924 Ramsay Macdonald formed Britain's first Labour Government.

Spain had come through the war unscathed but the power of the Spanish monarchy was threatened by a call for autonomy from Catalonia. In 1921 riffs killed 12,000 Spanish troops at Anual in Morocco. King Alfonso XIII was under growing pressure, and had to give tacit approval to General Miguel Primo de Rivera taking over on 13 September 1923. Once in power, de Rivera set himself up as a dictator, dissolved Parliament, suspended trial by jury, censored the press, imprisoned all democratic elements and put the country under martial law. He was forced to resign in 1930.

At the end of the Great War, in which she was on the losing side, the Ottoman Empire found herself on the point of being invaded by both Greece and Italy. But for many Turks the Sultan having to sign a humiliating peace treaty which reimposd European financial control was even more insufferable. Leader of the Young Turks in refusing to accept such a state of affairs was Mustafa Kemal (Kemal Ataturk) who not only drove out the French and Greeks, but forced the British to withdraw the imposed peace settlement and negotiate a new one as between equals. In 1923 Kemal became head of a Turkish republic which abolished the caliphate, secularised the law, abandoned the Moslem calendar and changed the old Islamic life of Turkey out of all recognition.

Right *Stanley Baldwin, British Conservative prime minister who resigned at the end of the year*

Above right *King Alfonso XIII of Spain from whom General Primo de Rivera took over power (with the monarch's permission) in 1923*

Far right *Calvin Coolidge, President of the United States*

DAILY HERALD

LATE LONDON EDITION

No. 2,488 (No. 1,495—New Series)   LONDON, WEDNESDAY, JANUARY 23, 1924.   ONE PENNY

FIRST BRITISH LABOUR CABINET

MR. MACDONALD NOW PREMIER

Rapid Developments Follow on Mr. Baldwin's Resignation

AUDIENCES WITH THE KING

Three Peers in the Government : Admiralty Provides a Surprise

WHY CABINET IS LARGE ONE

Plans for Working on Business-like Lines

MEETING TO-DAY

RAIL STRIKE LEADERS PROPOSE PARLEY

But Managers Insist on Acceptance of Wages Board's Award

"DISCUSS DIFFERENCES"

LENIN DIES SUDDENLY

POIGNANT SCENE IN THE SOVIET

A LONG SILENCE

MOSCOW MOURNS GREAT LEADER

A DAY OF QUICK CHANGES

Mr. MacDonald Shows He is Well Prepared

INDUSTRY SLOWS DOWN

How to avoid 'flu

1924

DAILY HERALD

LENIN DIES SUDDENLY

POIGNANT SCENE IN THE SOVIET

A LONG SILENCE

MOSCOW MOURNS GREAT LEADER

Nicolai Lenin (Vladimir Ilyitch Oulianoff) died at 6.50 on Monday evening at Gorky, in the hills near Moscow.

He had seemed to be recovering from his long illness—the aftermath of his attempted assassination in 1918; but suddenly on Monday afternoon he became worse. Paralysis of the respiratory organs set in. At 5.30 breathing became difficult. He lost consciousness, and died at 6.50.

The All-Russian Soviet Congress was in session yesterday morning at the Bolshoi Theatre in Moscow, when Kalenin—the President of the Republic—tears streaming down his face—told the news. The great assembly rose and stood for five minutes in silence, very many of them weeping. And from the theatre word spread through Moscow—already draped in black in honour of the heroes of 1905.

Right *Lenin and Sverdlov looking up to the Marx and Engels monument after its unveiling in Moscow in November 1918*

Master strategist of the Russian Revolution – code-name 'Lenin'

Secret agents and underground conspirators love code names. Vladimir Ilyich Ulyanov hid his true identity from the czar's police under the code name Lenin. When Mensheviks and Bolsheviks were contesting for the leadership of the Russian Revolution which overthrew the Czarist regime of the Romanovs in 1917, his forceful personality, backed by an iron will, formulated a definite plan of action to be executed not by 'the masses' but a small, fanatical Bolshevik minority. He wanted nothing to do with the provisional government of Alexander Kerensky, and cried, 'All power to the Soviets!' From then on he was the master strategist of the revolution, and Leon Trotsky the man who put the plans into action, urging world revolution while Lenin concentrated on the organisation of a Socialist Russia.

Lenin only had seven years to fulfil his mission. Leading a five-man Politburo (Lenin, Trotsky, Stalin, Kamenev and Bukharin) he set the pattern of the Union of Soviet Socialist Republics which has survived to today. In May 1922 he had a stroke and then two more. He died in January 1924 and was succeeded by the General Secretary of the Central Committee of the Communist Party, Josef Stalin.

Between the wars some 65 million people in America (population 130 million), and more than 20 million in Britain, went to the cinema every week. Tastes in films varied. Those who went to the cinema for romance never missed a film starring Rudolph Valentino who sprung to fame in 1921 in *The Four Horsemen of the Apocalypse* followed by *The Sheik* and *The Son of the Sheik*. For five years he had the world's female population at his feet, and when he died in 1926 his funeral was a national event.

Whatever their preferences however, two names outside a cinema attracted well-nigh everybody – Walt Disney and Charlie Chaplin.

'Creator of a new language of art who has brought the joy of deep laughter to millions' was the eulogy which accompanied Yale University's conferment of an honorary MA on the creator of Mickey Mouse and Donald Duck. 'By touching the heart of humanity without distinction of race, he has served as ambassador of international goodwill.' He made the first animated sound-film *Steamboat Willie* in 1928.

Charlie Chaplin, music-hall comedian from Kennington, made 71 short silent films in Hollywood between 1914 and 1923 when in 1925 he made his first full-length film featuring himself as the tramp, *The Gold Rush*. At the New York premiere the United Artists sales manager told him, 'Charlie, I guarantee that it will gross at least six million dollars.' And it did.

The following year a friend told Chaplin he had witnessed synchronisation of sound in films and predicted it would shortly revolutionise the whole film industry. Charlie thought MGM's full-length all-singing, all-talking *Broadway Melody* 'a cheap dull affair' but acknowledged it was a stupendous box-office success. 'That started it,' he wrote in his *Autobiography*; 'overnight every theatre began wiring for sound. That was the twilight of silent films.' But in that fading light he produced three more of them, *The Circus* (1928), *City Lights* (1931) and *Modern Times* (1936). But everyone else, from *The Jazz Singer* and 1928 onwards, was making talkies.

Charlie Chaplin

PICTURE SHOW, December 21st, 1929.   REGISTERED AT THE G.P.O. AS A NEWSPAPER

AL JOLSON AND BENITA HUME— ART PLATES INSIDE.

Vol. 22. No. 555.   DECEMBER 21st. 1929.   Every Saturday 2D

Picture Show

JOHN GILBERT

Have the Talkies Killed Screen Romance?

See page 10.

Rudolph Valentino and Wilma Banky in The Sheik

1925

Above *Douglas Fairbanks and Rudolph Valentino with Jackie Coogan*
Below *Charlie Chaplin has a bout with his* Gold Rush *partner burly Mack Swain*

Above *Mary Pickford, the World's Sweetheart, with her husband Douglas Fairbanks* Below *Starting work on* Modern Times, *Charlie Chaplin and Paulette Goddard, whom he married in 1936*

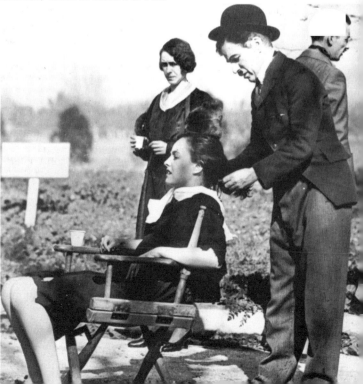

Mary Pickford with Ramon Navarro, star of the silent Ben Hur.

Walt Disney, creator of Mickey Mouse and Donald Duck

1926

North Mail

Newcastle Daily Chronicle

CITY EDITION.

No. 21,236. [Established 1858.] TUESDAY, MAY 4, 1926. PRICE ONE PENNY.

DELICIOUS FRENCH COFFEE.
RED WHITE & BLUE

ARTHUR WHITE & CO., "THE HANDYMAN STORE."

BIGGEST STRIKE IN BRITAIN'S HISTORY BEGUN.

N.U.R.'S FINAL INSTRUCTION.

"PERFECT ORDER" APPEAL.

CURTAILED SERVICE.

L.N.E.R COMPANY'S HOPE.

SOLDIERS' LEAVE STOPPED.

ACTIVITY IN NAVAL AND ARMY CIRCLES.

EMERGENCY STEP.

NEARLY 5,000,000 WORKERS INVOLVED IN STOPPAGE.

MR. J. H. THOMAS MAKES FINAL BUT FUTILE MEDIATION EFFORT.

PREMIER'S REPLY TO CHALLENGE

EMERGENCY PLANS OF GOVERNMENT.

SAFEGUARDING FOOD & TRANSPORT SERVICES.

APPEALS TO PUBLIC.

WIDE POWERS OF THE STATE.

LAND, WORKS, STORES CAN BE SEIZED.

COMPLETE CONTROL.

TRAMS, SHIPS, PORTS AND RAILWAYS.

The British Government were ready for the General Strike when it came in 1926. During the war, when labour was short, trade unions had become very powerful and high wages had given their members plenty of money to spend. In 1920 the Coalition Government passed a measure authorising the government of the day to make special regulations whenever an Order in Council declared a state of emergency. A national strike by coal miners seeking higher pay and shorter working hours was averted in July 1924 by the prime minister, Stanley Baldwin, offering to subsidise the coal industry with £10 million and set up a Royal Commission to report on its economic condition. But in April 1926 the mine owners still insisted that, whatever the commission found, they had to *reduce* wages or close the pits. The miners put their case in the hands of the Trades Union Council who, on 1 May 1926, called a strike of railways and transport workers, the printing and paper union members and many in the metal, engineering and building trades. On 3 May the compositors of the *Daily Mail* refused to set an article they considered insulting to the workers. Using the emergency powers provided by the 1920 legislation, the Government organised a fleet of private motors and lorries to keep public passenger, and goods, transport going. Clerks and undergraduates volunteered to drive buses and trains – amateur 'blacklegs'. Home Secretary Joynson-Hicks ('Jix') called for thousands of special constables to help the police control the crowds – 50,000 in London alone. He ordered two battalions of Guards and ten armoured cars to secure food supplies lying at London Docks being picketed by strikers; and authorised a submarine to be brought into the basin to generate current by her engines when the docks electricity supply was threatened. With no newspapers the Government published a daily *British Gazette*.

Though there was no violence or bloodshed the General Strike of 1926 was a direct and dangerous challenge to the authority of Parliament and Government. Sir John Simon declared it 'illegal' which the Labour Party vigorously contested. In the belief that the reorgansation proposed by the Royal Commission would be effectively adopted the TUC called off the strike on 12 May, though the miners were not to return to work until November.

Top *Striking railwaymen at St Pancras, London*

Centre *Special Constables are sworn in to help control crowds*

Far left *Home Secretary Joynson-Hicks organized mounted 'Specials' such as these to supplement the regular police force*

Left *Food convoy passes down Holborn, London*

1927

While the British Sir John Alcock and Arthur Whitten Brown were the first *couple* to fly the Atlantic non-stop (to Ireland only), the 25 year old American Charles Lindbergh was the first to fly non-stop *solo* – and with the extra distance of New York to Paris. It was eight years after Alcock and Brown's pioneering journey, and was spurred once again by the offer of a money prize – $25,000. Between 1924 and 1925 Lindbergh had been an instructor in a US Army Flying School, and in 1926 got a job as an airmail pilot between St Louis and Chicago. But he had his sights set on greater things, and when he heard about the prize for the first man to fly solo to Paris, he made the rounds of the St Louis business fraternity and persuaded them to put up the money to finance the project. Impressed by his enthusiasm and his obvious skill as an aviator, they gave him what he wanted. And on 20 May 1927 he took off in his monoplane *Spirit of St Louis* and won the $25,000 by successfully crossing the Atlantic non-stop on his own and landing safely in the French capital across the English Channel. It was a flight which captured the imagination of all America – indeed of all the world – and on his return to the USA he received a 'ticker-tape' reception as a national hero. The same year he was awarded the Medal of Honour.

He became technical adviser to a number of airlines, and once more hit the headlines when, in 1932, the Lindbergh Baby was kidnapped and later found murdered. Americans were less sympathetic when they learnt of his right-wing inclinations and his support for the Nazi German Government by which he was decorated in 1938. He flew some 50 combat missions in the Pacific during World War 2 however; he then became consultant to Pan American World Airways, and died in 1974.

Right *The* Spirit of St Louis *in which Lindbergh made the first non-stop solo flight across the North Atlantic*

Inset *American transatlantic airman Charles Lindbergh*

Below *Lindbergh at Croydon airport where British crowds acclaimed his feat*

1929

People left their native countries to settle in the United States of America to share in a standard of living far above any they were likely to achieve by years of hard toil at home. In the 1920s the image of America as the Land of Opportunity was justified, but the boom was largely artificial, fed by rash speculation in securities on the stock exchange and lacking sufficient cover. In 1928 businessmen began experiencing difficulty in obtaining short term loans, and sensed that the boom was about to end. Domestic prosperity and the confidence it engendered gave America ample capital for export, but when that confidence began to wane it had to call in the many loans it had made to Europe.

On 23 October 1929 fear of the probity of a number of firms led to panic selling on the New York Stock Exchange situated in Wall Street. Thirteen million shares changed hands in one day. Speculators lost their heads as share prices collapsed, and many more sober-minded citizens with family investments found they had been ruined overnight. No longer did the world have quite the same respect for, or confidence in, American business acumen. American overseas investment dried up. The Wall Street Crash of 1929 led to the Great Depression which lasted to 1932 and was world-wide, with the failure of banks, the collapse of industrial and commercial enterprises and millions of unemployed.

Where the crash that shook the world got its name – Wall Street, the site of the New York stock exchange

When the Fédération Internationale de Football Associations (FIFA) was formed in Paris on 21 May 1904, without the participation of the inventors of the game, Britain, its six founder members, Belgium, Denmark, France, Holland, Spain and Switzerland inserted a clause in its constitution stating that it alone had the right to organise a World Football Championship. But FIFA could not bring itself actually to stage one for 26 years, though throughout all that time the matter was frequently discussed. During the FIFA Congress in Amsterdam during the 1928 Olympic Games they thought they had hesitated too long; they would hold a tournament for a 'World Cup', they declared, in 1930. The European clubs took for granted that the first would be held in Europe, and made no bones of their astonishment at the association's choice of Uruguay on the other side of the world, which then could only be reached after a long and expensive sea voyage. When most of the European nations boycotted the tournament, the South Americans threatened to form their own association. Uruguay's selection was influenced by her proposal to celebrate in 1930 the anniversary of her independence from Spanish rule, and their offer to build a new Centenary Stadium for the event, which however, in spite of two year's notice, was not ready for the first match on Sunday 13 July between Mexico and France. Thirteen nations including the USA finally agreed to compete, and four of them were European – Belgium, France, Roumania and Yugoslavia.

France won that first match 4–1, despite having their goal keeper carried off. They lost to Argentina by the only goal scored after 80 minutes. When the referee blew his whistle with five minutes still to go and the teams had gone off, the crowd insisted on his recalling the players from their dressing rooms and finishing the game – but there was no more scoring. The stadium was ready for Uruguay's game against Peru on 18 July. Yugoslavia was the only European nation to get through to the semi-finals; Belgium failed to score against Paraguay; the USA teams won both their matches 3–0. The final between South American neighbours Uruguay and Argentina watched by a crowd of 90,000, was exciting, entertaining and surprisingly sporting. Uruguay scored first; by half time Argentina were ahead 2–1; in the second half Uruguay got three goals to be the first winners of the World Cup. The host nation, celebrating both its independence from Spain and its soccer triumph, turned Montevideo into a raving carnival.

Top *Jules Rimet presents the World Cup to the president of the Uruguayan Football Association at the end of the match*

Centre *Hugging 1930's style – Uruguayans celebrate victory*

Right *The Uruguay team who won the first football World Cup by beating Argentina in Montevideo in 1930*

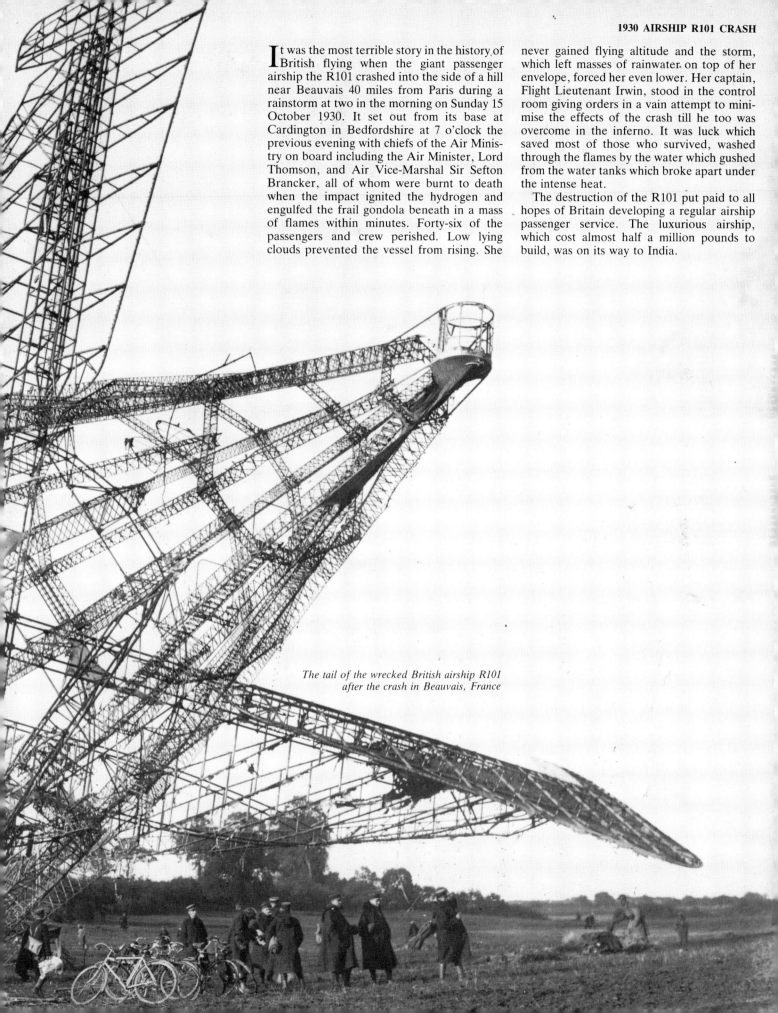

It was the most terrible story in the history of British flying when the giant passenger airship the R101 crashed into the side of a hill near Beauvais 40 miles from Paris during a rainstorm at two in the morning on Sunday 15 October 1930. It set out from its base at Cardington in Bedfordshire at 7 o'clock the previous evening with chiefs of the Air Ministry on board including the Air Minister, Lord Thomson, and Air Vice-Marshal Sir Sefton Brancker, all of whom were burnt to death when the impact ignited the hydrogen and engulfed the frail gondola beneath in a mass of flames within minutes. Forty-six of the passengers and crew perished. Low lying clouds prevented the vessel from rising. She never gained flying altitude and the storm, which left masses of rainwater on top of her envelope, forced her even lower. Her captain, Flight Lieutenant Irwin, stood in the control room giving orders in a vain attempt to minimise the effects of the crash till he too was overcome in the inferno. It was luck which saved most of those who survived, washed through the flames by the water which gushed from the water tanks which broke apart under the intense heat.

The destruction of the R101 put paid to all hopes of Britain developing a regular airship passenger service. The luxurious airship, which cost almost half a million pounds to build, was on its way to India.

The tail of the wrecked British airship R101
after the crash in Beauvais, France

1931

At the end of the 19th century Tsarist Russia sought to extend its influence over the Far Eastern borders of its vast empire, in particular Korea and Manchuria, and in doing so were in direct conflict with Japan. Between 1896 and 1900 the Russians built the Chinese Eastern Railway through Manchuria to Vladivostock, and, after the Boxer Rising of 1900, occupied Manchuria. In 1904, after 18 months fighting, the Japanese turned the Russians out; but by the Treaty of Portsmouth of the following year both Japanese and Russians agreed to give Manchuria back to the Chinese.

Under the treaty Japanese troops were allowed to guard the South Manchuria Railway, and in September 1931 they took it into their heads to seize the town of Mukden. Within five months, in spite of protests from the League of Nations, the Japanese had occupied the whole of Manchuria and expelled the Chinese authorities. The following February they set up the puppet State of Manchukuo which was at once recognised by Germany and Italy.

The invasion was the first major challenge to the authority of the League of Nations. The United States wanted to invoke the 9-Power Pact upholding the integrity of China, but Britain opposed the idea. Lack of collective action on this occasion encouraged the dictator countries to risk the aggression which snow-balled into World War 2. The Mukden Incident ended any pretence to party government in Japan and set the nation on its militaristic path which began so victoriously but ended in the defeat of 1945 when Manchuria was once more restored to China.

Low's prophecy

UNEASY STREET

Left *Refugees seek safety in the foreign concessions in Shanghai.* Above *Japanese tanks in Shanghai prepare for an attack.* Below left *A British armoured car patrols the streets of the International Settlement in Shanghai.*

The internationally acceptable means of exchange was gold – the 'gold standard'. In the 1930s all the countries of Europe and the United States struggled to keep the value of their currencies steady in relation to gold. In insisting on balancing their books however they took to deflationary policies which only had the effect of cutting demand and causing a drastic fall in industrial production. By 1933 all the major currencies except the French were off gold. Britain came off it on 21 September 1931 when the National Government, headed by Ramsay McDonald the Labour leader, formed to prevent Britain doing just that, had to bring in a law stopping anyone sending gold out of the country for six months. It suspended a 1925 Act which

required the sale of gold at a fixed price. From now on it could float and find its own level; control was removed. The rate of interest on loans – the bank rate – was raised one and a half points to six per cent. The stock exchanges were closed for the day to enable the brokers and jobbers to make the necessary adjustments. The public, most of whom had little idea what it was all about, were placated by the negative information that there would be no sharp increase in prices and no shortage of food. Maybe there was no need for alarm but, as one writer put it, it meant the dethronement of one old idol of liberal economics – 'the social gains of the 1920s, when many people's standard of living had improved, were wiped out.'

1932

The world's first motorways were in Germany – *autobahnen*. The planning and building of these great new highways was a proud achievement, and provided work for many thousands of Germans at a time when unemployment was still a serious threat to the consolidation of the new National Socialist dictatorship. Moreover they were the prototype for motorways elsewhere, and the Germans seized every opportunity to show them off to foreign visitors as an example of how the Third Reich was attending to the peaceful development of its economy, and what could be done with a disciplined workforce under state control. Britain was among the countries which showed an interest. After the committee of the Automobile Association had given His Excellency Joachim von Ribbentrop, the German Ambassador, honorary membership – like AA Secretary Sir Stenson Cooke he had once been a wine salesman — the AA received an invitation from Dr Todt, Inspector General of the German Highways, in April 1937 to join a road delegation to Germany composed of MPs, county surveyors and others to see the autobahn system at first hand. The AA thought British needs would be met however by improving and reconstructing the existing main arteries rather than building special roads in virgin country for the exclusive use of motor traffic.

Britain had to wait 20 years for its first *autobahnen*, with the opening of the Preston By-Pass and the M1 from London to Birmingham in the 1950s.

Hitler the autobahn builder

Britain's first 'Hunger March' was in October 1922, but the circumstances of the World Slump which prompted the second in 1929 were very much more serious. Stemming from the Wall Street Crash of that year, world trade rapidly declined and confidence in the international money market was undermined. In the two years following 1929 Britain's exports fell from £729 million to £309 million. Foreign assets held in London, the financial capital of the world, were withdrawn. With less demand for exports (particularly ships) and a fall in internal consumption, factories closed and industrial production fell.

There had been considerable unrest among the unemployed during the last years of Stanley Baldwin's premiership from 1924 to 1929 – the Liberal programme at the 1929 election was summarised in the pamphlet *We Can Conquer Unemployment*. The unemployed employed themselves in calling attention to their plight in the way they had done in 1922. One morning in January 1929 thousands of Glasgow workers gave a rousing send-off to 200 men representing Scottish coalfields, shipyards, textile mills and fishing who set out to walk to London, each with a haversack full of clothes and a blanket for sleeping at night. A banner reading 'Welcome to the Hunger Marchers' was slung across the plinth of Nelson's Column in Trafalgar Square for their arrival. Another group of marchers composed of unemployed shipyard workers from Jarrow arrived the next year.

The Depression wiped out most of the social gains of the 1920s by which the standard of living had been raised for so many. Unemployment was worst in America and Germany; but in Britain it reached three million in 1933, by which time all the major currencies, except France's, were off gold. Tragically the world was given no chance fully to recover from this deep-seated Economic Crisis before it was overwhelmed by a second World War.

Preis 20 Pfennig
Ausland: 35 Pfennig

8 JAHRGANG / FOLGE 40 / SAMSTAG, 7. OKTOBER 1935

JB Illustrierter Beobachter

VERLAG FRZ. EHER NACHF., 8/P MÜNCHEN 2 NO

Far left *Hunger Marchers pass through the village of Codicote en route for the seat of government*

Left *Jarrow marchers headed by a brass band march on London*

Above *Once in London, unemployed who had marched from Glasgow, Jarrow and other depressed areas staged demonstrations in Hyde Park*

1933

In the United States the depression was fast sinking into despair when in 1932 Franklin D Roosevelt won the first of four successive presidential elections on the strength of offering Americans not only hope but the promise of action. The confidence with which FDR put his ideas across convinced Americans that no economic problem was insoluble if tackled with courage and imagination. Wealthy and upper-class, Roosevelt, a Democrat (left wing), was on each occasion elected president by an absolute majority of the popular vote – the first time that had happened to a candidate of that party since the 1860s. If his 'New Deal' did not have all the answers, and the gloom had not been entirely dispelled by the time they came to the help of the Allies in a second World War, it revitalised capitalism and extended the power of the Federal Government in an unprecedented way. Under the New Deal millions of central government dollars were provided for public works such as the Tennessee Valley hydro-electric scheme. Finance was strictly regulated and unemployment relief introduced with insurance.

In the view of J M Roberts the New Deal 'changed the course of American constitutional and political history as nothing else had done since the Civil War'. Whatever else, the free world recognised intervention in the economy by the US federal government as a democratic alternative to fascist and communist dogmas, which gave hope to more than the Americans.

CLOSE OF PLAY EDITION LATE NIGHT FINAL

Evening Standard

No. 34,020 LONDON, FRIDAY, SEPTEMBER 1, 1933 ONE PENNY

NEW PROCLAMATION BY HITLER

To 20,000 Nazis at "Congress of Victory"

FIERY ATTACK ON THE JEWS

Discovery of Two Communist Plots

TWENTY thousand Nazis at the party "Congress of Victory" at Nuremberg to-day heard a proclamation from Hitler in which he declared that he would continue his attack on enemies until they were "entirely destroyed."

The Nuremberg police declare that they have discovered in a Communist's house a parcel posted in Berlin containing enough typhus bacilli to cause terrible havoc among the population of the city.

Another Communist "plot," it is suggested, is responsible for large quantities of high explosives found near two bridges over the Rhine at Dusseldorf.

Nazis arriving in Nuremberg by train for to-day's great Hitlerite Congress.
—Picture by Wire.

VISCOUNT SNOWDEN DENIES STORY OF INTRIGUE

"Unmitigated Lie" Reply to Commander Kenworthy

VISCOUNT SNOWDEN to-day denounced as an "unmitigated lie" a story of an intrigue for leadership of the Labour Party told by Lieutenant-commander Kenworthy in an interview.

Gold at New High Record To-day:
£6 10s. 8¼d. an Ounce

From Our City Correspondent

THE price of gold rose to a new high record to-day—£6 10s. 8¼d. per fine ounce.

This is 1s. 1¼d. higher than yesterday's figure.

Liner Passenger With Suitcases Full of Opium

Sent to Prison and Fined £250

From Our Own Correspondent
SOUTHAMPTON, Friday.

Adolf Hitler, now ruler of Germany, outlines his plans for recovery and revenge in a first broadcast to the German people

Above left *The Reichstag in flames*

After the German elections of 1930 the National Socialists (Nazis, for short) became the country's second largest political party. In 1932, when they won 230 seats, their leader (*Führer*) Adolf Hitler came second to Field Marshal Hindenburg in the presidential election. Their success was largely due to the belief that with six million unemployed and the Weimar republic doing nothing to bring them relief, a group of communists were planning to mount a revolution, an event which could only be prevented by a firm Nazi government.

When only a month after Hindenburg had reluctantly named Hitler chancellor, fire destroyed the parliament building in Berlin (the Reichstag) on 27 February 1933, the new government claimed it was the work of communist arsonists as the first move in the revolution which they had forecast. A half-witted Dutchman called Van der Lubbe, who was found wandering round the ruins, was arrested, tried and condemned to death. When a Bulgarian called Dimitrov was also tried for complicity in the burning of the Reichstag, he saved himself by brazenly accusing his accusers of starting the blaze to provide themselves with an excuse to pass decrees against 'the reds'.

Whatever the spur, with their Enabling Act of 24 March 1933 the Nazi regime at a stroke deprived parliament of all control over legislation, the budget, the constitution and foreign policy, and made Germany 'totalitarian' in the fullest sense of the word, with total suspension of democratic liberties.

The burnt-out ruins of the German Parliament building (Reichstag) in Berlin

THE DAILY MIRROR, Friday, January 12, 1934.

Daily Mirror

Broadcasting - Page 12

THE DAILY PICTURE NEWSPAPER WITH THE LARGEST NET SALE

HUNTING A RADIO MONSTER —Page 2

No. 9,401 Registered at the G.P.O. as a Newspaper.   FRIDAY, JANUARY 12, 1934   One Penny

PARIS NIGHT OF WILD RIOTING

700 Arrests—Hundreds Hurt

M.P.s ALSO HAVE ANGRY SCENES

IN wild Stavisky rioting outside the French Parliament last night police arrested 700 people. Hundreds of police and demonstrators were injured.

Inside the Chamber there were also scenes of disorder. "Graft" charges were made.

The Public Prosecutor, brother-in-law of the Premier, was accused, and the Premier retorted: "I will see justice is done without consideration of family ties."

The debate is being resumed to-day, but it is believed that the Government is now safe from defeat.

Trees as Weapons

Five thousand people—including women and boys—took part in the rioting.

A column of demonstrators in the Boulevard Saint Germain tried to reach the Chamber. They were driven back by the police, but re-formed and were driven back a second time, says Reuter.

Railings around young trees were torn up by the rioters and thrown on to the tramlines. Trees, too, were uprooted and used to trip up the police.

In the Boulevard Raspail the demonstrators demolished a workmen's shelter, and erected a barricade in the centre of the road.

At the corner of the Rue de Sevres and the Boulevard Raspail another pitched battle occurred, and several police were injured.

Another report says that the rioters charged towards the Chamber with cries of "Down with the thieves" and "Assassins."

They were loudly cheered by the spectators in the windows and on the balconies as they were hustled into police vans.

So serious did the position become that the police, in order to prevent their lines being broken, had to call upon the fire brigade to turn their hoses on the crowd.

"Thanks to Graft"

The scene inside the French Parliament was scarcely less exciting during the seven-hour debate on the Stavisky fraud.

Every deputy was in his place—for the first time for about four years—and many of them were in ugly mood. At one time the Chamber was in complete disorder.

M. Lagrange started the attack. He blamed the judicial authorities for delaying the proceedings against Stavisky, says the Exchange.

"How could Stavisky, during six years and even when he was on bail, succeed in dazzling Paris and in stealing millions?" asked M. Lagrange. "Thanks to graft," he replied.

M. Bonnaure, the withdrawal of whose Parliamentary immunity has been asked for by the examining magistrate, when he tried to speak, says the Exchange, was greeted with cries of "Go and pay your tailor." (Stavisky had paid his tailor to the tune of £187, comments Reuter.)

Premier's Pledge

M. Dommange demanded to know what the finance section of the Prosecutor's office did. If Stavisky had not been left at liberty he would not have been able to carry out so many swindles.

If he was at liberty at the end of last year it was because the Public Prosecutor had not done his duty, he said.

Turning to M. Chautemps, says the Central News, he declared: "If there is an inquiry you cannot preside, for one thing because of your

(Continued on page 3)

Police arresting demonstrators in Paris last night. Right: A seat wrenched up and placed across tramlines

Firemen with one of the pieces of railing torn up and used as weapons by the rioters.

DUCHESS OF ALBA DIES AT 34

One of Most Beautiful Women in Spain

Reputed to be one of the most beautiful women in Spain, the Duchess of Alba, wife of the Duke of Alba and Berwick, died yesterday in Madrid at the age of thirty-four, says the Central News.

She was well known in London and was married to the Duke, at the Spanish Embassy here, by Cardinal Bourne in October, 1920.

There is one daughter, Cayetana, who is heiress to sixty titles of nobility.

The Duchess has been in indifferent health for some years. She was the daughter of the Duke and Duchess of Aliga.

A very distant relation of Mr. Winston Churchill, the Duke of Alba is a descendant of a sister of the first Duke of Marlborough.

Last year the Republican Government of Spain confiscated the great estates, houses in Madrid and country seats owned by the Duke of Alba.

The Duchess of Alba.

The exposure of corruption and inefficiency in French government circles brought about by the Stavisky Affair in 1934 took France to the brink of civil war. Exploited by French communists, fascists and royalists, all of whom were equally disgusted at the inability of the weak, left-wing administration of radical Edouard Herriot to cope with the worsening economic situation, there was non-stop rioting in the streets of Paris by the ex-servicemen terrorists the Croix de Feu in the first week of February 1934 which led to a general strike. For it appeared that in his many dubious speculative activities, Serge Stavisky, a small-town French company promoter of Russian-Jewish origin, had the protection of several government ministers and deputies who made sure he was never prosecuted. When he was accused of issuing fraudulent bonds on the security of the municipal pawnshop in Bayonne, the government refused to hold a parliamentary enquiry. When a high official in the Public Prosecutor's Office in Paris was found murdered, it was said he had been killed to prevent the truth coming out about others in high places. When Stavisky himself committed suicide, it was rumoured he had been shot to stop him making any further scandalous disclosures.

Top left *A witness is cross-examined on the fourth day of the Stavisky trial*

Top right *The mayor of Bayonne defends himself vigorously during the sensational procès Stavisky*

Bottom left *Serge Stavisky, accused of issuing fraudulent bonds, had government protection*

Bottom right *Arlette Stavisky, wife of the financier at the centre of the scandal, in court with her counsel*

With the death of Sun Yat-sen in 1925, China entered a period of some confusion. He had wanted to broaden the basis of the Chinese Nationalist Party (Kuomintang) to include Communists, in which event it was likely to come under Russian control. But in 1926 the man who had been his chief-of-staff, Chiang Kai-shek, broke with Soviet Russia and dismissed their advisers. In 1927 Chiang set up his own government in Nanking, supported by Chinese businessmen and foreign bankers in Shanghai; but those who favoured communism retained their identity and continued to take their orders from Moscow. Their leader was Mao Tse-tung who had become a communist convert while a student at Peking University and now organised a peasant revolutionary army in the south of China. But by successfully subduing the remaining warlords in the north and west of China, by 1928 Chiang's Kuomintang government was in undisputed control of the whole country. He introduced a new constitution with himself as president acting through a State Council, and the provinces governed by councils under chairmen appointed by Peking. In 1931 he had no alternative but to concede Manchuria to the Japanese who overran the country with little difficulty.

Mao Tse-tung's communism meant rural revolution. He could never have persuaded town dwellers to embark on a Long March, the tactic he decided to employ when, after proclaiming a Chinese Soviet Republic in the southern province of Kiangsi in 1931, the forces of General Chiang Kai-shek's Kuomintang surrounded them. The only thing to do

was to break out of the cordon if they were not to surrender themselves and the ideas which had inspired the Revolution. Three years of harrassment by the general's army led them near to capitulation but their spirits were raised, and their future ensured, when in 1934 Mao led 90,000 of them out on the 8,000 mile trek which became a central part of Chinese Communist legend.

They set out northwest for the Shensi province on the Yellow River but after a year's gruelling slog through the mountains only 20,000 arrived. At Yenan they consolidated

and continued to resist the Kuomintang until 1937 when they agreed on a truce to allow the two sides to join forces in repelling China's common enemy, Japan.

Above Mao Tse-tung (second from left) with fellow communists in 1927. **Right** Chou En-lai joins Mao on the Long March to Yenan. **Right inset** General Chiang Kai-skek, whose Kuomintang forces encircled the communist followers of Mao Tse-tung in south China. **Left inset** The young revolutionary – Mao Tse-tung in 1925. **Below** Sun Yat-sen, who died in 1925, with his daughter

1935

Evening Standard

To-morrow's Weather —
Unsettled; strong winds.

Lighting-up Time
To-day, 7.36 p.m.

No. 34,666   LONDON, WEDNESDAY, OCTOBER 2, 1935   ONE PENNY

ITALIANS IN ABYSSINIA
Emperor Announces Invasion is Begun

MUSSOLINI CALLS VAST TEST MOBILISATION TO-NIGHT

Abyssinian Chiefs Ordered to Prepare to March Immediately

"VIOLATION" WARNING TO LEAGUE

THE ABYSSINIAN GOVERNMENT ANNOUNCED TO-DAY THAT ITALIAN TROOPS HAD ENTERED ABYSSINIAN TERRITORY AT THE MOUNTAIN MUSSA ALI, CLOSE TO FRENCH SOMALILAND.

THEY PROTESTED TO THE LEAGUE AGAINST THIS "VIOLATION OF THE FRONTIER," AND ASKED FOR A COMMISSION TO BE SENT AT ONCE TO ESTABLISH THE VIOLATION.

THE EMPEROR, IT IS LEARNED, HAS WARNED HIS PRINCIPAL CHIEFTAINS TO PREPARE TO MARCH "AT A MOMENT'S NOTICE."

MINISTERS AT THE PALACE

Two Meetings at Downing-Street

IMPORTANT EVENTS IN THE ABYSSINIAN CRISIS TO-DAY WERE:

Two meetings of Cabinet Ministers were held at 10, Downing-street.

Sir Samuel Hoare, Foreign Secretary, and Viscount Halifax, Secretary for War, were received by the King at Buckingham Palace before the first meeting.

It is understood that the Cabinet were concerned with steps to be taken in the event of war in Abyssinia, which is now regarded as inevitable (writes the "Evening Standard" Political Correspondent).

Later the Prime Minister summoned a number of Ministers to a further meeting, which was attended by the heads of the

'Collective Security' was the in-phrase of the 1930s. The League of Nations who coined it had an opportunity of showing it was no empty phrase when in October 1935 Italian forces invaded Abyssinia (Ethiopia). Mussolini, the Italian leader, knew he was chancing his arm in trying to realise his dream of a new Roman empire, because he rightly reckoned that he would be opposed by France, Britain – and the League. But an adventure in Colonial Expansion was consistent with his view of Italy as a Big Power – and perhaps at the same time it would secure some of the Ethiopian raw materials which Italy lacked.

Britain committed herself firmly to Collective Security, and led the League in urging economic sanctions against Italy to deny her the means of waging war. The agreement specifically excluded oil however, and could do little to stop the advance of the Italian tanks and air bombers against the ill-armed and terrified Abyssinians. Their emperor, Haile Selassie, fled to Britain whose foreign secretary, Sir Samuel Hoare, agreed with Pierre Laval of France to allow Italy to keep two-thirds of its ill-gotten African Empire – the notorious Hoare-Laval Pact. The outcry which followed publication of the agreement forced Sir Samuel to resign. By May 1936 however the Duce's risky venture in 20th century imperialism had paid off, and he had secured the whole Abyssinian prize by force of arms.

Though Abyssinia/Ethiopia in the north east corner of Africa had been Christian for 14 centuries, until 1930 it had failed to keep

Haile Selassie, Emperor of Abyssinia, broadcasts a plea for help as his country is overrun by Fascist Italy

The Emperor Haile Selassie with the Duke of York on his last visit to London in 1929

Italian carabinieri and colonial troops make their way over the Tacasse river near Ogaden

abreast of 20th century civilisation. If they had lost the battle of Adowa in 1896 they might have become an Italian colony as other parts of the African continent had become German, British, French, Belgian, Spanish and Portuguese colonies in the great 'Scramble' for Africa. But as it was, they defeated the Italians at Adowa, and Ethiopia was for years the only independent people in Africa – and

suffered from it in terms of general backwardness both politically and socially.

But when in 1930 the Empress Zandito died she was succeeded by the 32-year old Haile Selassie who a year later introduced a new and more liberal constitution. He signed a treaty of friendship with Mussolini's new regime in Italy whose warlike watchwords 'Combattere, Obbedire, Credere', did not bode well for the

new relationship. Frontier incidents from neighbouring Italian Somaliland grew more frequent, culminating in a serious clash at the oasis of Walwal in December 1934 in which 100 Ethiopians and 30 Italian colonial troops were killed. The Italian army invaded Abyssinia, and in May 1936 captured the capital, Addis Abbaba. Haile Selassie went into temporary exile in England.

There was little resistance to the Italians' advance into the interior of Ethiopia – apart from the rivers

Italian colonial infantrymen captured during the final attack on the Abyssinian capital are marched through Addis Abbaba

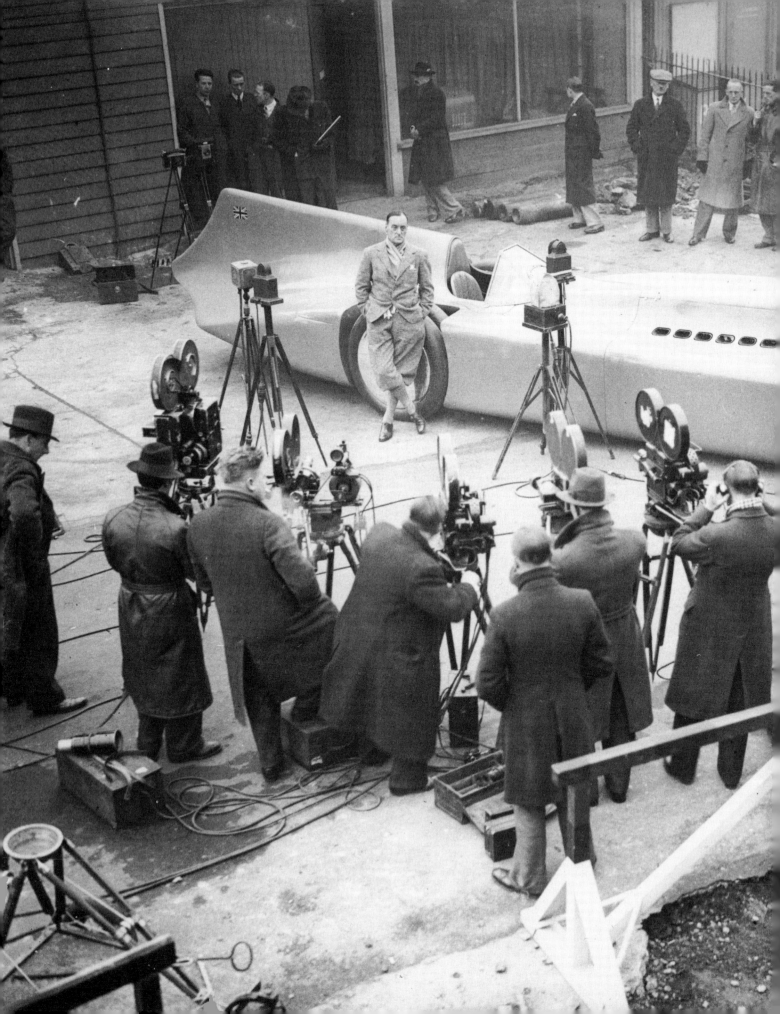

Sir Malcolm Campbell's first attempt to establish a land speed record in a specially built racing car caused a sensation in 1924, and it never ceased to be headline news as eight times again between that year and 1935 he set out to beat his own record – and never failed. By 1935 he had driven his monster 'Bluebird' at an official speed of 272 miles an hour, and in the latest version of the motor, which had an engine capable of developing 2,450 horse power (and no rockets), he hoped once more to go even faster – at least 300 mph. The eyes of all the world therefore – and of all the world's film news cameramen – were on him when he took the car across Bonneville Salt Flats near Salt Lake City, Utah, USA in that year on several runs at an average speed of 301.13 miles an hour. He then decided to call it a day, and to leave the beating of his last world land speed record to any other contender – and turned to boats. After 1935 Sir Malcolm Campbell broke the water speed record three times, raising it to 141.75 mph. He died in 1948 – in bed.

Left Bluebird, *the 2450 horse power motor car which Sir Malcolm Campbell drove at more than 300 miles an hour*

Sir Malcolm's car is towed to Bonneville Salt Flats in Utah, USA, before raising the world land speed record yet again

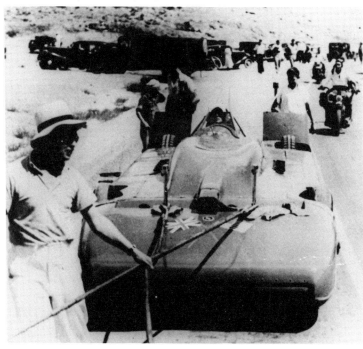

1936

Evening Standard

CLOSING CITY PRICES — FINAL NIGHT

No. 35,036   LONDON, THURSDAY, DECEMBER 10, 1936   ONE PENNY

THE KING ABDICATES
Duke of York Monarch

THE following message from his Majesty King Edward VIII. was read in the House of Commons this afternoon by the Speaker:

AFTER LONG AND ANXIOUS CONSIDERATION I HAVE DETERMINED TO RENOUNCE THE THRONE TO WHICH I SUCCEEDED ON THE DEATH OF MY FATHER, AND I AM COMMUNICATING THIS, MY FINAL AND IRREVOCABLE DECISION.

REALISING AS I DO THE GRAVITY OF THIS STEP, I CAN ONLY HOPE THAT I SHALL HAVE THE UNDERSTANDING OF MY PEOPLES IN THE DECISION I HAVE TAKEN AND THE REASONS WHICH HAVE LED ME TO TAKE IT.

I WILL NOT ENTER NOW INTO MY PRIVATE FEELINGS, BUT I WOULD BEG THAT IT SHOULD BE REMEMBERED THAT THE BURDEN WHICH CONSTANTLY RESTS UPON THE SHOULDERS OF A SOVEREIGN IS SO HEAVY THAT IT CAN ONLY BE BORNE IN CIRCUMSTANCES DIFFERENT FROM THOSE IN WHICH I NOW FIND MYSELF.

I CONCEIVE THAT I AM NOT OVERLOOKING THE DUTY THAT RESTS ON ME TO PLACE IN THE FOREFRONT THE PUBLIC INTERESTS WHEN I DECLARE THAT I AM CONSCIOUS THAT I CAN NO LONGER DISCHARGE THIS HEAVY TASK WITH EFFICIENCY OR WITH SATISFACTION TO MYSELF.

I HAVE ACCORDINGLY THIS MORNING EXECUTED AN INSTRUMENT OF ABDICATION IN THE TERMS FOLLOWING:—

I, EDWARD VIII. OF GREAT BRITAIN, IRELAND, AND THE BRITISH DOMINIONS BEYOND THE SEAS, KING, EMPEROR OF INDIA, DO HEREBY DECLARE MY IRREVOCABLE DETERMINATION TO RENOUNCE THE THRONE FOR MYSELF AND FOR MY DESCENDANTS, AND MY DESIRE THAT EFFECT SHOULD BE GIVEN TO THIS INSTRUMENT OF ABDICATION IMMEDIATELY.

IN TOKEN WHEREOF I HAVE HEREUNTO SET MY HAND THIS TENTH DAY OF DECEMBER, NINETEEN HUNDRED AND THIRTY-SIX IN THE PRESENCE OF THE WITNESSES WHOSE SIGNATURES ARE SUBSCRIBED.

EDWARD R.I.

MY EXECUTION OF THIS INSTRUMENT HAS BEEN WITNESSED BY MY THREE BROTHERS, THEIR ROYAL HIGHNESSES THE DUKE OF YORK, THE DUKE OF GLOUCESTER, AND THE DUKE OF KENT.

I DEEPLY APPRECIATE THE SPIRIT WHICH HAS ACTUATED THE APPEALS WHICH HAVE BEEN MADE TO ME TO TAKE A DIFFERENT DECISION, AND I HAVE, BEFORE REACHING MY FINAL DETERMINATION, MOST FULLY PONDERED OVER THEM.

BUT MY MIND IS MADE UP.

MOREOVER, FURTHER DELAY CANNOT BUT BE MOST INJURIOUS TO THE PEOPLES WHOM I HAVE TRIED TO SERVE AS PRINCE OF WALES AND AS KING, AND WHOSE FUTURE HAPPINESS AND PROSPERITY ARE THE CONSTANT WISH OF MY HEART.

I TAKE LEAVE OF THEM IN THE CONFIDENT HOPE THAT THE COURSE WHICH I HAVE THOUGHT IT RIGHT TO FOLLOW IS THAT WHICH IS BEST FOR THE STABILITY OF THE THRONE AND EMPIRE AND THE HAPPINESS OF MY PEOPLES.

I AM DEEPLY SENSIBLE OF THE CONSIDERATION WHICH THEY HAVE ALWAYS EXTENDED TO ME BOTH BEFORE AND AFTER MY ACCESSION TO THE THRONE, AND WHICH I KNOW THEY WILL EXTEND IN FULL MEASURE TO MY SUCCESSOR.

I AM MOST ANXIOUS THAT THERE SHOULD BE NO DELAY OF ANY KIND IN GIVING EFFECT TO THE INSTRUMENT WHICH I HAVE EXECUTED, AND THAT ALL NECESSARY STEPS SHOULD BE TAKEN IMMEDIATELY TO SECURE THAT MY LAWFUL SUCCESSOR, MY BROTHER, HIS ROYAL HIGHNESS THE DUKE OF YORK, SHOULD ASCEND THE THRONE.

EDWARD R.I.

The Prime Minister told the House how King Edward came to his decision—See Page Two

It was on 3 December 1936 that the world was informed that the King of England was enamoured of the American divorcee Mrs Wallis Simpson. Edward VIII had been proclaimed the first bachelor king since George III on 22 January, two days after the death of his father George V. Mrs Simpson whose divorce from her second (English) husband Ernest Simpson, a member of the Baltic Exchange, was still pending, was from then on a constant guest at royal dinner parties. In August she accompanied His Majesty on a cruise down the Dalmatian coast in a chartered steam yacht. Her divorce came through on 27 October, and three weeks later Edward told the prime minister Stanley Baldwin, and his mother Queen Mary, that there would be no coronation, as he intended abdicating. He was not going to be allowed to remain king with a morganatic wife, as he had expected.

The day after the public announcement of the king's intended abdication, Wallis Simpson left England for an American friend's villa in France. Both Houses of Parliament heard a formal message from the king announcing his abdication on 10 December, and the following night he boarded the destroyer *Fury* for France. His brother, the Duke of York, who succeeded him as George VI made him Duke of Windsor. In June 1937 Edward married Wallis, who became Duchess of Windsor but without the title 'Her Royal Highness'.

Top and bottom left *A news-stand and street banner at the time of the Abdication Crisis.*

Top right *The king tells his subjects over the 'wireless' the circumstances which led him to make his difficult decision*

Bottom right *The Abdication Crisis over, His Royal Highness the Duke of Windsor begins a new life with the woman he loves*

Left *Ex-King Edward VIII, now the Duke of Windsor, with ex-Mrs Simpson whom he married in 1937, honeymooning in Venice*

Below *Edward VIII in London shortly before announcing his wish to abdicate*

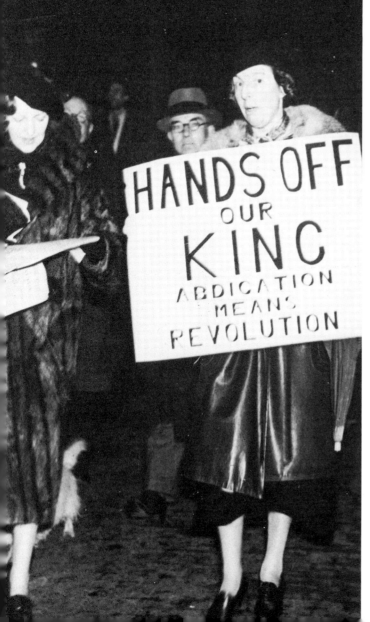

"HOW MUCH WILL YOU GIVE ME NOT TO KICK YOUR PANTS FOR, SAY, TWENTY-FIVE YEARS!"

Evening Standard

To-morrow's Weather— Bright periods; showers.

Lighting-up Time To-day 6.19 p.m.

No. 34,799   LONDON, SATURDAY, MARCH 7, 1936   ONE PENNY

GERMAN TROOPS ENTER RHINELAND

Hitler Denounces Locarno

OFFERS AN ALL-ROUND PEACE PACT

And Proposes To Re-enter the League of Nations —on Conditions

GERMAN TROOPS TO-DAY MARCHED INTO THE DEMILITARISED RHINELAND ZONE.

NEWS OF THE *COUP D'ETAT*, WHICH SMASHES LOCARNO AND THE VERSAILLES TREATY, WAS RECEIVED FROM BERLIN AND TOWNS IN THE ZONE AN HOUR BEFORE HITLER ADDRESSED THE REICHSTAG.

Herr Hitler simultaneously handed to the Ambassadors of Britain, France, Italy and Belgium, the guarantor Powers, a Note

BRITAIN'S AIR PACT PROPOSAL TO GERMANY

IT was learned in London this afternoon that Mr. Anthony Eden saw the German Ambassador yesterday and informed him that Great Britain was anxious to enter into discussion for a western air pact.

This step was taken with the full knowledge of the French Government and before there was any knowledge in London of the contents of the declaration which Hitler made to-day.

The German Ambassador gave no indication of Germany's attitude to the proposal, but confined himself to taking note of the British suggestion.

Simultaneously with the declaration of Herr Hitler in Berlin to-day the Ambassador called at the Foreign Office in London and handed to Mr Eden the memorandum dealing with the denunciation of Locarno and the Seven Point Pact proposals.

Afterwards Mr. Eden saw separately the French Ambassador, the Italian Ambassador and the Belgian Charge d'Affaires. This

It was the riskiest gamble of the four year old Nazi regime when on 7 March 1936, against the advice of his generals and of the injunctions of the Treaty of Versailles, the Führer sent a lone division of the newly re-armed German Reich to re-occupy the demilitarised zone on its south-west frontier with France, which had 90 divisions to defend it with. 'The 48 hours after the march into the Rhineland were the most nerve-racking in my life' Hitler told Paul Schmidt. But not a single French soldier was sent to stop him – as he had reckoned. No one moved while a single battalion crossed the Rhine into what the French called Aix-la-Chapelle and the Germans Aachen, and two others into Trier and Saarbrucken. On the same day the German Foreign Minister denounced the Locarno Pact which guaranteed the inviolability of the frontiers of France and Belgium with Germany, on the grounds that it was now incompatible with the recently announced Franco-Soviet alliance. Behind the offer of a 25 year Non-Aggression Pact to take its place, was the implication that Germany and France were now equal. Hitler at once started building fortifications along the frontier. 'All of us, and all peoples, have the feeling that we are at the turning point of an age' he told a rally at Breslau. 'No event marks a clearer stage in the success of Hitler's diplomatic game than the re-occupation of the Rhineland' was the verdict of historian Alan Bullock in 1952.

When thousands of foreigners flocked to Berlin for the Olympic Games in August 1936, the opportunity was taken to impress and dazzle them with a show of theatrical flag-waving, massed bands and precision marching to demonstrate the stuff which the re-born and re-armed, confident, National Socialist Germany was made of. For those round the world who could not attend in person, the Führer had a lengthy film made of the occasion by actress-turned-director Leni Riefenstahl who had just finished her film of the 1934 Nuremburg rally *Triumph of Will*.

Right *German mounted troops riding through Cologne to occupy Germany's southern 'Rhineland' frontier with France*

Far right *The 1936 Olympic Games in Berlin open with a runner placing a torch, lit on Mount Olympus, into a brazier in the Lustgarten*

1937

DAILY TIMES
357,857
CHICAGO'S PICTURE NEWSPAPER
LATE NEWS PICTURES
Vol. 3 No. 258   FRIDAY, MAY 7, 1937   TWO CENTS   80 Pages

34 KILLED!
Zep Crash Shocks World

Was the conflagration which destroyed LZ-129 Zeppelin *Hindenburg* at Lakehurst aerodrome in America on 6 May 1937 sabotage or an accident? The *Hindenburg* was the first zeppelin designed specifically for the North Atlantic route. It was 800 ft long and weighed 242 tons. It was the culmination of 25 years of experience with passenger airships, and was going to be ready in time for the first years of the new National Socialist government which came into power in 1933. It was to be the pride and boast of the Third Reich. In March 1935 the new Air Minister, Hermann Goering, formed Deutsche Zeppelin Reederei in which the German national airline Lufthansa was the dominant partner. The seven million cubic feet giant vessel was completed by Christmas 1935. Its first flight on 4 March 1936 without a name gave rise to the rumour that Dr Hugo Eckener, director of the Zeppelin Company, was still resisting the new regime's wish that the previously chosen name *Hindenburg* should be changed to *Hitler*. In fact the only setback had been the inability of the US Government to sell the Germans the safe helium gas for filling the envelope. The Helium Control Act of 1927 had forbidden the export of this light, fireproof gas. So the *Hindenburg* was filled with hydrogen instead. And that was its undoing.

Eckener obtained permission from the US Navy Dept to make ten round trips to Lakehurst in 1936, and then made ten more to Rio de Janeiro. This was followed by a ten-hour, showing-the-flag cruise over New England with 72 American businessmen, industrialists and pressmen aboard. A plan was hatched to form an American Zeppelin Transport Corporation to operate two airships under the German flag and two under a US flag on a transatlantic service. It was to take 64 hours westbound and 52 hours eastbound.

On the first of 18 scheduled flights from Frankfurt to the US base at Lakehurst, it was down on the ground approaching the mooring mast at the end of its flight when several noted a blue flame – St Elmo's Fire? – flickering along the airship's back, and a minute later hydrogen escaping from the front gas cells was ignited, and the whole ship went up in flames, killing Ernst Lehmann, flight director of the Reederei, 21 crew and 13 passengers. It was not a communist or Nazi plot, but some kind of electrical discharge which brought disaster. But a sister ship the LZ-130, 837 ft long, was in the hanger waiting to take over.

German airship Hindenburg in flames on exploding as it neared its moorings at Lakehurst airfield USA after a flight from Frankfurt

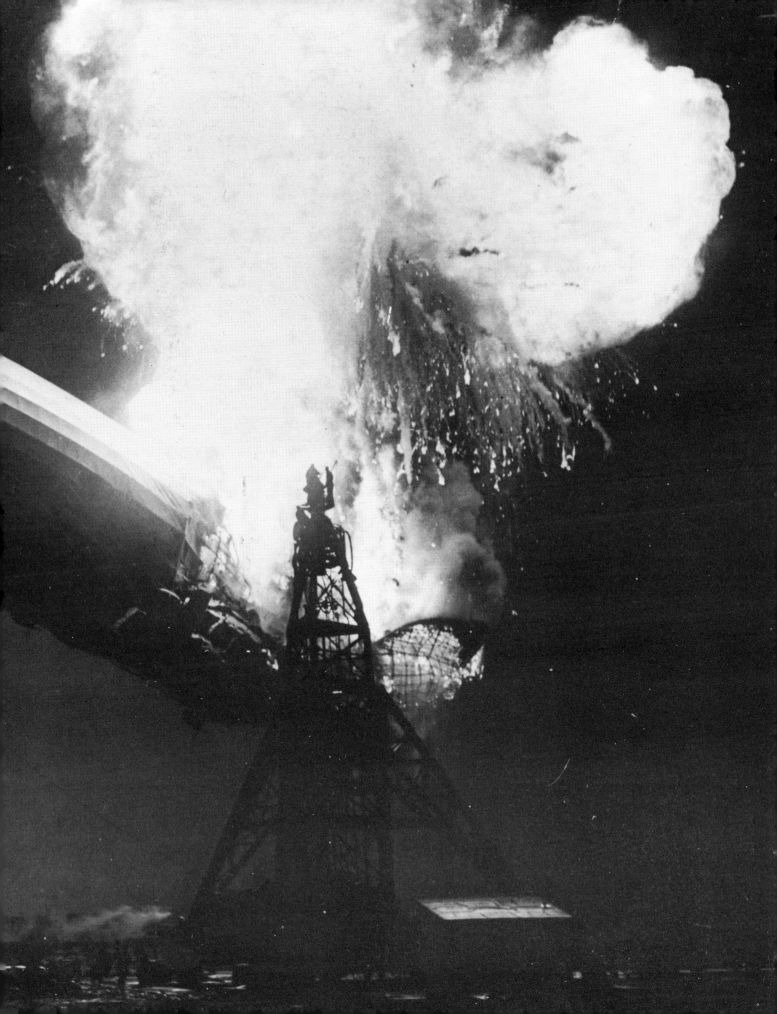

DUBLIN EVENING MAIL

New Horror In Battle For Madrid

REBELS THREATEN TO USE GAS

REPORTS OF GOVERNMENT GAINS ERRONEOUS?

FIERCE BAYONET FIGHTING

GAS warfare is the latest horror threatened in Spain's civil war, which enters its 118th day to-day.

The insurgents apparently already have the possibility of its use against Madrid in mind, for a message received in Lisbon to-day quotes insurgent officers as saying that the Government troops are already using gas bombs and that as a result "we may be forced to use gas as well."

The latest messages from Reuter correspondents at the front seem to indicate that the military position around Madrid has hardly changed in the last 24 hours.

War at close quarters on the Guadarrama Front showing the open nature of the fighting

Manoeuvres may be useful combat training but nothing compared with the Real Thing. The leaders of Germany's National Socialist government took the opportunity provided by the Spanish Civil War to try out techniques of dive bombing and to test the staying power of their Stukas, their pilots and gunnery, and the accuracy of their bombsights, in 'unofficial' attacks on troops and installations in all kinds of terrain.

The military commanders who revolted in Spanish Morocco in July 1936 were led by General Francisco Franco who in October was proclaimed 'Chief of the Spanish State'. Many towns such as Cadiz and Seville rallied to his cause and gave support to his insurgent 'nationalists' who aimed to overthrow the elected Popular Front Republican Government of President Azana.

By the end of 1938 Franco's rebel forces held half of Spain, but failed to capture the capital, Madrid, where an International Brigade had firmly dug itself in. On 21 June 1937 the ancient Basque town of Guernica was completely destroyed by German and Italian airmen on instructions from their Nazi and Fascist masters. After the death of some three quarters of a million people on both sides, the government's forces collapsed in 1939, and Madrid surrendered to Franco's rebels on 28 March.

In a Spain torn by civil war cavalry clatter through the streets of Barcelona

I'M BRINGING PEACE TO THE POOR SUFFERING BASQUES

Nineteen thirty eight was the year of the British Record Breakers – on the railway, on the cricket field.

On 3 July Driver Duddington drove the Gresley A4 Pacific no 4468 *Mallard* locomotive of the London & North Eastern Railway 126 miles an hour – the highest speed ever reached by steam power in any part of the world. The designer of the streamlined engine which was only a few weeks old, Sir Nigel Gresley, the company's chief mechanical engineer since 1923, was in the dynomometer car to record the feat achieved for 185 feet on its journey from Newcastle to London's King's Cross when descending from Stoke Summit towards Peterborough. The 240-ton, seven-coach train maintained an average speed of 120.4 miles an hour for five miles on this stretch. Thirty-five A4 Pacific steam locomotives were built at Doncaster between 1935 and 1938, and the record-breaking *Mallard* continued in service until 1963, having run 1,426,260 miles in 25 years. No steam train since *Mallard* has ever travelled at a greater speed. It remained the fastest train of any kind for 35 years – until, in June 1973, British Rail's diesel-electric High speed train prototype reached 131 miles an hour between Darlington and York, and a few days later set up a world record for diesel trains by achieving 143 mph.

England's cricket score of 903 runs for seven wickets declared in the 5th Test March against Australia at The Oval in August 1938, and their margin of victory – an innings and 579 runs – were records which are still unbeaten. It is the only instance in Test History of a side exceeding 850. The 13 hour innings in that match of the 22 year old Yorkshire cricketer Len Hutton, in which he made 364, was also a record. It stood for 20 years until Sir Garfield Sobers got 365 not out in ten hours against Pakistan in Jamaica in 1958. When Hutton exceeded the previous England-Australia Test highest number of runs, Sir Don Bradman, the Aussie captain, was the first to go and shake him by the hand – it was his record of 334 which had just been broken. Before finally being caught by Hassett, Hutton had run six miles and made 211 shots off 836 balls. Sir Leonard Hutton was the second professional cricketer to be knighted and the first to be regularly appointed captain of England.

The 22 year old Len Hutton during his 13-hour innings against Australia at the Oval cricket ground in London

The LNER steam locomotive Mallard *which Driver Duddington coaxed to a record speed of 126 miles an hour this year*

Daily Herald

No. 7061   SATURDAY, OCTOBER 1, 1938   ONE PENNY

MR. CHAMBERLAIN DECLARES "IT IS PEACE FOR OUR TIME"

5,000 British Troops Will Be Sent To Sudetenland

PRAGUE'S DAY OF SORROW

To a frenzied welcome from tens of thousands of Londoners, Mr. Neville Chamberlain came home last night and announced to all the world: "I believe it is peace for our time."

GERMANS WILL MARCH AT NOON

ORDERS were given yesterday by General Brauchitsch, Chief of Staff for the German Army, to begin the march into Czechoslovakia at noon to-day (reports the British United Press).

"Our forces step into the liberated region," he said, "with the proud joy of being the bearers of German discipline and order."

The first Sudeten areas to be occupied will be the area north of Passau and Linz, in Upper Austria.

The Czech Government last night ordered evacuation to start immediately. It will be continued over the week-end.

INSIDE PAGES

2 News broken to Czechs: W. N. Ewer's story from Munich. Daladier's welcome in Paris. Chamberlain-Hitler "No More War" agreement.

3 After the Crisis. What happened in England.

5 Hannen Swaffer tells of Downing Street scenes. Stories from Buckingham Palace and Heston Airport.

7 General Sirovy's broadcast from Prague: Text of Munich Agreement and Map.

8 Editorial comment: Pen Portraits of International Commission.

BACK PAGE & PAGE 6
After the Crisis pictures.

Result of the **HOLIDAY MUSIC PROGRAMME COMPETITION** will be announced in the Daily Herald on Monday. Order your copy now as there is certain to be an extra demand.

The Premier had two agreements in his pocket:

1.—The Munich Four-Power Pact for the transfer of Sudetenland from Czechoslovakia to Germany; and

2.—An Anglo-German declaration of the "desire of our two peoples never to go to war with one another again."

Mr. Chamberlain's welcome in Downing Street was overwhelming. Women in tears cried "Thank you, thank you." Police strove in vain to hold back the throng.

"The Second Time"

From a first-floor window of No. 10 the Prime Minister spoke to the crowd.

"My good friends," he said. "This is the second time in our history that a statesman has come back from Germany to Downing Street with peace with honour. [The first was in 1878, when Disraeli returned from the Congress of Berlin.] I believe it is peace for our time."

Nearly 5,000 British troops will leave during the next few days for the policing of Sudetenland.

They will be battalions of the Coldstream Guards, Grenadier Guards, Scots Guards and Welsh Guards, together with two battalions of line regiments. One of these will be the Gordon Highlanders; the other had not been decided last night.

The men will travel by way of Brussels and Germany, and last night the War Office and Foreign Office were busy completing the arrangements for their transport.

The first draft of men are expected to travel to-morrow and the remainder on Monday and Tuesday.

One of the points still to be fixed is the uniform in which the men will travel.

Cabinet Meeting

A short meeting of the Cabinet was held last night, at which Mr. Chamberlain gave a brief report of the Munich negotiations.

No arrangements have been made for a further Cabinet meeting, and it is expected that the Premier will spend a quiet week-end in the country.

Parliament meets again on Monday, when it is expected the Munich agreement will be debated. Mr. Attlee, Labour's leader, and Mr. Greenwood, deputy-leader, have cancelled their week-end meetings so as to remain in close touch with the situation.

Before the House assembles, the National Council of Labour, the Executive of the Parliamentary Labour Party, and Labour M.P.s will meet.

The Prime Minister's homecoming was one long triumphal procession.

At Heston there were 10,000 people to welcome him. And there were cries of "Well done!" when Mr. Chamberlain pulled from his pocket the Anglo-German agreement and said to the crowd: "Here is a paper which bears Hitler's name upon it as well as mine."

The Premier held the document, typewritten on foolscap paper, high above his head for the crowd to see. Beneath the typescript could be seen the names "Neville Chamberlain" and "Adolf Hitler."

"I want to say," Mr. Chamberlain stated "that the settlement of the Czechoslovak problem is only a prelude to a larger settlement in which all Europe may find peace."

"Superior Force"

From Heston the Prime Minister drove through miles of cheering streets to Buckingham Palace. Here again his reception was overwhelming. Tremendous crowds shouted "We want Chamberlain" and sang "For he's a jolly good fellow."

The crescendo of cheering reached its climax as first the King and Queen and then Mr and Mrs Chamberlain stepped out on to the floodlit balcony.

From a Window at No. 10

Mr. Chamberlain speaking from an upstairs window at No. 10 Downing Street, to the great crowd which gathered to welcome him home.

Czechs Cry "We Want To Fight"

And so to Downing Street—and more frenzied applause.

London's West End last night was filled with jubilant crowds. Traffic was at times almost at a standstill.

In contrast to all this rejoicing, Prague yesterday was a city of sorrow. Tens of thousands of people paraded the streets shouting, "We want the whole Republic! We want to fight!"

The city authorities, fearful lest Germany might seize this pretext for an invasion, ordered a "black-out" to get the crowds off the streets.

General Sirovy, the Czech Premier, broadcast a message to the nation in which he said: "We have accepted unheard-of sacrifices. . . . . Superior force has compelled us to accept. . . . But the nation will be stronger and more united."

What They Will Lose

It is now clear that the Czechs, under the terms of the annexation, will lose:

(a) The radium mines of Joachimsthal;
(b) Large seams of bituminous coal and lead deposits;
(c) Rich belts of timber;
(d) Ironworks, glassworks and breweries;
(e) The famous spas of Karlsbad, Marienbad and Franzenbad.

They will not, however, lose the famous Pilsen brewery or the great Skoda munition works.

Examination of the detailed plan (given in full on Page 7) shows great modifications by Hitler of the demands made in his Godesberg ultimatum.

Many questions which Hitler then said would be decided by Germany unilaterally, are now to be referred to the International Commission, which held its first meeting in Berlin yesterday.

Also, Hitler will now guarantee the new Czechoslovakia if a minority agreement is reached with Poland and Hungary; and provision is made for exchange of populations.

BUT—

Poles Rush Ultimatum

BY OUR OWN CORRESPONDENT
WARSAW, Friday night.

WITHIN 24 hours of one threat of an immediate war on the Czechs being averted, Poland to-night handed a new ultimatum to Prague.

Imposing a 24-hour time limit, the ultimatum insisted on an immediate answer to the demand that all Czech territory inhabited by Poles shall be evacuated at once.

A Warsaw Foreign Office spokesman announced that the Note would reach Prague by ten o'clock to-night.

An official communiqué explained that Czechoslovakia's answer to the Polish Note, sent last Tuesday, containing a detailed plan of frontier adjustments in Teschen Silesia, reached Warsaw at 1 p.m. to-day, but had been found unsatisfactory.

The Polish Government had therefore sent another Note requesting a "clear and precise" answer and the cession of the territory.

The answer to the Note is expected by noon to-morrow.

If the ultimatum is rejected, the threat was one of Germany, France, Italy, Britain, Rumania and the United States, and the Hungarian Minister.

"will resort to measures which may have the gravest consequences."

Suggestions were made that Polish troops would enter the Teschen district of Czechoslovakia to-morrow at the same time that the Germans occupied the areas ceded to them.

The official wireless broadcast to-night declared: "The hour is approaching when Polish troops will free the Poles in Czechoslovakia with their fixed bayonets."

Reports were circulated in Warsaw to-day of alleged "incidents" on the Czech border.

An urgent meeting was called, attended by General Smigly-Rydz, virtual Dictator of Poland, President Moscicki, the Premier, vice-Premier and Foreign Minister.

Colonel Beck, the Foreign Minister, dozed off.

Relief at the reprieve from war which the 'Munich Agreement' brought the people of Europe may not have been universal but was certainly widespread. The possibility of armed conflict had come and gone when in March 1938 German troops invaded Hitler's homeland Austria, which was thereupon proclaimed a province of the German Reich – the 'Anschluss'. The next step in the reclaiming of Germany's Lost Territories and reversing the Treaty of Versailles was directed at the three million German-speaking people in Bohemia, part of the Czechoslovakia which had been artificially created after the great War – the Sudeten Deutsch. Hitler insisted that as German stock outside the Reich the Sudetens belonged to Germany and that he would fight for their right of self-determination.

On 14 September 1938 Neville Chamberlain the British prime minister flew to see the German chancellor at Godesburg where Hitler suggested partitioning the Czech state, but later (when Chamberlain saw him a second

Below left *Joachim von Ribbentrop, German ambassador in London, escorts Neville Chamberlain on his journey to Munich to resolve the Sudetenland crisis*

Below *British prime minister Neville Chamberlain, on arrival at Heston Airport after visiting the German Chancellor in Munich, waves the piece of paper signed by Hitler which, he said, meant 'peace for our time'*

time) changed his mind. Sudetenland he then said, must be wholly occupied by German troops – 'the last territorial demand I have to make in Europe.' On 24 September Britain, France and the Czechs rejected the proposal, and Chamberlain told Hitler that if France went to war with him Britain would support her. On 27 September the British fleet was mobilised and the Auxiliary Air Force mustered. It was the very verge of the precipice.

To seek a way of appeasing the Führer the prime ministers of Britain, France and Italy met Hitler in Munich, but without any representative of Czechoslovakia or her ally Russia. The agreement made at Munich was that German troops should occupy Sudetenland on 1 October, the frontiers to be settled by a Four-Power Commission after a plebiscite. Before he left Munich Chamberlain persuaded Hitler to sign a short declaration which he had had typed out, expressing the 'desire of our two peoples never to go to war with one another again.' It was this piece of paper which he held up when he stood at the top of the steps of the aircraft in which he flew back to England. It meant, he told those who assembled to welcome him home, peace with honour. 'I believe it is peace for our time.'

Europe had withdrawn from the verge, but the precipice still yawned.

Right *Von Ribbentrop and Chamberlain*

1939

Winston Churchill

Anxious crowds await the formal declaration of war they knew was now inevitable – London, 3 September 1939

Daily Mirror

DAILY MIRROR, Monday, September 4, 1939

No. 11,152 — ONE PENNY
Registered at the G.P.O. as a Newspaper

BRITAIN'S FIRST DAY OF WAR: CHURCHILL IS NEW NAVY CHIEF

BRITAIN AND GERMANY HAVE BEEN AT WAR SINCE ELEVEN O'CLOCK YESTERDAY MORNING. FRANCE AND GERMANY HAVE BEEN AT WAR SINCE YESTERDAY AT 5 P.M.

A British War Cabinet of nine members was set up last night. Mr. Winston Churchill, who was First Lord of the Admiralty when Britain last went to war, returns to that post.

Full list of the War Cabinet is:—

PRIME MINISTER: Mr. Neville Chamberlain.
CHANCELLOR OF THE EXCHEQUER: Sir John Simon.
FOREIGN SECRETARY: Viscount Halifax.
DEFENCE MINISTER: Lord Chatfield.
FIRST LORD: Mr. Winston Churchill.

SECRETARY FOR WAR: Mr. Leslie Hore-Belisha.
SECRETARY FOR AIR: Sir Kingsley Wood.
LORD PRIVY SEAL: Sir Samuel Hoare.
MINISTER WITHOUT PORTFOLIO: Lord Hankey.

There are other Ministerial changes. Mr. Eden becomes Dominions Secretary, Sir Thomas Inskip goes to the House of Lords as Lord Chancellor, Lord Stanhope, ex-First Lord, becomes Lord President of the Council, Sir John Anderson is the Home Secretary and Minister of Home Security—a new title.

None of these is in the Cabinet, which is restricted to the Big Nine. These are the men who will be responsible for carrying on the war.

But Mr. Eden is to have special access to the Cabinet.

The Liberal Party explained last night that although Sir Archibald Sinclair had been offered a ministerial post, the Party had decided at this moment not to enter the Government.

Petrol Will Be Rationed

The first meeting of the new war Cabinet took place last night. Mr. Churchill was the first to leave and the crowd broke into a cheer as he walked out. Mr. Hore-Belisha was driven away by a woman chauffeur in uniform.

The Premier went from Downing-street to Buckingham Palace where he stayed with the King for three-quarters of an hour.

It was announced last night that as from September 16 all petrol will be rationed. In the meantime all car owners are asked not to use their cars more than is vitally necessary.

POLES ATTACK

POLISH troops are fighting on German territory, according to a Warsaw message.

A Polish counter-attack pushed back the Germans and penetrated East Prussia near Dewisch Eylau, it was claimed.

The Polish Embassy in London described a Nazi report that troops had cut the Corridor as "entirely false."

Later according to the Havas Agency, the Polish Radio announced that Poland had retaken the frontier station of Zbaszyn.

The German News Agency claimed that Nazi troops, operating on the Southern front had taken the town of Radomsko. Radomsko, north of the industrial region round Katiwitz, is about forty miles from the Polish frontier.

1,500 Raid Casualties

The Poles' latest estimate of casualties in German air raids was issued last night in Warsaw.

It is alleged that 1,500 people were killed or injured in German air bombardment of open towns and villages during Friday and Saturday. A considerable proportion of the victims were women and children.

(The German Government had secured from

"BREMEN IS CAPTURED"
—French Report

The £4,000,000 German liner Bremen was reported to have been captured yesterday and taken to a British port.

A report from a high French source stated that the Bremen was captured at 4 p.m., but the area in which the liner was captured was not mentioned.

A French Government radio station broadcast the report which was picked up by the Mutual Broadcasting System of America.—Associated Press and British United Press.

Contd. on Bk. Page, Col. 1

The King to His People

"The task will be hard. There may be dark days ahead. . . . But we can only do the right as we see the right, and reverently commit our cause to God. If one and all we keep resolutely faithful to it, ready for whatever service or sacrifice it may demand, then, with God's help, we shall prevail."

These words were broadcast by the King last night. And to every household in the country a copy of his message, bearing his own signature facsimile, will be sent as a permanent record. The full speech is on page 2.

To-day all banks throughout Britain will be closed.

Australia yesterday declared war on Germany. "Where Britain stands, stand the people of the Empire and the British world," said Prime Minister Menzies in a broadcast message last night.

New Zealand has cabled her full support to Britain. There is a rush of recruits in Canada. At Toronto a queue of 2,000 men lined outside the Recruiting Office.

Japan has renewed Britain of her neutrality in the present war.

Britain's last two-hour ultimatum to Germany was revealed to the people of Britain in a memorable broadcast from Downing-street by Mr. Chamberlain at 11.15 yesterday morning. By that time

cont'd in Col. 4, Back Page

'In spite of the hardness and ruthlessness I thought I saw in his face, I got the impression that here was a man who could be relied upon when he had given his word.' Thus Neville Chamberlain on Adolf Hitler in the British premier's account of his leave-taking of the Nazi leader at Munich in September 1938. He had given Hitler hope that maybe he could lay the foundations of the Thousand Year Reich without war. In *Mein Kampf* however, for all to see and note, the future führer had written 'we move through the world as a peace-loving angel, but one armed in iron and steel'.

After Austria and Czechoslovakia the angel moved into Poland. No excuse was needed for implementing this latest stage of the New Order for Europe, the March to the East. But the iniquities of the 1919 Versailles settlement were trotted out once more to justify recovery of the Polish Corridor which separated East Prussia from the East of Germany, and the port of Danzig.

Stalin offered Poland Russian troops to counter the German threat, but the Poles would not admit them. It would mean losing their souls, they said, whereas conquest by the Germans would only mean losing their freedom. Then, to everyone's surprise, on 23 August 1939 extreme right and extreme left sunk their differences, and Nazis and Com-

Top left and right *This time it was to be orderly mobilisation by official call-up*

Above *Families who heard that Britain and France were at war with Germany while holidaying in Europe and hurried back home, arrive at Victoria Station, London – glad to have escaped in time*

munists signed a pact to share Poland, which was promptly overrun by both German and Russian forces. German troops and aircraft began sweeping in on 1 September; Russian forces on 17 September. In the meantime, on 3 September 1939, Britain declared war against Germany, and France followed suit.

'Close your hearts to pity!' called the man whom Chamberlain thought could be relied upon. 'Act brutally! Eighty million people must obtain what is their right!' Nothing would now deter him from attempting to fulfil his theories of race superiority and risking all to gain what he wanted most: the power of domination.

The day war broke out – a false air-raid alarm sends workers scuttling for shelter in Whitehall

1940

LATE SPECIAL

Evening Standard

This is the Gin
Gordon's
Stands
Supreme

No. 36,093   LONDON, FRIDAY, MAY 10, 1940   ONE PENNY

NAZIS INVADE HOLLAND, BELGIUM, LUXEMBURG: MANY AIRPORTS BOMBED

Allies Answer Call for Aid: R.A.F. Planes are in Action

HITLER HAS INVADED HOLLAND, BELGIUM AND LUXEMBURG. HIS PARACHUTE TROOPS ARE LANDING AT SCORES OF POINTS AND MANY AIRPORTS ARE BEING BOMBED.

THE DUTCH HAVE OPENED THEIR FLOODGATES AND CLAIM TO HAVE BROUGHT DOWN A DOZEN BOMBERS.

It was confirmed in official quarters in London shortly after 8 a.m. to-day that appeals for assistance have been received from both the Belgian and Dutch Governments, and that these Governments have been told that H.M. Government will, of course, render all the help they can.

Every airport in Belgium has been attacked by Nazi airplanes, it is announced in Brussels.

BRUSSELS IS BEING "BOMBARDED TERRIFICALLY," SAYS A NEW YORK MESSAGE.

A Zurich report states that casualties in the first raid over Brussels amounted to 400 dead and wounded.

Lyons Airport Bombed

Other reports say that Antwerp and the airport at Lyons (France) have been bombed.

THE BELGIAN ARMY IS RESISTING THE GERMAN INVASION. IT IS OFFICIALLY ANNOUNCED IN PARIS. GENERAL MOBILISATION HAS BEEN PROCLAIMED.

BRUSSELS RADIO ANNOUNCE THAT ALLIED TROOPS ARE ON THE WAY TO BELGIUM'S AID.

French, Belgian and British airplanes have been sighted over Holland, states an official Dutch announcement.

"These airplanes," it was added, "belong to our Allies and they are enthusiastically greeted as a sign of friendship."

You Must Carry Your Gas Mask

A.R.P. Should Be On Alert

—*Says Ministry*

The Minister of Home Security states that in the light of to-day's events in Holland and Belgium, it is very necessary that all civil defence and A.R.P. services should be on the alert.

The carrying of gas masks by the public is once more necessary. They should acquaint themselves with the position of shelters and first aid post in their neighbourhoods.

Householders are recommended to overhaul their domestic preparations against air attack.

Anti-aircraft guns over a wide area around the mouth of the Thames were in action at dawn to-day when five German airplanes, believed to be Heinkel bombers, flew over the coast and passed over several towns.

The sound of heavy firing awakened thousands of people, who hurriedly dressed and went into the streets to catch a glimpse of the raiders.

No air raid warning was sounded, but wardens were on duty and leadership exercise ordered.

Five airplanes, flying in an arrowhead formation, were seen. They were flying at about 10,000 feet. Their course was clearly marked by the puffs and flashes of the bursting shells from the anti-aircraft batteries.

They were flying due east. A few ...

The Dutch Legation in London announce: "Our appeal for aid sent to the Allied Governments has been answered. Britain and France are going to our assistance immediately."

Belgium, too, appealed for help. The Luxemburg Government have fled.

(Continued on PAGE TWO)

HITLER IS FOLLOWING THE SCHLIEFFEN PLAN — SPECIAL ARTICLE AND MAP, PAGE SEVEN.

(Continued on Back Page Col. Three)

A soldier standing in the debris is the only sign of life in this Belgian town blasted in the Nazi blitzkrieg of 1940

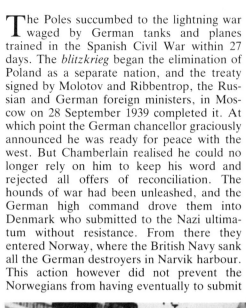

The Poles succumbed to the lightning war waged by German tanks and planes trained in the Spanish Civil War within 27 days. The *blitzkrieg* began the elimination of Poland as a separate nation, and the treaty signed by Molotov and Ribbentrop, the Russian and German foreign ministers, in Moscow on 28 September 1939 completed it. At which point the German chancellor graciously announced he was ready for peace with the west. But Chamberlain realised he could no longer rely on him to keep his word and rejected all offers of reconciliation. The hounds of war had been unleashed, and the German high command drove them into Denmark who submitted to the Nazi ultimatum without resistance. From there they entered Norway, where the British Navy sank all the German destroyers in Narvik harbour. This action however did not prevent the Norwegians from having eventually to submit

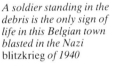

to German occupation and rule by Vidkun Quisling. Their despised countryman's name became synonymous with traitors everywhere.

The neutrality of the Dutch and Belgians could not save them from invasion on 10 May. Holland capitulated after five days; King Leopold of the Belgians panicked and surrendered on 28 May. The remnants of the British and French armies which had tried to stem the onslaught of massed panzer divisions and devastating air power were rescued from the Dunkirk beach line in an epic operation that succeeded in bringing off 215,000 British and 120,000 French.

The 'Phoney War' was over.

Below *Devastation of a French village in the early days of the German occupation*

Bottom *Troops of a German Panzer Division armed with machine guns and trench mortars are halted by a road block and anti-tank guns*

Norway was powerless to withstand the Nazi onslaught – German soldiers in Oslo

German sentries on patrol in Irun on the border of German-occupied France and neutral Spain

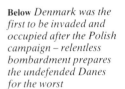

Below *Denmark was the first to be invaded and occupied after the Polish campaign – relentless bombardment prepares the undefended Danes for the worst*

Fighter Command Sector Operations Room during the Battle of Britain

Left *Some of 'The Few' who saved Britain from conquest and occupation in 1940 – RAF pilots run to their planes 'somewhere in Kent'*

Spitfire *pilots return after attacking the enemy off the south coast of England*

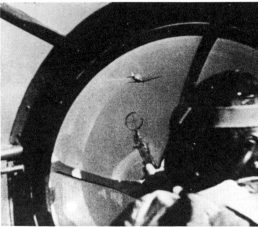

The newspaper front page reproduced:

DAILY HERALD

No. 7672 MONDAY, SEPTEMBER 16, 1940 ONE PENNY

175 NAZI PLANES DOWN

Buckingham Palace Is bombed third time

By JOHN SLEE. "Daily Herald" Reporter

They Saved St Paul's

SUICIDE SQUAD DIG OUT TON LIVE BOMB: MAD DRIVE TO HACKNEY TO EXPLODE IT

By A. L. EASTERMAN, "Daily Herald" Reporter

Hitler's Moves Seen

By REGINALD FOSTER, "Daily Herald" Reporter ON SOUTH-EAST COAST, Sunday

RAF Triumphs In Biggest Air Battles Of War

GOERING'S AIR FORCE HAD LOST 175 MACHINES UP TO TEN O'CLOCK LAST NIGHT FOLLOWING A DAY WHICH SAW FOUGHT THE FIERCEST AIR BATTLES OF THE WAR. FIGHTERS BROUGHT DOWN 171 AND A.A. FIRE FOUR.

RAIDERS CHASED BACK TO THE CHANNEL

RAIN OF SHRAPNEL

RAF PUTS GOERING IN SHADE

STOP PRESS
BOMB SCARE IN NEW YORK

NAZIS HOLD UP FRENCH TRAIN

TWO ITALIAN PLANES RAID LONDON

RAID VICTIMS IN NEW HOMES

"Tell Daddy I've gone to Boots"

You can rely on Boots

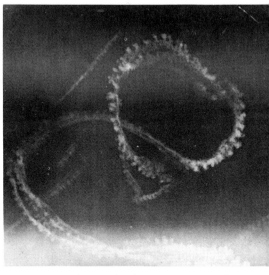

Top and centre *As seen by the enemy – view of a* Spitfire *diving through a bomber formation from the pilot's seat of a German* Heinkel

Above *Frozen exhaust gases from* Hurricanes *and* Spitfires *in deadly combat with their German counterparts trace patterns over Dover*

What the British newspapers called The Battle of Britain, which lasted from July to September 1940, was really the battle *for* Britain and was intended by the Germans as the softening-up exercise preparatory to the invasion, subjugation and occupation of the island across the channel. For Operation Sea Lion, as they called it, the Germans assembled 13 divisions in the north of France. Hermann Goering, Air Minister since 1933 and creator of the Luftwaffe (the German Air Force), had first to gain control of the English Channel, secure landing places for the invaders – and destroy the Royal Air Force which in July 1940 had 45 squadrons of (propeller) *Hurricane* and *Spitfire* fighter planes.

The battle began with heavy air raids on England's south coast; and the second stage was large-scale attacks on RAF airfields and factories. The newly created Reich Marshal Goering, confident that he could put the RAF out of action in four weeks, launched his air attack on 15 August. He had not reckoned on the skill and bravado of the few young men, mostly from public schools and universities, whom he had been led to believe were decadent and lacking the aggressive spirit. Their daring and persistence turned the tables on the would-be conquerors of Britain whose notion of a quick campaign was soon in disarray. As the man who had become prime minister after the collapse of Norway told the House of Commons on 20 August 1940, 'never in the field of human conflict was so much owed by so many to so few'. Some 700 British pilots and crews were killed or wounded.

Contributing to this great victory in the air was the British invention which enabled the defenders of Britain to plot the approach of enemy aircraft well before they reached their targets – radar.

The failure of Goering's Luftwaffe to achieve its mission and the permanent weakening of Germany's air strength in the Battle of Britain made a German sea-borne invasion impossible; and on 17 September Hitler ordered its indefinite 'postponement'. The daylight raids gave way however to night bombing, and London and other cities were severely damaged in the Blitz, which was not lifted until November.

The flag still flies from the US battleship Arizona *destroyed as she lay in Pearl Harbor, Hawaii on 7 December 1941*

Below *Burning oil streaming from shattered fuel tanks turns part of US Naval Base Pearl Harbor into a sheet of flames*

Japanese aggression was in full flood in the late 1930s – against China. By July 1937 its forces had overrun the whole Tientsin-Peking area, and by November Shanghai, by December Peking and Nanking, where in 1940 they established a puppet government. They then aped their Nazi German partner in the 'Axis' by announcing a 'New Order for East Asia', the whole of which would, by military conquest, be subordinated to Japanese domination. They saw an easy prey in the east asian colonial territories of the British, French and Dutch whose attention was now diverted by the conflict in Europe.

As the Japanese started to put the plan into action, first with French Indo-China, then Siam (Thailand), they realised the need to appease the still neutral United States, whose 'lend-lease' gesture to the Allies and the 'Atlantic Charter' revealed an attitude which was far from rigid isolationism.

Japanese prime minister Konoye, and the emperor, wanted peace, and negotiations with the US government were in progress when the hawks in Japan's armed forces persuaded them that a quick, knock-out blow would force America to accept Japan's terms. So, without formal declaration of war, early on Sunday 7 December 1941, Japanese carrier-borne aircraft attacked the main US naval base in Hawaii, Pearl Harbor.

In two hours they sank or disabled five battleships and 14 other ships, destroyed 120 aircraft and killed 2,400. Congress declared war on Japan on 8 December; Germany, Italy and Japan (the AXIS) on the United States three days later. The disaster at Pearl Harbor enabled the Japanese to complete the rest of their New Order by overrunning the whole of East Asia, including Singapore, the Dutch East Indies and the Philippines, which gave them access to vital war materials.

Mussolini's Fascist Italy did not join Hitler's Nazi Germany in the war to create the New Order for Europe until 11 June 1940. At first however Italy's forces were employed stirring up trouble outside Europe. From their African base in Abyssinia they attacked British Somaliland, and from Libya they invaded Egypt, for long a British protectorate but since 1922 independent under its own King Farouk. The Anglo-Egyptian Treaty of 1936 provided for the gradual withdrawal of British troops but the events of 1940 had postponed the operation.

After Somaliland had been liberated early in 1941 and the Emperor, Haile Selassie, had been put back on the throne of Abyssinia, Italy's Axis partner felt obliged to bring her aid in the form of an Afrika Corps commanded by Marshal ('Desert Fox') Rommel who promptly re-captured Libya (except for Tobruk). In July 1942 however Rommel's advance to the Nile was halted by British and Commonwealth forces under General Sir Claude Auchinleck only five miles from Alexandria at El Alamein. It was a rehearsal so-to-speak for the second Battle of El Alamein which took place between 23 October and 4 November when General Sir Bernard Montgomery's 8th Army (the 'Desert Rats') forced the Germans to retreat.

If Egypt had fallen Hitler would have had the whole of the Middle East as part of the German Reich. As it was, Monty's triumph was the beginning of a victorious advance across Libya in which his army covered 1,400 miles in 18 weeks. By May 1943, with the aid of US forces and the British First Army advancing from Algiers to Tunis and Cap Bon, the Axis troops were cleared from the whole of North Africa.

Left *General Sir Bernard Montgomery, whose Eighth Army forced the Germans to retreat at El Alamein in 1942*

German soldiers captured during the first two days' fighting at El Alamein wait for trucks to take them to Prisoner-of-War 'cages'

General Montgomery

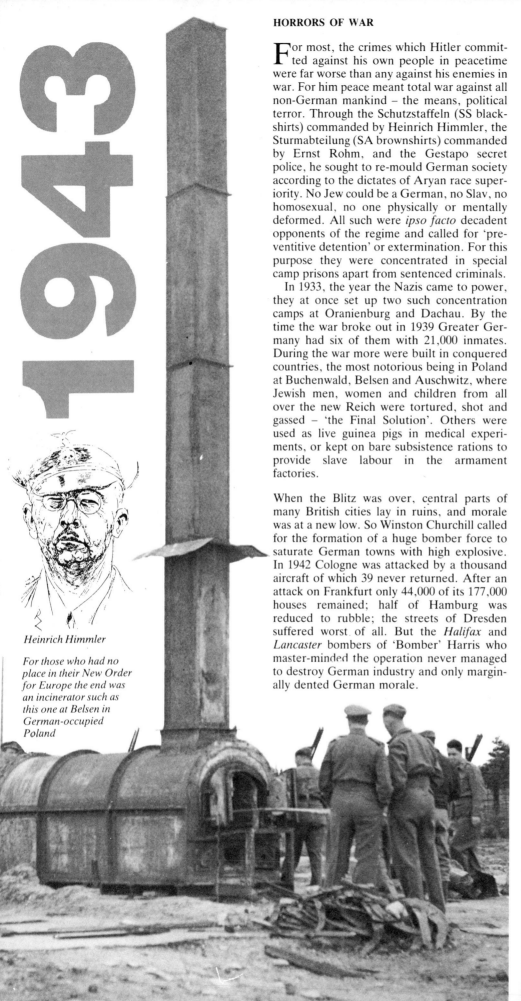

1943

Heinrich Himmler

For those who had no place in their New Order for Europe the end was an incinerator such as this one at Belsen in German-occupied Poland

HORRORS OF WAR

For most, the crimes which Hitler committed against his own people in peacetime were far worse than any against his enemies in war. For him peace meant total war against all non-German mankind – the means, political terror. Through the Schutzstaffeln (SS blackshirts) commanded by Heinrich Himmler, the Sturmabteilung (SA brownshirts) commanded by Ernst Rohm, and the Gestapo secret police, he sought to re-mould German society according to the dictates of Aryan race superiority. No Jew could be a German, no Slav, no homosexual, no one physically or mentally deformed. All such were *ipso facto* decadent opponents of the regime and called for 'preventitive detention' or extermination. For this purpose they were concentrated in special camp prisons apart from sentenced criminals.

In 1933, the year the Nazis came to power, they at once set up two such concentration camps at Oranienburg and Dachau. By the time the war broke out in 1939 Greater Germany had six of them with 21,000 inmates. During the war more were built in conquered countries, the most notorious being in Poland at Buchenwald, Belsen and Auschwitz, where Jewish men, women and children from all over the new Reich were tortured, shot and gassed – 'the Final Solution'. Others were used as live guinea pigs in medical experiments, or kept on bare subsistence rations to provide slave labour in the armament factories.

When the Blitz was over, central parts of many British cities lay in ruins, and morale was at a new low. So Winston Churchill called for the formation of a huge bomber force to saturate German towns with high explosive. In 1942 Cologne was attacked by a thousand aircraft of which 39 never returned. After an attack on Frankfurt only 44,000 of its 177,000 houses remained; half of Hamburg was reduced to rubble; the streets of Dresden suffered worst of all. But the *Halifax* and *Lancaster* bombers of 'Bomber' Harris who master-minded the operation never managed to destroy German industry and only marginally dented German morale.

On coming to power in 1933 Hitler had an encampment built at Dachau to house 'non-Aryans'

Right *Rescued just in time. Another day at Belsen might have been his last*

The western powers refused to believe the stories of wholesale genocide of non-Aryans until in 1945 they discovered mass graves such as this at Belsen

Below right *The body of one of the hated SS guards, lynched by his victims the moment the Americans entered Dachau concentration camp, lifted from the moat* **Below** *The killing continued up to the last day*

The greatest blow to German morale came on the Eastern front. In 1942 Hitler was determined to capture Stalingrad (renamed Volgagrad by Kruschev). In November the German general Paulus predicted the early fall of the city, but the Soviet army counter-attacked, and on 31 January 1943 Paulus's beleaguered army surrendered – only 91,000 left alive to be marched away to captivity out of the original 285,000.

Having re-captured Tunisia, in July 1943 the Allies landed on the Italian mainland – or more precisely in Sicily. It was the beginning of the end for the Fascist regime, and on 25 July the Italian king Vittorio Emanuele, who constitutionally was still Head of State, dismissed Mussolini as his prime minister and put him under arrest. The Germans took control of Rome, and the Italians became their enemies along with British and Commonwealth troops, the French and the Americans.

Above German tanks advance on Stalingrad. Below Any factory the Germans captured on the outskirts of Stalingrad had already been destroyed by the Russians

Below Infantry and a tank in the streets of Panchino during the British advance through Sicily in the summer of 1943

It was in 1928 that an accident led the Scottish bacteriologist Sir Alexander Fleming to discover the bacteria-killing properties of the fungus *Penicillium notatum*. Some of it had fallen into a jar containing a culture of microbes which he had put aside to throw away. Though he noted that no bacteria grew around the spores of the natural mould, he was unable to isolate the anti-biotic substance. It was many years later that the researches of the British chemist of German origin Ernst Chain into micro-organisms, prompted a re-investigation of Fleming's discovery. In 1943 Chain succeeded in isolating the anti-biotic and called it *Penicillin*. In 1945 Sir Alexander Fleming, Lord Florey and Ernst Chain all shared a Nobel Prize for this revolutionary breakthrough in medical science.

Penicillin, which chemists later learnt to synthesize, came to play a special part as a therapeutic agent in the treatment of pneumonia, septicaemia and meningitis. But during the war the so-called Wonder Drug was of the greatest value for a range of conditions extending to more than half the possible total of cases requiring emergency treatment. Because of the small and slow production, Penicillin became highly prized – the merchandise of the notorious fictional Harry Lime in the famous film *The Third Man*. As a germ-killer it certainly saved thousands of soldiers' lives on the battlefronts of the world. Larger scale production was soon under way in the safer laboratories of North America.

Penicillin saving our wounded

PENICILLIN has been given to soldiers wounded in North Africa and Sicily by Professor N. W. Florey and Brigadier Hugh Cairns, who have now reported to the War Office on the results.

Their report is for "official use only" but the British Medical Journal tells how this new drug works in the front line.

There can be little doubt that the prevention of infection with pyogenic cocci or the control in war wounds is within reach is the conclusion reached as the result of an intensive all-out trial lasting only three months.

Wounded only

"Pyogenic cocci" are the germs that infect wounds and make them septic, and sometimes destroy life and limb.

THE professor and the brigadier wanted to find out if penicillin would work if it was applied to the wound only—up to now it has usually been dropped straight into the blood. They put it into the wound as a powder, as a solution, and as a cream, and sometimes combined with sulphanilamide.

Badly infected wounds were stitched up—an unheard of procedure in pre-penicillin days—and one or two fine rubber tubes were put into the wound between stitches.

Twice a day

Through these rubber tubes penicillin was run into the wound twice a day for four days.

Only seven cases out of 171 failed to clear up. An Army doctor comments: "With penicillin the obstacles of infection have been practically overcome."

The men get out of hospital three to six weeks sooner than they used to.

[...]

Sir Alexander Fleming, who in 1928 discovered by chance the bacteria-killing properties of the fungus Penicillium notatum

Twenty-five pounders of a British Royal Artillery Field Regiment push on up Sicily through a deserted Aci Sant'Antonio

Below *Wartime production of* Penicillin, *the germ killer, in an American laboratory in Pennsylvania*

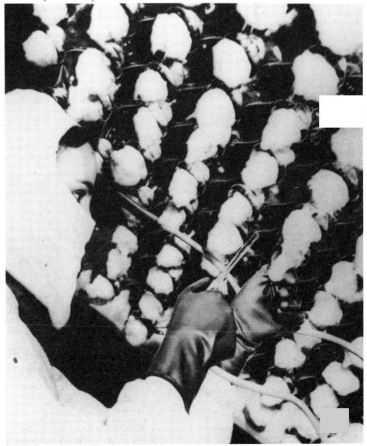

1944

The Evening News

NO. 18.485   LONDON, TUESDAY, JUNE 6, 1944   ONE PENNY

LATE EXTRA

Montgomery Leads British, U.S., Canadian Force

WE WIN BEACHHEADS

4,000 Ships, 11,000 Planes in Assault on France: 'All Going to Plan'—Premier

THE KING ON RADIO AT 9 P.M.

"ALLIES ARE PENETRATING DEEPER INLAND"

D-Day parachutists descend on Nazi-occupied France on 6 June 1944

Right *Within two months of the Normandy landings and after very heavy fighting, the Germans are surrendering in droves – but there was still a long way to go before final victory*

Below *D-Day infantry wade on to Normandy beaches from a cross-Channel landing craft in the opening stages of Operation Overlord*

DAILY HERALD

The V2 Rocket Comes To Southern England

1,000 Tanks In Third Army's Loraine Drive

BUILDING NEW WEST DEFENCES

'COMETS' THAT DIVE FROM 70 MILES

Antwerp Under Fire—

Ten-ft. Parts Recovered

Above left *No matches and nothing to drink, only a not very saucy postcard was available at a Bayeux café.* **Left** *One of the sinister, pilotless V-1 flying bombs – 'Doodlebugs' – which the Nazi enemy launched from pads in occupied France, crosses the south coast of England.* **Below** *A flying bomb reached its target in the heart of London's West End – Glasshouse Street, off Piccadilly. Civil defence workers and nurses remove the victims*

The Allies' re-entry into the top part of Europe across the English Channel, Operation Overlord, in 1944, has been described as the greatest seaborne expedition in history. Josef Stalin, who had been calling for a Second Front to take the heat off the eastern campaign, declared 'the history of wars does not know of any undertaking so broad in conception, so grandiose in its scale and so masterly in its execution.'

For the planners The Day the invasion fleet set off (6 June) was 'D', the next day D + 1, the next D + 2 etc. Inevitably that first day became known as D-Day. Hitler guessed the landing would be in Normandy, out his generals predicted the Pas-de-Calais, and told him the D-Day attack was a diversion and so delayed deploying their panzer (tank) divi-

sions – a mistake which enabled the Allies to consolidate on the beaches.

American General Dwight Eisenhower was the Supreme Commander. Two ingenious engineering feats made important contributions to the success of the invasion, PLUTO (the Pipe Line Under The Ocean) which carried oil supplies across the Channel, and the prefabricated Mulberry Harbours which were towed across the Straits of Dover to replace harbours destroyed by the enemy.

By 15 June General Montgomery, who was in command of the British and Canadian contingent, had established a headquarters in Normandy, and his troops were on their way to Caen, with the Americans breaking through on their right. French resistance fighters, alerted by secret code signals broadcast

by the BBC, played havoc behind the German lines.

But 13 June saw the first appearance across southern England of Hitler's secret weapon, the V-1 pilotless flying bomb which, launched from sites in France, inflicted heavy but indiscriminate damage and casualties. If they had come earlier they might have changed the outcome of the war. Britain's Frank Whittle invented the jet engine, and its application to RAF fighters by the last months of the war certainly increased aircraft speed and manoeuvrability – and caused widespread disbelief of those who insisted they had just seen a plane fly by without a propeller. But jet fighters also came too late to have any marked effect on the outcome of the war.

1945

The Daily Telegraph

and Morning Post

No. 28,043   LONDON, THURSDAY, MAY 3, 1945   Printed in LONDON and MANCHESTER   PRICE 1½d.

BERLIN FALLS: GARRISON LAYS DOWN ARMS

HITLER AND GOEBBELS COMMITTED SUICIDE

TOTAL SURRENDER IN ITALY: 1,000,000 PRISONERS

RESISTANCE IN HOLLAND REPORTED ENDED

BERLIN, "THE HEART OF GERMAN AGGRESSION," AND THE CAPITAL WHICH THE NAZIS SAID WOULD NEVER CAPITULATE, HAS FALLEN TO THE RED ARMY. AN ORDER OF THE DAY FROM MOSCOW, ANNOUNCING THIS LAST NIGHT, SAID THAT THE REMNANTS OF THE DEFEATED GARRISON SURRENDERED AT TWO P.M. B.D.S.T. YESTERDAY.

'MAGNIFICENT TRIUMPH' —F-M. ALEXANDER

EISENHOWER EXPOSES NEW "FUEHRER"

Himmler's Version of Hitler's Death

ITALY TALKS BEGAN THREE WEEKS AGO

PREMIER SAYS ITALY WILL AID OTHER EVENTS

MUSSOLINI WAS TO SIGN CAPITULATION

OFFER MADE THROUGH MILAN ARCHBISHOP

Adolf Hitler

S oon after the Normandy landings the Russians entered Poland, which, with the Italian campaign, meant Germany was now fighting on three fronts. In March 1945 British and American armies were crossing the Rhine and on 25 April the Russians, who had already occupied Vienna, met up with the Americans on the Elbe.

Hitler saw no reason to withdraw his troops from Denmark and Norway, Italy or Austria, to defend the homeland now in desperate need of every gun, tank and soldier it could lay hands on if it was not to be overwhelmed by the superior forces of the Allies. But since January 1945 the 56-year old führer had been living in the unreal world of a concrete bunker in the garden of his Chancellery in Berlin, a broken man with trembling hands, twitching arms and a dragging leg, 'a stooped figure with a pale and puffy face' who now saw his dream of a New Order for Europe crumbling about his head. On 29 April, with the Russians in the suburbs of Berlin, he handed over power to Admiral Doenitz and married his mistress Eva Braun. On the afternoon of 30

Right *The war in Europe is over – German officers surrender to Monty*

Far right *Russians show Allied officers the underground bunker below the Reich Chancellery in Berlin from which Hitler tried to command his retreating armies. Rather than be captured alive, he committed suicide*

April the two of them killed themselves rather than fall into the hands of the dreaded Reds. On 2 May Berlin surrendered; on 7 May General Jodl made the final capitulation of Germany to General Eisenhower near Rheims, and the following day Wilhelm von Keitel surrendered to the Russians near Berlin.

The Third Reich was over. The victors celebrated 8 May 1945 as V.E. Day.

Right *The end of the Thousand Year Reich and all hopes of imposing a New Order of Terror on a submissive Europe – the Reich Chancellery in Berlin, where it was to be master-minded, in ruins*

Below *The Rhineland frontier with France, once brashly reoccupied by Hitler's armies, is now freed – German civilians surrender at Trier*

Above *The atomic bomb dropped on Hiroshima on 6 August 1945. Better surrender now, said the Japanese after a second had devastated Nagasaki, than have the same thing happen to Tokyo*

Centre *The Allies not the Axis won the race to make the first atomic bomb – or else this death-dealing cloud could have mushroomed over London not Hiroshima*

Right *Chasing four million fanatical Japanese soldiers out of the Pacific Islands and China would have meant the death, maiming and torturing of vast numbers of Americans. The knock-out blow to Hiroshima brought instantaneous death to 160,000, and radio activity blistered the bodies of thousands of others like this. Who is to say which was 'worse'?*

Victory in Europe – V.E. Day (8 May 1945) – did not mean victory in any other part of World War II's huge arena. The would-be creators of the New Order for East Asia were determined to accomplish it in spite of the defeat of their two Axis partners, but by August 1945 the Japanese government knew there was no hope of ever completing their grandiose plan. Many of the lands they had conquered and occupied had been re-captured and their towns pulverised by American bombers. At the Yalta Conference in February 1945 the ailing US President Roosevelt saw the defeat of Japan dependent on Russian aid and gave Stalin considerable concessions in China and the Balkans. Vice-President Harry Truman who succeeded him when he died on 12 April was of the same opinion, and was advised by his chiefs-of-staff that American casualties would be very high if they were to dislodge the four million Japanese still defending the Pacific islands and parts of China.

But on 16 July 1945 an experimental bomb was exploded in the deserts of New Mexico with a potential for mass destruction on an unprecedented scale. It was a device which worked not by dynamite or high explosive but nuclear fission, the secret of which had been solved by the American and British scientists of the so-called 'Manhattan Project'.

Three weeks later (6 August) President Truman approved the dropping of an atomic bomb on the Japanese city of Hiroshima, killing and wounding 160,000 people at one blow. The USSR then (for the first time) declared war on Japan and invaded Manchuria. On 9 August an American aircraft dropped a second atomic bomb on Nagasaki with equally devastating effect. On the 14th the Japanese government, rightly fearing a third drop, ordered their forces to end all resistance. On 1 September General Macarthur took the Japanese surrender in Tokyo and Lord Louis Montbatten in Singapore.

The Second World War was over.

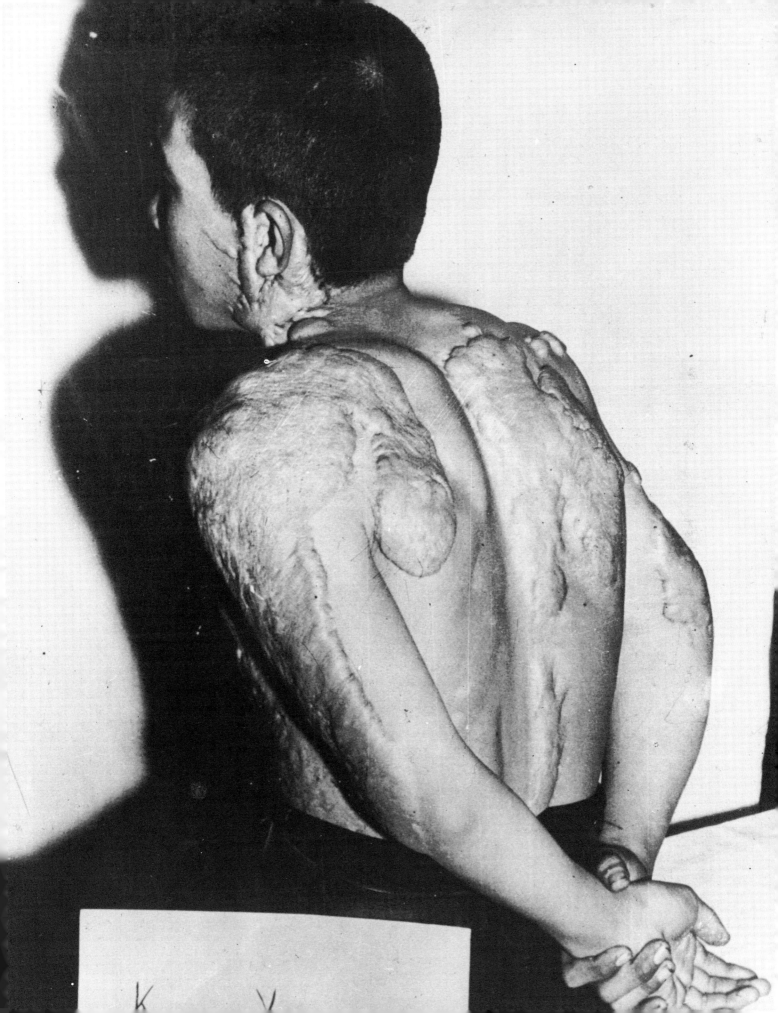

1945

Those in high places who gambled on what they considered the inevitability of Hitler's Nazi Germany winning the war which it had started and wanted, paid with their lives when they lost out. The retribution of those whose deprivations and humiliations had been rewarded with a decisive defeat of the hateful enemy, was swift and merciless.

Pierre Laval, a lawyer, first became prime minister of France at the age of 48 in 1931, and for the second time in 1935. He was out of office however when France declared war against Germany in 1939, and after his country's defeat in 1940 he entered the government of Marshal Pétain as Minister of State. He persuaded the Government to remain on French soil and accept an armistice with the enemy with whom it could negotiate terms and hopefully a peace treaty. He also persuaded the Assembly to dissolve itself, thus ending the Third Republic on 10 July 1940 and replacing it with a new constitution. Convinced of an ultimate German victory, he saw France's best way of assuring herself a role in the New Order which would come with a Nazi-imposed peace, was to collaborate with the potential victors to the fullest extent. He began negotiations on his own – and was dismissed by the government. Returning in 1942, he courted unpopularity by agreeing to provide French workers for German industry, asking for volunteers in a speech in June 1942 in which he asserted positively that he *wanted* Germany to win. He began losing his grip on being forced to work with extremists like Marcel Déat, and on repeated confrontation with the Resistance.

When the German armies surrendered and he realised he had backed the wrong horse, he fled to Spain to prepare his defence for the trial which he knew awaited him in Paris. He returned to face the music in July 1945; was tried for treason by a hostile court and heckling jury, and after failing to procure his own end by poison was executed as a traitor to France on 15 October.

The treachery in similar circumstances of Vidkun Quisling, the Norwegian army officer and diplomat, was more calculated and more despicable. In 1933, the year Hitler came to power, he formed in Norway the Nasjonal Samling (National Union) Party which advocated the suppression of communists and trade unionists. It contested several elections but none of its candidates were ever elected to the Norwegian Parliament – which should have told him something about his countrymen's dislike of right-wing policies. Norway was not involved in the war which Britain and France declared against Germany in September 1939, but Quisling chose to go and see Adolf Hitler in December 1939 and to urge him to occupy Norway as soon as possible. He suggested he was appointed head of a government friendly to the Nazis. After the German invasion of Norway in April 1940, and the chaos that followed, he proclaimed himself head of a new regime composed of his own supporters. But he had overplayed his hand, and within a week it had collapsed. Instead, in February 1942 he became 'Minister President' under Reich Commissioner Josef Terboven. Like Laval, he sealed his fate in the event of a German defeat, by heavy-handed, public attempts to convert the church, the schools and young people in Norway to National Socialism. Worse, he was held responsible for sending at least a thousand Norwegian Jews to die in concentration camps. Within days of Norway's liberation and the end of the war in Europe, he was arrested, tried for treason and many other crimes, found guilty and executed. He was 58. The infamy of his behaviour made 'Quisling' synonymous with 'Traitor' throughout the world.

Vidkun Quisling

Pierre Laval

Right *Pierre Laval, one time prime minister of France, takes his seat in the Paris courtroom to be tried for treason – and found guilty*

Far right *All eyes are on the would-be leader of a Norwegian Nazi government, Vidkun Quisling, as he enters the court to try to justify his treachery.*

THURSDAY, OCTOBER 4 1945 **Evening Standard** FINAL NIGHT EXTRA*

BOOTHS DRY GIN

ONE PENNY

Lawyers cry 'It is blackmail': Shouts from the public gallery
LAVAL TRIAL UPROAR
Judge threatens to throw him out —AND MAKES HIM APOLOGISE | Bevin to speak next week | *Express 40 mph too fast over the crossing*

'If we fail [in stopping Hitler from introducing his New Order] then the whole world, including the United States, including all that we have known and cared for, will sink into the abyss of a new Dark Age made more sinister, and perhaps more protracted, by the lights of perverted science.' Thus the British prime minister Winston Churchill.

The Allies did not fail and, as R W Cooper has written, 'it was perhaps in an instinctive urge to retain its sanity and moral values that the civilised world, represented by the four victorious powers, set out on 20 November 1945 on the great Nuremburg Trial – the first trial to call aggressive war mass murder.'

Half way through the war there had been established a United Nations War Crimes Commission, and an International Conference had drawn up the Charter which listed three categories of crime: Crimes against Peace, War Crimes, and Crimes against Humanity. Adolf Hitler, Heinrich Himmler and Joseph Goebbels had all killed themselves, but 21 leading members of the Nazi hierarchy (plus the absent Martin Bormann) were all arraigned including Goering, von Ribbentrop and Rudolf Hess. A British high court judge was president of the tribunal and was supported by American, French and Russian members.

After sitting for a year the tribunal sentenced eleven to death plus Bormann, seven to terms of imprisonment and acquitted economist Schacht, diplomat von Papen and Hans Fritzsche. The eleven were to be hanged on the night of 16 October 1946 and all were, with the name of the fatherland on their lips, except for Hermann Goering who took cyanide of potassium in his cell shortly before they came for him. By the time the doctor arrived he was dead.

Above Behind the scenes at the Nuremburg Trial. In each cell sits a Nazi leader waiting to be tried for war crimes. **Below left** Wearing headphones to hear the German translation, Goering, Hess, Ribbentrop and their Nazi colleagues, in the dock in the Nuremburg courtroom. **Below right** Frau Oberhauser one of the doctors who conducted human experiments in a German concentration camp receives her sentence **Right** Hermann Goering

1947

Mahatma Gandhi

Top centre *The streets of Bombay are lit with elaborate illuminations and fireworks to celebrate Britain's handing over of power in India*

Top right *The Governor General of the new Moslem Dominion of Pakistan, Mr Jinnah, with the Mountbattens at Government House, Karachi*

Right *Part of the huge crowd which greeted Lord and Lady Mountbatten on their state drive through New Delhi on 15 August*

The British Raj and his memsahib in their topis, with punka wallahs in constant attendance waving their outsize fans, have for long been comic Establishment figures. The princedoms of India remained backward and undeveloped, but it is unlikely that 20th century India would have acquired a similar level of political and economic stability without the dedication which members of the Indian Civil Service gave to a country so alien in lifestyle and culture to that they knew at home. 'Self-determination' had been partly achieved in 1935 with the Government of India Act which, by a new federal constitution, had given self-government to the provinces. But it was not enough for Mahatma Gandhi's Congress Party who refused co-operation in Britain's struggle with Germany and Japan unless India was given complete independence. Both hindus and moslems rejected Sir Stafford Cripps's 1942 proposals for yet another constitution, and continued civil disobedience in spite of the Japanese already occupying Burma, Siam and Malaya and on the point of invading India.

After the war, Clement Attlee's Labour government was set on an early realisation of self-government in India, and in March 1946 sent over a mission to decide on the terms of independence, on which however they found the hindus and moslems could not agree. To bring matters to a head Attlee announced that, come what may, Britain was quitting India not later than June 1948, and dispatched Lord Mountbatten as the last viceroy.

Jinnah, the moslem leader, insisted on a separate state for the 42 million moslems (out of a total population of 330 million) and the hindu Congress Party had reluctantly to agree to partition. British rule came to an end on 15 August 1947. In its place came the independent moslem Pakistan (sliced into a western and an eastern portion) and the independent hindu India.

Where did the people who lived in the Polynesian Islands come from? To find out the answer – and prove that theirs was the right one – Norwegian scientist Thor Heyerdahl and five companions built themselves a raft out of locally available balsa logs at Callao, Peru. In 1947 they sailed it from the west coast of South America to islands east of Tahiti to demonstrate the possibility that some ancient tribe of people living on the South American continent could have done as they were doing and been the first human beings to settle on Polynesia. Sailing – or rather drifting – across 5,000 miles of ocean for three and a half months, and landing up in Polynesia was proof enough he claimed that the Polynesians probably came from South America and not, as his fellow-ethnologists insisted, from South East Asia. He called the balsa raft with the single sail 'Kon-Tiki' after a legendary Inca god. It has been preserved in a museum in Oslo.

Thor Heyerdahl's Kon-Tiki Expedition was only the first of a series of similar 'drifts'. In 1969 he sailed from Africa to America in a papyrus boat *Ra II*, based on Egyptian and American Indian designs. Whatever man can do to the land, he cannot change the nature of the oceans; and by this voyage he hoped to show that the ancient Egyptians could well have crossed the Atlantic all those thousands of years ago.

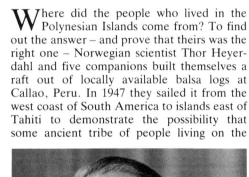

Thor Heyerdahl, instigator of the Kon-Tiki Expedition

1948

The Daily Telegraph and Morning Post, Thursday, July 1, 1948 — featuring headlines: "NO BERLIN SURRENDER SAYS MR. BEVIN", "200 BRITISH PLANES A DAY FOR BERLIN", "U.S. TO RELEASE JUGOSLAVIA'S GOLD RESERVES", "LAST BRITISH TROOPS SAIL FROM HAIFA", "£7,000,000 PLAN TO HARNESS THE NILE"

Top *Dividing the capital in half did not make instant 'communists' of those whose houses fell in the Eastern Zone. Berliners demonstrate outside the bombed Reichstag, and tear the Russian flag from the Brandenburg Gate*

Bottom left *The Russian blockade came in the coldest September for 50 years, and the lack of fuel caused the greatest hardship – these Berliners have been collecting wood in the Grunewald Forest*

Centre *Flour is unloaded from a huge Globemaster aircraft at Gatow airfield during the Berlin Airlift*

Bottom right *Forced to admit that the Berlin Airlift, which they never expected, had undermined their blockade, the Russians lifted it – convoys surge through the checkpoint between eastern and western zones to bring supplies*

The Hot War military alliance of the USSR and 'The West', which defeated Nazi Germany, soon gave way to a Cold War in which the communist state retreated within its own ideological frontiers and failed to respond to overtures from their erstwhile associates to share in the reconstruction of battered Europe. The position of the Allied armies on the day the Germans surrendered hardened into 'zones' which the Russians were anxious should remain, opposing the creation of a united Germany with a thriving economy over which they had no control. Unfortunately the United States decided that their recovery scheme known as 'Marshall Aid' should apply only to the zones occupied by The West. Into these were introduced new currencies without the assent of the USSR, and all hope of an integrated scheme disappeared. More unfortunately still, Berlin, the capital of Germany, which housed the HQ of the Allied Control Council, was in Russia's Eastern Zone (the old Prussia) and was itself partitioned into zones.

In 1947 the victors were still trying to formulate a peace treaty to present to defeated Germany; and by 1949 the western powers had got round to suggesting a federal constitution for the French, American and British zones under an occupation statute. But the Russians would have none of it, and imposed a blockade to prevent access to the western zone of Berlin (population 2 million) from western Germany.

So France, the USA and Britain organised an 'Airlift' to bring supplies through the narrow air corridor allowed by the Russians to the airfield the French had built at Tegel and to the strip which the British had enlarged at Gatow. Before long planes were landing every five minutes at the US Templehof aerodrome. There was a daily delivery of 5,000 tons of coal, but the principal supplies were food. As if in defiance of the Russians, few were tempted to buy goods in the Russian Zone, then not yet divided from them by a wall. More than 50 were killed in crashes in the fog and on icy runways that winter.

The expensive Berlin Airlift (total cost £100 million) was kept up for nearly a year. Finally however the Russians lifted the blockade.

A West German parliamentary election was held in August 1949 which was won by the Christian Democrat Union whose leader, Konrad Adenauer, formed the government of what the Allies called the Federal Republic of Germany (West Germany). In reply the Russians turned their zone into the German Democratic Republic (East Germany). Allied Control remained in Berlin, but Germany has remained disunited.

1949

When dropping the atomic bombs on Hiroshima and Nagasaki in August 1945 brought a sudden surrender of Japan, there were two Chinas – Nationalist China (Chiang Kai-shek's Kuomintang) and Communist China (Mao Tse-tung's CCP). With the removal of the external enemy, for the defeat of whom the two factions had temporarily combined, the fight for mastery of China was resumed. In spite of its inertia and corruption, the KMT had the military support of the United States in re-asserting authority over the areas which the Japanese were now evacuating. But the Chinese themselves, particularly the peasants, showed signs of favouring an extension of the kind of government which was lowering rents and instituting land reform.

In 1945 Mao had a Communist army of a million, and in the next three years waged a steady war of attrition against the KMT, aided by their fellow-communists of the USSR who had invaded Manchuria just before the Japanese surrender. Their cause was strengthened by the growing American disillusionment with Chiang Kai-skek's corrupt regime. In 1947 the USA withdrew its forces from China and cut down financial aid to the KMT. Civil servants began to co-operate with Mao's regime in greater numbers, and on 10 October 1949, by which time few Nationalist forces remained on the mainland, Mao inaugurated the People's Republic of China in Peking which, with 300 million, was the largest com-

Mao Tse-tung, Chinese communist leader, addresses a political meeting in 1945

munist state in the world. Recognised by Britain in 1950, it was however excluded from the UN Security Council. In December Chiang Kai-shek withdrew to Formosa off the coast, which he re-named Taiwan (population 8 million).

DAILY TELEGRAPH

BATTLE AFTER FALL OF SHANGHAI

NATIONALISTS TRYING TO ESCAPE BY SEA

FROM OUR OWN CORRESPONDENT
SHANGHAI, Wednesday.

Mao Tse-tung's "People's Liberation Army," which entered Shanghai at 7.30 this morning [as reported in the later editions of THE DAILY TELEGRAPH], had occupied practically the whole of the city to-night.

Although Shanghai, the world's fourth largest city, had surrendered, the battle continued in the Woosung area, due north. Unconfirmed reports said Nationalist troops were embarking in 40 craft at the mouth of the Wangpoo in an effort to escape to Formosa.

It is thought that it will take the fugitive troops two days to embark—if they can. Meanwhile it is clear that Communists are making a heavy attack, from both sides, on Woosung fort to cut off their escape.

The Nationalists blew up arms and fuel dumps at Kiangwan Airfield. To cover their retreat northwards they defended the bridges across Soochow Creek. The Communists attacked with mortar fire.

Then Communist units moved around the western suburbs and took the north side railway station. This meant that the Nationalists were outflanked.

This evening the area south of Soochow Creek was completely in the Communists' hands. North of the creek Nationalist soldiers were reported to be changing into mufti.

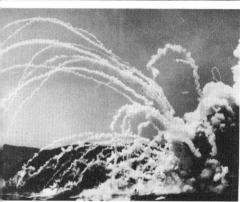

For years both China, on whose continent it lay, and Japan, who faced it, claimed the peninsula of Korea as a legitimate 'sphere of influence'. In 1875 Korea had become an independent state not subject to China, but in 1910 it was annexed by Japan. After 1945 the future of the country lay with the victorious Allies as part of the collapsed Japanese Empire. At first both Russia and America seemed amenable to the idea of a four-power trusteeship for the whole country. Under this a Russian occupying army was to take over the industrial north of the country, and an American force the agricultural south, under a Joint Commission administering the country as a single unit. But the USSR had second thoughts, and, once their forces had arrived, set up a *government* for their area, which was not part of the agreement. They made the 38th line of latitude their 'frontier' with the American area, chopping the peninsula into two. Moscow had hoped that Washington would meekly allow the communist government of North Korea jurisdiction over the whole country, whereas the Americans at once sought a ruling on what best to do with the country from the United Nations.

When the UN organised a fact-finding mission to visit Korea, the Russians refused to allow it north of the 38th parallel; and when it recommended the holding of a free election throughout the whole country, the Russians proclaimed their North Korea to be a People's Republic with a capital at Pyongyang, which moreover they held had sovereignty over the whole of Korea. The southern Koreans thereupon declared their territory to be a separate republic with its capital in Seoul, and this was reluctantly supported by the USA. Russian and American forces then withdrew.

When in 1950 the People's Republic's army suddenly crossed the frontier with the south, the UN Security Council (which the USSR were currently boycotting) declared the action a breach of the peace, and voted for the recall of the American troops to resist the aggression in the name of the UN. Other western forces joined the UN force, and Chinese 'volunteers' came to the aid of North Korea in 1951, driving back General MacArthur's UN army which had almost reached Manchuria. General Ridgeway, who replaced the dismissed MacArthur, then re-occupied the South, and an armistice was signed between the two Koreas in July 1953. Some 120,000 Americans fell in the Korean War and, like after the Battle of the Somme, there were many to ask what on earth they had died *for*.

Above left *American tanks moving up to the front cannot distract these Korean women from the daily clothes wash.* **Inset** *Phosphorus shells explode when a Korean munition dump is hit.* **Left** *Telling a North ('red') Korean, who was your enemy, from a South Korean, who was your ally, was no easy matter. A dismounted member of the US 8th Cavalry Regiment takes no chances*

1950

1951

Holland Toffee *Best on Earth*

NEWS CHRONICLE

No. 33,611   SATURDAY, FEBRUARY 27, 1954

FUHRER McCARTHY

Americans say it—and probe the prober

His body is broken, his spirit —NEVER

MORRISON OPENS FIRE

THE fight against McCarthyism in the two leading nations of the Free World. Last night's get-tough news :

IN AMERICA the storm over the Army-Senator feud blows right up to the doors of the White House. And a great newspaper hits out : This is the way Germany went under Hitler. The Republicans order an all-in probe of Senate investigations. That includes (and is directed against) McCarthy's own Star Chamber.

IN BRITAIN, where five million people were shocked to see the Senator in action on TV this week, Herbert Morrison made a forthright attack. He spoke of 'curious and objectionable activities,' and declared : I know what would happen here if we were afflicted with such a chairman as McCarthy.

From STANLEY BURCH : New York, Friday

JOSEPH McCARTHY was called an American Hitler and the Administration accused of an American Munich today by two of the nation's greatest newspapers. Both appealed to President Eisenhower to speak out at last against the senator.

'There is only one man in the country,' the Liberal Washington Post asserted 'with stature and votes to speak out in clarion tones for the things decent American believe in. That is President Eisenhower himself.

HURTING THE GOOD NAME OF AMERICA

CommunistRussia had been an ally of Capitalist America throughout World War II, and Stalin and Roosevelt had presumably exchanged information of the highest confidentiality when meeting at Yalta, Potsdam and elsewhere to plan the future of the post-war world. After the death of Roosevelt and the end of the war, the US government was insistent that no other country should learn the secrets of nuclear fission discovered by the Manhattan Project, even for the peaceful applications seen as so valuable for the advance of civilisation. In 1946 they passed the MacMahon Act forbidding the communication of atomic information to any foreign power. Thus anyone who conscientiously believed that such formulae should be disclosed to all who wished to use them for the benefit of mankind could not do so without being considered a traitor.

Did the USA harbour any 'traitors'? President Truman said they should find out, and Congress set up an Un-American Activities Committee to root out 'security risks' in public life, in business, in the arts (Hollywood particularly), and in sport. Many felt obliged to resign their jobs. Julius and Ethel Rosenburg were convicted of passing atomic secrets to the Russian Government; Alger Hiss of the State Department was condemned for lying about his previous Communist connections.

Joseph McCarthy, senator for Wisconsin, declared the State Department a nest of Communism and launched an hysterical campaign against 'communists' in the way the authorities had once hunted down deranged old women as 'witches'.

Dwight Eisenhower succeeded Truman as right-wing Republican president in 1952. As such he felt unable to show too much disaproval of McCarthyism. However the Democrat-controlled Senate had no hesitation in passing a vote of censure on the Senator when in 1954 he sent his agents Roy Cohn and David Schine to denounce 'communists' in American embassies and consulates overseas. He had, they said, brought their house into disrepute. McCarthyism was dead. So, too, three years later was McCarthy.

Senator Joseph McCarthy waves and smiles as he leaves the Federal Court in New York after a public session of his investigations sub-committee

King Farouk of Egypt posed in May 1951 with his 17-year-old bride Narriman for their first formal portrait before setting sail in the royal yacht for what the London *Sunday Express* described as 'the most fabulous honeymoon of modern times'. It took in Venice, Capri and Cannes, where the king lost £75,000 in two nights' gambling. A year later, they set sail from Egypt again – into exile. Local newspaper headlines proclaimed: 'There goes the shame of Egypt. There goes Farouk the First – and Last'. The king's extravagance had proved his downfall. Initially, his style had won him the hearts of a nation long dominated by the Ottoman Empire, the French and the British. He came to the throne at 16 in 1936, mixed freely with his people, especially at times of disaster, showed himself a devout Moslem and stood up to his country's most recent occupiers, the British. But it all got out of hand. He began to believe himself the spiritual head of Islam while at the same time building up immense wealth. He is reputed to have owned 250 cars, 25 of them Rolls Royces.

He led his country to defeat in the first Arab-Israeli war in 1948 and divorced his first wife, the popular Queen Farida, who had borne him three daughters but no sons. Finally, on 23 July 1952, Army officers dismayed at the war defeat and continued incompetence of the service led a successful siege of Army headquarters in Cairo. They found overwhelming support in a country eager to be rid of a corrupt king and army. On 26 July, King Farouk announced his abdication – and with it the end of the Egyptian monarchy – and left the country the same evening.

Right *No longer a king, 43 year old Farouk is more in his element in a night club chatting up a young Italian singer Irma Capece Minutolo whom, according to Irma, he was shortly to marry – a picture taken in 1953.* **Below right** *Still the ruler of Egypt, King Farouk entertains, at the Koubba Palace in Cairo, HRH Prince Philip, and Ernest Bevin, Britain's Foreign Secretary, on his way home from the 1950 Colombo Conference.* **Below** *More youthful and less bloated Farouk – duck shooting in 1939*

THE PEOPLE

Narriman's baby is Egypt's new King

FAROUK ABDICATES

She sends a message to the women of Britain

A tearful farewell—after shots outside Palace

HE FIGHTS IKE

Britain's rockets can chase bombers

JET GENIUS WHITTLE WAS SACKED

1953

THE DAILY TELEGRAPH and MORNING POST, WEDNESDAY, JUNE 3, 1953.

24-PAGE PICTURE SUPPLEMENT

The Daily Telegraph

and Morning Post

No. 30,548   LONDON, WEDNESDAY, JUNE 3, 1953   Printed in LONDON and MANCHESTER   Price 3d.

ELIZABETH II IS CROWNED

SPLENDOUR IN ABBEY SEEN BY MILLIONS

QUEEN 4 TIMES ON PALACE BALCONY: VAST CROWDS

ROYAL BROADCAST: PLEDGE TO SERVICE OF HER PEOPLES

WITH THE SPLENDOUR AND SOLEMNITY OF AN HISTORIC RITUAL INSIDE WESTMINSTER ABBEY, WITH TRADITIONAL POMP AND COLOUR AND PAGEANTRY ALONG THE ROYAL ROUTE OUTSIDE, ELIZABETH II WAS YESTERDAY CROWNED QUEEN AMID THE AFFECTIONATE ACCLAIM OF MILLIONS OF HER PEOPLE IN THIS COUNTRY AND THROUGHOUT HER GREAT COMMONWEALTH OF NATIONS.

Some 8,000 people witnessed the traditional crowning ceremony of Britain's latest monarch in Westminster Abbey in the nation's capital on 2 June 1953, and heard the youthful Queen Elizabeth II in her magnificent robes give the ancient coronation oath dedicating herself to the service of her subjects – who also heard and saw her, together with millions of others round the world, on their television screens. It was the first time the actual service had been televised from inside the church.

Hundreds of thousands thronged the decorated streets of London to watch and cheer the colourful procession of coaches, horsemen and foot soldiers as it wended its way to the abbey (in pouring rain) and back again to Buckingham Palace (in near sunshine). Her Majesty, and her husband, Prince Philip, Duke of Edinburgh, accompanied by her children Prince Charles (not yet proclaimed Prince of Wales) and Princess Anne, later appeared on the balcony of the palace to wave to crowds who packed the Mall below; and in the evening she broadcast to the Commonwealth assuring her listeners of her determination to be worthy of their trust. Her lasting memory of that day, she said, would be not only of the beauty and solemnity of the ceremony but the inspiration of their loyalty and affection.

Coronation Night was then celebrated with feasting, dancing and singing in streets, homes, pubs, restaurants and night clubs throughout her United Kingdom which had just ended food rationing, and in the independent nations and colonial territories of the Commonwealth. Everyone looked to what hopefully would be a new Elizabethan Age in which Britain and the world would put the effects of the recent war finally behind them, and give a New Look not only to fashion but every aspect of modern living.

Right *The scene inside London's ancient Westminster Abbey as the newly crowned Queen Elizabeth II proceeds down the nave to the west door after the ceremony.* **Inset** *The new sovereign shows herself to her subjects from the balcony of her London home*

Below *No amount of rain could tarnish the splendour of the coronation procession through London. The state coach moves out of Hyde Park by the gates (since removed) at Marble Arch (which once stood outside Buckingham Palace)*

It was one of the wettest Junes for many years – people who waited all night got soaked

1953

No human being had ever stood on top of the 29,002 feet high Mount Everest in the Himalayas, the world's highest, until 1953. On 1 June in that year, the day before the Coronation of Queen Elizabeth II in London, a 34 year old New Zealand bee farmer Edmund Hillary (he was later knighted for his achievement), and the 38 year old leader of the Sherpa guides and bearers Tensing Norgay, reached the summit after a slow climb at less than ten steps a minute up the final three hundred yards from their last Camp Eight. Together they plunged a Union Jack into the hard snow. On receiving the news the next day while preparing for the great ceremony that lay ahead, the Queen at once sent a cable of congratulation on what all the papers called the Crowning Glory.

The climb to the top, which had defeated seven previous attempts (backed by three reconnaissance expeditions), was the result not only of superhuman endurance and persistence, but of the careful planning and teamwork of the whole British expedition led by Colonel Sir John Hunt, and the superb performance of the sophisticated equipment. To enable the climbers to breathe and walk in the thin air each had to carry a 26 lb cylinder of extra oxygen lasting five hours. The two who finally succeeded gained from the experience of men like Mallory and Irvine who disappeared without trace within sight of their goal. Tensing had gone to within 800 feet of it only the previous year with Raymond Lambert of a Swiss expedition, before having to turn back. That Hillary and Tensing should make it, after the mountain had defied conquest for so many centuries, certainly shook the world that coronation week.

Below Some of the Everest Expedition porters with their loads moving off from Bhatgaon, their temporary supply headquarters

Right The conquerors of Everest – Edmund Hillary and Tensing Norgay – enjoy a snack at Dulaghat, 40 miles from Khatmandu, on their return to base

Medical student Roger Bannister finishes his record mile

The Everest Expedition forward reconnaissance group pitched this tent on the edge of a 2000 ft ravine separating them from the Khumbo glacier seen towering in the background

In 1954 for the first time since records had been kept, a mile was run in under the round figure of four minutes set by athletes throughout the world. On 6 May in that year 25 year old Roger Bannister accomplished this feat by clocking three minutes 59.4 seconds in an athletic meeting between Oxford University and the Amateur Athletic Association at the Iffley Road track.

1954

Front line news photographer takes a front page picture of the first wounded being evacuated from Dien Bien Phu by helicopter to Louang Prabang

'Where do we go from here?' Anywhere but forwards. No future for the French in Dien Bien Phu

Part of the New Order which Japan managed to impose on East Asia between 1941 and 1945 was the merger of the French Colony of Cochin China with her protectorates of Annam and Tonking in a single state under the Emperor of Annam, to which they gave the name 'Vietnam' – the Annamese name for Annam. During that time an underground movement chivvied both the French administrators and the Japanese intruders – the Vietnam Independence League known as 'Vietminh', dominated by Ho Chi Minh, head of the local communist party.

With the dismantling of the New Order on the defeat of Japan, France moved to reestablish her sovereignty over the area, but before she could do so Ho Chi Minh had taken over the palace of Hanoi and proclaimed a Democratic Republic of Vietnam, which they had to recognise.

In the north of Indo-China the Japanese surrendered to the Chinese Nationalist army of Chiang Kai-shek; in the south they surrendered to the British who handed the territory over to the French, who then made an agreement with the kings of the rest of French Indo-China, Cambodia and Laos. The Vietminh, who had the protection of Chiang Kaishek, occupied the centre of the country, and to prevent them attacking Laos the French installed a large garrison at Dien Bien Phu.

In 1954 Ho Chi Minh's forces launched a savage attack on the French garrison at Dien Bien Phu and captured it after a long siege. It was the signal for France to withdraw from Indo-China entirely, and at the Geneva Conference that year they agreed to stop the war.

DAILY SKETCH
WEDNESDAY, OCTOBER 31, 1956   2d

War flashes 4.30 is zero hour ★ Ike says

WE'RE GOING IN

By GUY EDEN and SKETCH WAR BUREAU

BRITISH troops are poised this morning to reoccupy the Suez Canal bases, they left in 1954.

An Anglo-French force of Marines, Commandos and assault troops was lying off Port Said early to-day in a huge fleet of landing craft supported by warships and aircraft carriers.

President Nasser has rejected outright the Anglo-French 12-hour ultimatum given him at 4.30 p.m. yesterday.

Air, sea armada poised

In 1954, Egypt, the location of the Suez Canal once so important to the maintenance of what had been the British Empire, had been a British sphere of influence for 80 years. But in that year the Tory government of Sir Winston Churchill made a reappraisal of its Middle East strategy, and agreed with Colonel Nasser, Egyptian head of the new United Arab Republic who had seized power from King Farouk in 1952, to withdraw British troops from the Canal Zone.

When the Colonel asked for a loan of $1,300 million to heighten the old British-built Aswan Dam on the Nile, the USA offered $50 million and Britain $14. To help make up the rest the USSR, which had been supplying Egypt with arms when Britain, France and the US had refused, offered to lend Nasser another $100 million. On hearing of the Soviet deal the US government withdrew their offer, which so incensed Nasser that he said he would get the money by diverting to Egypt the revenues of the international Suez Canal Company, which he thereupon appropriated. It was a provocative act reminiscent of Hitler's re-occupation of the Rhineland in 1936. Would the world let Nasser 'get away with it', as it had let Hitler?

Egypt refused to attend the 22-country conference called to sort matters out on 11 August 1956, and rejected its proposals. Mr Kruschev warned Britain that coercion

Colonel Nasser greets Anthony Nutting, British Under Secretary for Foreign Affairs (Foreign Secretary Anthony Eden's no 2) in Cairo to discuss the Suez Pact in 1954

might lead to Russia's intervention to uphold Egypt's stand. The United Nations were not prepared to act; neither was the United States. But France was determined to stop Egypt helping those who were revolting against French rule in Algeria; Israel was always pleased for another excuse to humiliate Nasser; Britain could not be seen to be taking the nationalisation of the Suez Canal lying down.

Israel struck first; on 29 October her troops crossed the Israeli frontier and their *Mystère* fighters supplied by France swept into the desert. Within four days the Egyptian army had collapsed, with 6000 taken prisoner. On 31 October the British Royal Air Force destroyed the Egyptian airforce on the ground. In another two days Egypt's resistance ceased and the Canal Zone was re-occupied. On 3 November Nasser sunk vessels in the canal to stop the passage of all traffic, which was effective up to April 1957 when they were raised by a UN team of experts. By then Britain and France had handed over the Canal Zone to an international force.

British commandos raise a white ensign over Navy House, Port Said, ten minutes after capturing the building on 8 November 1956

Men of the Duke of Wellington's Regiment, en route for the Middle East, pass rifles along the line before 'emplaning' into a Hermes at Blackbushe on 12 August 1956

Daily Mail

MORNING SPECIAL

NO. 18,833 TWOPENCE   FOR QUEEN AND COMMONWEALTH   MONDAY, NOVEMBER 5, 1956

A dying nation's last SOS. It reached Vienna from a Hungarian reporter. His full story is in Page 5

good bye we do not forget you   the russian are too near   good bye friends good bye friends   save ou souls

BUDAPEST CRUSHED—Red troops storm into Parliament

The MURDER OF HUNGARY

Comment *Nagy marched out*
MONDAY, NOV. 5, 1956   *at gunpoint*

HUNGARIAN TRAGEDY

From JEFFREY BLYTH: On the Austro-Hungarian Frontier, Sunday Night

HUNGARY, the little country that dared to defy Russia, was murdered today. Russian troops struck at the freedom fighters all over the country. More than 1,000 tanks surrounded Budapest. Soviet soldiers stormed into the Parliament building after Premier Nagy had just broadcast to the world an agonised cell for help.

COMMANDOS EMBARK: FIRST PICTURE

GET OUT! IKE URGES BULGANIN

And U.N. says 'Get out' too

Coast defences attacked

CYPRUS TROOPS BOARD THE INVASION SHIPS

From T. F. THOMPSON: Allied H.Q., Monday, 1 a.m.

TWELVE hours after some of the toughest units in the British and French armies embarked yesterday on the invasion fleet at a Cyprus port, Allied Headquarters announced this morning that coastal defences "well clear of Alexandria " were being attacked.

Israel plane shot down

Not every Russian satellite state was as securely in orbit round the Marxist Communism of the USSR as the rulers would have liked. As early as 1948 they had resented the liberties which Marshal Tito was taking with orthodoxy in Yugoslavia. To show their disapproval they withdrew their advisers from Belgrade and expelled Yugoslavia from the Cominform. It was not the sort of behaviour the new Mother Russia expected from her offspring, but instead of crushing this display of independence with an iron fist Kruschev went to apologise to Tito for Russia's attitude.

The incident encouraged nationalistic, anti-Soviet elements to riot in East Berlin in 1953, and in Poland in 1956. In October 1956 however occurred demonstrations which alarmed the Kremlin more than any other, and became what was justifiably called the Hungarian Revolution.

A Hungarian worker stands guard with a machine gun at the entrance to his strike-bound factory on Csepel Island outside Budapest

Those who stage-managed the uprising were doubtless encouraged by the denunciations which Kruschev made that February to the Twentieth Party Congress of Stalin's 'intolerance, brutality and abuse of power'. The Hungarians drove communist ministers Rakosi and Gero from office, and installed an administration composed of all shades of political opinion, including outright anti-commun-

'Hands up for democracy! Hands up for a free Hungary!'

Hungarians risked immediate shortages and breakdowns in the longer term interest of ridding their country of the Soviet yoke – a Budapest boy, sent by his parents to collect food brought in by the Danish Red Cross, takes home a crust of bread and soup for all to share

The price of 'deviation' – a district of Budapest after the rioting

ists. They put one Imre Nagy at its head.

The people of Hungary then rose in revolt, hanged communist leaders from the trees of Budapest, and lynched known members of the secret police. Many took the opportunity to leave Hungary for ever, escaping with the minimum of possessions to Britain, France, Holland and elsewhere in the West, en route for some of them to Canada. The iron curtain was not raised for long; in November Russian tanks and infantry moved into the ancient capital and quelled the uprising with terrible ferocity, killing 20,000 including the brave Imre Nagy.

Kruschev's de-Stalinisation went slower from then on, and satellites were less keen to step out of line after so unequivocable a demonstration of how the Kremlin would be likely to deal with any further signs of 'deviation' – and how unlikely it was, as in the case of Hungary, that the United States or any other western power would dare to interfere.

Demonstrators topple a huge statue of Stalin near Budapest's national theatre

America may have stolen a march on Russia by perfecting the world's first atomic bomb in 1945, but any thoughts they may have had that they were way ahead of the USSR in all matters of technology were severely shattered when on 4th October 1957 they, and the world, heard of the launching into space by rocket of the unmanned, artificial satellite, 'Sputnik I'. It was the world's first, and established once and for all that space travel was possible. It orbited the earth transmitting radio signals. The race for the control of space was on and 'Sputnik I' gave Russia a spectacular lead. It meant they knew how to make an inter-continental missile capable of reaching America. The United States had nothing like it and felt very vulnerable. 'Whoever gains that ultimate position [of controlling space],' stated Senator Lyndon B Johnson, 'gains control, total control, over the earth, for purposes of tyranny or for the service of freedom.' Secretary of State Foster Dulles had to admit that US prestige had been damaged.

The United States had begun exploring the possibility of space travel in 1955. Announcements came from both Washington and Moscow of the intention to solve all problems for International Geophysical Year (1957–8), but only the USSR were able to put their words into action. Not only that, but within a month of Sputnik I they had rocketed Sputnik II into space, a half-ton container carrying a black and white dog as passenger, Laika. It circled round and round the world for all to see for six months. After a failure in December 1957, America's tiny, three-pound 'Vanguard' was finally shot into space in March 1958 – and is still there.

Before it was launched by rocket into space – the Soviet unmanned satellite Sputnik 1

Once free of the obligation of becoming compulsory members of Hitler's New Order for Europe, the western powers set about implementing their own plans for integration. In 1948, the year Winston Churchill told an audience in Zurich, 'We must build a kind of United State of Europe,' Belgium, Netherlands and Luxembourg ('Benelux') formed a customs union, a conference at The Hague called for a European Parliament, and an Organisation for European Economic Cooperation was instituted. The following May ten countries, including Britain, signed the Statute of the Council of Europe which had its headquarters at Strasbourg but no power. Britain refused however to take part in the European Coal and Steel Community when it was set up in 1951, with Jean Monnet as president.

Further economic cooperation came in March 1957 when the six member countries of the ESSC signed the Treaty of Rome creating the European Economic Community – 'the Common Market' – and the European Atomic Energy Community.

The military North Atlantic Treaty setting up NATO had been signed by nine European countries, including Britain, with the USA and Canada in 1949. The Soviet Union had replied with the Warsaw Pact, a 20-year treaty of mutual defence signed in 1955 between the USSR, East Germany, Czechoslovakia, Poland, Hungary, Rumania, Bulgaria and Albania.

The signatures of the heads of state beneath the Treaty of Rome of 25 March 1957 which created the European Common Market

The historic scene in Rome when representatives of six countries signed the document which set up the EEC and EURATOM

CASTRO COUP

The American State Department had frequently expressed its disapproval of the corruption and oppression of the Batista regime in Cuba, so welcomed its overthrow in 1958 by Dr Fidel Castro who made a favourable impression by at once implementing a programme of building schools and hospitals and introducing land reform. In 1959 Castro was installed as Prime Minister of a revolutionary Cuba which being 'humanistic' and not communist was supported by America where he became a romantic hero. But when he continued to delay restoring the democratic constitution of 1940, started interfering with American business interests and nationalised the sugar factories, the US broke off diplomatic relations with what had become a communist dictatorship.

Climax of the Cuban Revolution – Che Guevara (in the sombrero) watches out for trouble as Fidel Castro (in the peaked cap) harangues the crowds on arrival in Havana at the head of his rebel caravan on 1 January 1959

DAILY EXPRESS

FRIDAY JANUARY 2 1959

General Election will be in May

Express man-on-the-spot Ian Aitken sees the revolution win in Cuba

HAVANA GOES WILD

Blood and brandy riots after victory

From IAN AITKEN, Havana, Cuba, Thursday

COBBOLD FAILS TO STOP CITY ROW

By FREDERICK ELLIS

Prince sues ex-M.P. over £7,000 racehorse

GUNMEN KILL FOR A 'DARE'

From RONALD SINGLETON, Hollywood, Thursday

The Sceptre to go up for sale

By GEOFFREY WAREHAM

A fifth race dog poisoned

Daily Mail MORNING SPECIAL

NO. 19,574 © Associated Newspapers Ltd., 1959. FOR QUEEN AND COMMONWEALTH MONDAY, MARCH 30, 1959 PRICE 2½D.

FLASHBACK to 1956—Mao Tse-tung plays host to the Panchen Lama (left) and the Dalai Lama during their visit to Peking, capital of Red China.

Comment
MONDAY, MARCH 30, 1959

HUNGARY OF

TIBET RULER'S STAFF SEIZED
Then Chinese send picked force to seek him
out on mountain escape route from Lhasa

FLIGHT OF THE LAMA

Until the bridge they are building is ready, Chinese troops float their transport across the torrential river on heavy rubber dinghies to hasten their advance into the interior of Tibet

At the beginning of the 20th century Tibet had been part of the Chinese Empire of the Manchu dynasty but not under direct Chinese rule. Though the country became effectively independent in 1912 it was a status which received no international recognition. Chiang Kai-shek's Kuomintang followed the emperors in repressing minority races such as the Tibetans, but the communist regime of Mao Tse-tung was at first more tolerant. In 1950 however he decided to move into Tibet and occupy this remote and backward country in the mountains of north India. Its ruler, the Dalai Lama, was obliged to sign a treaty by which he officially recognised Tibet as part of China. In 1954 a new constitution incorporated the principle that 'the national autonomous areas are inalienable parts of the People's Republic of China'.

The Chinese communists tried to enlist the help of the local government, the monasteries and the nobles in modernising Tibet, but without success. Sporadic anti-Chinese guerilla attacks became a full-scale revolt in 1959 which was severely crushed by Chinese forces, and the Dalai Lama fled to India.

Left Once in Lhasa the Chinese invader invites the Tibetans to switch their allegiance from the departed Dalai Lama to their puppet Panchin Lama

125

1960

Every government has its intelligence gathering organisations but none can afford admitting it. Discovering what stage a potential enemy had reached in developing space missiles needed more sophisticated methods, but it was still 'espionage', an emotive word which made the situation worse when a nation's spy had the misfortune to be caught in the act, like Gary Powers, the pilot of a US U-2 aircraft shot down over Russia by Soviet missiles on 1 May 1960.

Powers was uninjured and had to admit he was on a photo-reconnaissance mission from Pakistan to Norway. The US government of President Eisenhower at once publicly justified such flights as necessary for national security. But the event seriously retarded the growing detente between the US and the USSR, and the Russian leader Nikita Kruschev angrily denounced American 'aggression' in sending over U-2s to spy on Russia. Eisenhower promised there would be no more missions, but Kruschev was not to be placated. The US Senate Foreign Relations Committee censured the 'grave mishandling' of the incident. Francis Gary Powers had to stand trial in public in a Moscow courtroom, and was sentenced to ten years imprisonment. Russia withdrew from the disarmament discussions at Geneva.

The U-2 Incident had certainly made the headlines, but had little effect on the intensity with which every government in the world continued their inevitably risky 'intelligence' operations.

DAILY EXPRESS

No. 18,753   SATURDAY SEPTEMBER 10 1960   1 a.m. forecast: Mainly bright; warm   Price 2½d

Action pictures of battle on road to Katanga

LUMUMBA'S INVADERS

Belgians fly to stop them

From DANIEL McGEACHIE
ELISABETHVILLE Friday

LUMUMBA'S invasion troops —300 strong— have advanced 10 miles into the breakaway province of Katanga tonight.

Rifles above their heads, they waded the Luika River near the border a few hours ago.

They are believed to be the advance guard of a larger force—some reports say 2,000 men—aiming at

Foot may go back on list

Express Political Correspondent

MICHAEL FOOT, knocked out of the short list by a shock vote, may be back in the running next week as prospective Labour candidate for Ebbw Vale, Aneurin Bevan's old seat.

The vote that cut Mr Foot out of the list was taken by the local party executive of 18 men and 12 women.

But next Saturday the general management committee of about 200 meets to confirm the executive decision.

And there the rumpus that is going on in the valleys over the selected few will come right into the open.

200 to decide

The "short" list may be made longer. Michael Foot's name—he was sixth in Thursday night's voting—may reappear. And all the other rank-and candidates with him.

There on September 24 final selection will be made by the 200 delegates.

While the row was going on

Death is the dust for two tribesmen. They died because they stood in the way of the terror march of Lumumba's troops through Kasai province, last bastion before breakaway Katanga

Colonel Joseph Mobutu, Congolese Army Chief of Staff, who in August 1960 announced that the army were taking over supreme power in Belgian Congo until the end of the year

In 1958 President de Gaulle offered independence to any French colony that wanted it. A conference of African independence movements in Accra was attended by Patrice Lumumba, leader of the largest political party in Belgian Congo. In 1960 the Belgian government agreed to give Congo independence with Congolese in political control but Belgians continuing to run the administration and public services. Lumumba was installed as head of an independent coalition government on 30

Indian troops of the United Nations force called to the driver of this car to stop, and in the confusion opened fire on it. Inside it were three Belgians, two of whom were killed. A tragic mistake in a tragic country

June 1960, and the Belgian army withdrew. A few days later however the Congolese army mutinied against its Belgian officers and the Belgian troops returned, soon to be replaced by a United Nations force of 3000. When Tshombe, president of Katanga province, rich in copper mines, declared it independent, the United Nations refused to allow Lumumba to use them to attack the province and subdue the revolt. So Lumumba looked for help from Russia who demanded the resignation of Dag Hammarskjold, UN Secretary General. At this Kasavubu, President of Zaire (as the Congo had been re-named), with the support of the army, dismissed and imprisoned Lumumba who, a few month later, was killed.

This disastrous beginning to the Congo's independence extended into 1961 with fierce fighting between UN and Katanga forces, which were not routed until the following year when Tshombe's independent Katangan government was overthrown. It was while on his way to a meeting with Tshombe in September 1961 that Hammarskjold's plane crashed and he was killed. In 1965 General Mobutu, army C-in-C, deposed president Kasavubu in a bloodless coup.

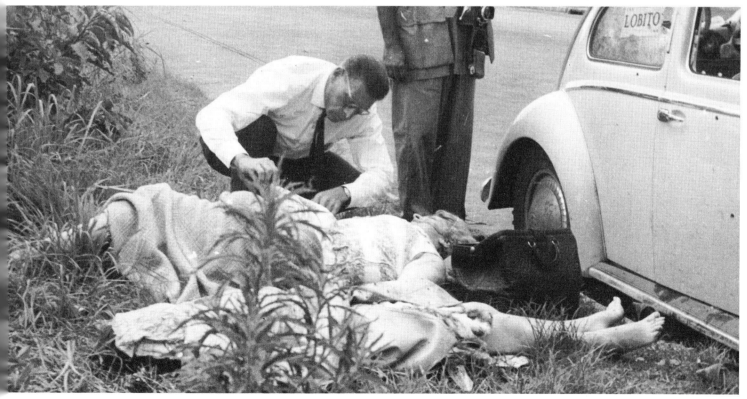

1961

When in 1946, Winston Churchill coined the phrase 'Iron Curtain' to describe the division between the communist and non-communist world, he never envisaged that within 15 years Soviet Russia would erect a physical barrier inside Berlin severing relations between east and west so emphatically. On his tour of Europe in May 1961 the new President of the US, John Kennedy, had met the Russian leader Kruschev in Vienna, and perhaps given him the impression he was young and immature, and on the defensive. However that may be, that August the Soviets decided to build the Berlin Wall making the Russian Zone an enclave within the German capital to which none would have unauthorised entry. It was the climax of Russian objections to the way Berlin had been organised which they had been airing ever since 1948 and became intensified after 1958. In that time more and more refugees were making their way out of East Germany through the western zone of Berlin and into West Germany, especially skilled workers whom Russia could ill afford to lose. Some 140,000 crossed over in 1959, another 200,000 in 1960 and 100,000 in the first half of 1961. With the building of the Berlin Wall the escape route was sealed. But the western powers were not to be provoked into abandoning the capital. 'We do not want to fight,' President Kennedy warned Kruschev, 'but we have fought before. We cannot and will not permit the communists to drive us out of Berlin either gradually or by force.' The temperature of the Cold War had risen.

Left *Escape at your peril! – the barricades are up around the Russian zone of Berlin*

Above *The two zones are finally separated. The East German police fix the last strands of barbed wire*

Right *Think of what a wall down the middle of Whitechapel Road would have meant to Londoners! – it happened to Berliners in August 1961*

Below *Berlin's stone curtain – Ernst Lemmer, West German Minister for All-German Affairs, views with dismay, on 20 November 1961, the Russian built walls in front of the Brandenburg Gate*

SUNDAY EXPRESS

APRIL 23 1961   Lighting-up Time 8.40 p.m. to 5.16 a.m. (Mon.)   Founded by LORD BEAVERBROOK   Moon D Rises 12.14 p.m. Sets 3.22 a.m. (Mon.)   PRICE 5d.

Police squads guard President's palace in Paris

GENERALS GRAB ALGIERS THEN DE GAULLE ACTS

Rebels' supplies cut off, iron grip put on France

Sunday Express Reporter: PARIS, Saturday

FRENCH paratroops of the Foreign Legion, led by a junta of four retired generals opposed to de Gaulle's soft-pedal policy in Algeria, today took command of the great city and port of Algiers without a shot being fired.

Tonight, President de Gaulle is taking the first counter-measures. He decided to cut off all supplies—and pay—to the rebels; and with France once again on the brink of civil war, he has ordered what amounts to a state of national emergency to prevent the insurrection spreading to the mainland.

It was just after dawn that soldiers surrounded the key points of Algiers, including the Summer Palace, seat of the chief Government official in the city, the Delegate-General, M. Jean Morin. He and the Algerian Commander-in-Chief, General Gambiez, are reported to be prisoners there.

Algiers radio then broadcast an "order of the military command" proclaiming a state of siege over the entire area of French North Africa.

Mr. K may try a

Milan says £100,000 for Haynes

MILAN have stepped up their offer for Fulham and England Soccer captain Johnny Haynes to £100,000. Fulham chairman Tommy Trinder said yesterday: "It is entirely up to Johnny now. If he feels that he has got to go to Italy, then he must go.

"But if we can keep him in this country and playing for Fulham we shall probably break ourselves in the attempt."

Mr. Trinder read a telegram he received yesterday from the Italian club. It said: Making firm offer of

DALI PAINTING

In 1961 Algeria was not a French colony or mandate (like Syria and Lebanon) or a protectorate (like Tunisia and Morocco), but an integral part of France. The first French civil government had been set up in the 1870s after 40 years of military campaigning. Political power was in the hands of the *colons*, the French Algerians who regarded themselves as superior to the moslem majority who were not classed as citizens. But in 1947 the French created an Algerian Assembly elected equally by *colons* and moslems. But soon the moslems were demanding full independence from France, organising themselves into a Front de Libération Nationale which began a series of violent demonstrations. But while in 1956 France gave her Overseas territories wide concessions, she insisted that she could not surrender the *colons* of Algeria to the Moslems, quite apart from wishing to exploit the oil which had just been discovered below the desert.

The Algerian Crisis reached a climax in May 1958 with a call for an emergency government to be set up in France under the old wartime leader of the Free French, General Charles de Gaulle, now in retirement and aged 67. He alone, it was thought, would 'save Algeria' where the FLN was demanding independence and the *colons* and the army wanted the country to be integrated with France. De Gaulle accepted the challenge, and in September 1959 decided that he would not impose a settlement on Algeria, but the country must choose for itself whether to secede from France or remain integrated with her. A referendum would be held in 1961, so long as there was an immediate cease-fire. Inevitably neither side welcomed the proposal, and the extreme Organisation de l'Armée Sécrète (OAS) resorted to violence, committing disgusting outrages on the moslem population. The OAS campaign reached a climax in March 1962 when a cease-fire was arranged and an agreement concluded by which a provisional government was set up and French troops were to quit Algeria within three years.

Recalled to solve the Algerian Crisis which threatened to tear France apart, the 67 year old wartime leader of Free France, General Charles de Gaulle, is garlanded at a French reception on Bastille Day 1961

Daily Mirror

3d. Thursday, April 13, 1961 • No. 17,828

TODAY the Mirror celebrates
the greatest story of OUR lifetime..
the greatest story of OUR century

.. MAN IN SPACE

ay morning. A
nily man. Yuri
und the world
nd continents.
. I feel well."
ssia just before
ritons. His first
ies or bruises."
ty achievement?
l the Wild Duck.

MAJOR YURI GAGARIN—his name means WILD DUCK.

Top centre *Major Yuri Gagarin joins Mr Kruschev, Mr Brehznev and other Soviet leaders in Red Square, Moscow, on 15 April 1961 to take the march past of workers celebrating his pioneering space flight.* **Right** *Yuri in his space suit*

The Space Age began with the Russians launching the unmanned satellite they called Sputnik 1 in October 1957, programmed to circle the earth emitting radio signals. America then put the first communications satellite in orbit, also unmanned, and the following year the Russians capped this with orbiting and retrieving the 4½ ton Sputnik V carrying two dogs. But the real sensation was when on 12 April 1961 a Russian rocket took off bearing the spacecraft Vostok 1 with 27 year old test pilot Yuri Gagarin on board – the first man to travel in space. He flew round the world in an hour and a half. He then landed without mishap, having sped in his tiny capsule 188 miles above the earth at 17,400 miles an hour. The *Daily Mirror* had no hesitation in calling it 'the greatest story of our lifetime, the greatest story of our century'.

Overnight the name Gagarin had become known throughout the civilised world. Three days later the famous major appeared in the uniform of the Russian airforce beside USSR political leaders Nikita Kruschev and Leonid Brezhnev on the Lenin-Stalin Mausoleum tribune in Red Square, Moscow, to take the salute at a celebration march past of workmen carrying flags and posters. He then made a world tour – this time with his feet on the ground. When he came to London on 13 July 1961 he laid a wreath on the Cenotaph.

1962

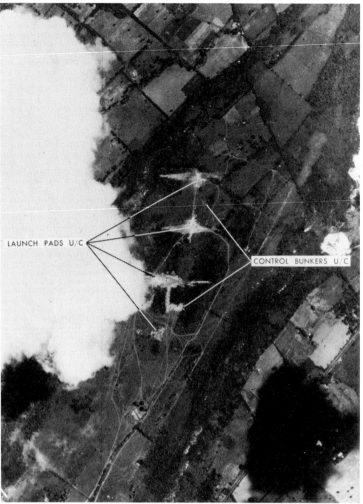

LAUNCH PADS U/C

CONTROL BUNKERS U/C

President Kennedy had good reason to be alarmed – Soviet Russia were actually building missile launching pads and control bunkers on Cuba, as these air photographs prove

The Soviet ship Anosov *returns to Russia carrying eight missile transporters with canvas-covered missiles which were intended for Cuba*

DAILY SKETCH | **CUBA** | SENSATIONAL MOVE BY KENNEDY

BLOCKADE!

Ultimatum to Kruschev 'Move those missiles'

When Cuba declined inclusion in President Kennedy's ten-year plan to raise living standards in Central and South America announced in March 1961, the US hoped that an invasion, under the auspices of the Cuban Revolutionary Council of exiles which it had sponsored in Miami, would trigger off another revolution and remove the unsettling Castro. But when on 16 April a force of less than 2000 without air cover landed on Cuba's south coast at the Bay of Pigs, most of them were captured and all expectations of an anti-Fidel rising were abandoned. Castro seized more American property in reprisal, but Russia feared that the American reaction would be another, more determined, attempt to oust the communist leader. To prevent this the Kremlin ordered the building of missile sites on Cuba from which rockets could threaten the American mainland, only 90 miles distant. Kruschev hoped the sites would be completed before America discovered them, but on 10 October 1962 Senator Keating of New York made public his belief that such sites were under construction. When Kruschev pooh-poohed the allegation, aerial photographs taken five days later revealed six sites each with four medium-range ballistic missiles with a range of 1200 miles, which could reach Washington, 42 jet bombers, military equipment and Russian troops. On 22 October President Kennedy said the secret and swift build up of these missiles was 'deliberately provocative', and that the launching of a missile from Cuba would be treated as an attack from the Soviet Union.

The bases were not yet usable, but Russian ships were on their way to Cuba with supplies which might well make them so, and Kennedy imposed a naval blockade of Cuba to stop them putting into Havana and unloading their threatening cargo. On 24 October, Kruschev, impressed by the 'immature' Kennedy's determination to stand up to him – he had ordered troops to Florida and had 156 rockets aligned on Russia – ordered the missile ships to slow down, and then turn back. The missile sites were destroyed, though the Russian troops remained.

A 'hot line' telephone was installed between the White House and the Kremlin in the hope that its use might prevent a recurrence of that nerve-wracking exercise in brinkmanship which had the world glued to the news headlines of those dramatic five days.

The motivation behind the events at Dallas of 22 November 1963 still remains a mystery. The presidential election was to take place the next year, in which John Kennedy's opponent would almost certainly be the right-wing Barry Goldwater. Anxious to win votes in the south where his racial policies were most criticised, he decided on a tour, accompanied by his wife Jacqueline, first to Texas, then to Fort Worth and Dallas. From the plane the party got themselves seated in the open limousine at the airport which then drove off into the town, with its accompanying motor cars full of officials and security agents. Shortly afterwards, as the motorcade was leisurely moving down Elm Street, a rifleman fired from a window high up in the Texas School Book Depository and shot the president in the back. With a second shot he wounded Governor Connally who was sitting beside the president; with a third he put a bullet through John Kennedy's head.

The assassin was almost certainly one Harvey Oswald an alleged 'communist', from whom however the purpose of his deed was never extracted, for a few days later he too fell victim to murder by one Jack Ruby.

Kennedy was succeeded by his vice-president Lyndon B Johnson.

John Kennedy, President of the United States of America 1961–1963

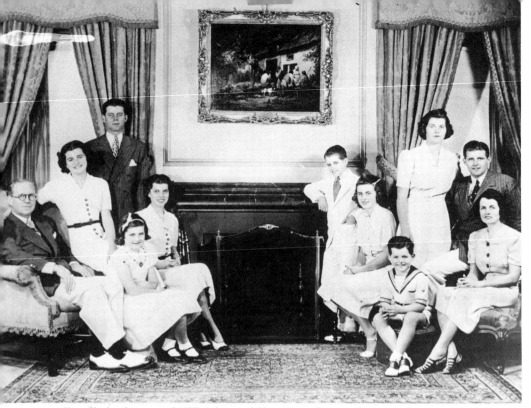

Above *Kennedy family group of 1937: John, aged 20, stands on the left with his sister and father, Joseph Kennedy, American ambassador to Britain*

Below *Emotional moment for Jacqueline Kennedy, centre, as she views the coffin at the state funeral of the assassinated president in Washington*

Above *Queen Elizabeth entertains President Kennedy to dinner at Buckingham Palace on 6 June 1961*

'I have a dream!' was the repeated cry at all his mass rallies of the tall Rev Dr Martin Luther King, the American negro with the spell-binding way of public speaking who, like Gandhi, insisted on using only non-violent means and passive resistance to plead his cause – the granting of full civil rights to his fellow negroes. It was a stance which in 1964 won him the Nobel Peace Prize.

A Baptist minister in Alabama in the deep South, his first success was in organising a negro boycott of all public transport in 1956, which led the federal government to pass a de-segregation law which allowed black to sit with white passengers in buses, trains and coaches. This encouraged him to press home his campaign with a series of huge non-violent marches and demonstrations in Washington and elsewhere in support of President Kennedy's civil rights laws. As head of the Southern Christian Leadership, he gave full support to the National Association for the Advancement of Coloured People. The Gentle Giant's dream of equality for blacks with whites was well on the way to fulfilment when he fell victim to an assassin's bullet in Memphis Tennessee in 1968; and the urgency of maintaining the momentum of his Negro Civil Rights movement was kept alive in books such as *Why We Can't Wait*.

The killing of Dr Martin Luther King provokes mass demonstrations.

Inset *His dream came true – American negro leader Dr Martin Luther King*

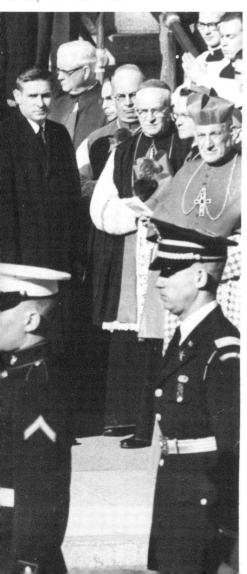

1964

The assassination of President Kennedy in November 1963 and the automatic succession of his Vice-President Lyndon Johnson, brought a change of mind regarding America's commitment in Vietnam. Johnson prepared secret contingency plans to escalate the war, and when in August 1964 two US destroyers were fired on by North Vietnamese

Left *An American soldier ducks from the back blast of his recoil-less rifle.* Left inset *Men of the US Navy Medical Corps and Marines carry a wounded comrade from a fire fight near Dong Ha, Vietnam.* Right inset *Pushing his air mattress in front of him loaded with combat gear, an American soldier swims a monsoon-flooded river in Hau Nghia Province, Vietnam*

gunboats in the Gulf of Tongking, he got the excuse to carry them out. The US Senate gave him authority to bring help to anyone who asked for it in defence of its freedom and to resist armed attack. Accordingly more American servicemen were flown out to the war-ravaged country, and in February 1965 they began bombing North Vietnam, which did little to undermine civilian morale however. A ground combat unit of US marines landed in March, and the end of the year saw 150,000 American troops in South Vietnam, rising to 500,000 by 1969. The 'communist' enemy, the Vietcong, had no aircraft, tanks or artillery, but kept the more sophisticatedly armed Americans at bay with crafty guerilla tactics

Scout dog Sandy accompanies Marine Corporal Kaplan of New York on patrols in the rice paddies of Da Nang, Vietnam

for month after month. The fact that the Vietcong had no uniforms to distinguish them from harmless South Vietnam villagers led to atrocities such as the My Lai incident in which 109 unarmed civilians of both sexes were slaughtered 'by mistake'. The object of it all was stated to be the prevention of South Vietnam and other states in South East Asia from falling into the hands of 'communists'.

A hovering US Army sky crane lowers a steel bridge to fill a hole blasted in the road to Ca Lu, Vietnam, by the Vietcong

Daily Mirror

Goodbye, Britain—Hello New York

3d. Saturday, February 8, 1964 • No. 18,704

Fans on a roof at London Airport wave goodbye to the Beatles yesterday.

YEAH! YEAH! U.S.A!

That old Beatlemania hits New York . . . . a screaming girl tries to get nearer the Beatles.

Paul, Ringo, George and John answer questions at the Press conference.

FATHER FLIES TO GET IRENE

PRINCESS Irene of Holland, whose romance has started a constitutional crisis, is going home today.

It was announced last night that her father, Prince Bernhard, would fly to Spain to pick her up.

And in Madrid, five Spanish statesman, Irene's secretary stated early today that her engagement to a Spanish nobleman will be announced by "the Dutch Royal House in Holland."

'Engagement news soon'

Irene—who recently became a Roman Catholic—is second in line to the Dutch Throne after her sister Beatrix.

Marry

But there were strong rumours in The Hague, the Dutch capital, last night that 24-year-old Irene will give up her rights of succession to the throne and marry the man she loves.

Yesterday Prince Bernhard flew his own plane to Austria and took Beatrix and her younger sister, Princess Margriet, home to Holland. They had been on holiday, watching the winter Olympics.

Their arrival in The Hague strengthened reports that the Dutch Royal family is gathering for an important meeting when Irene arrives today.

The announcement that Irene would be returning home today said that she had been spending several days in a "house of retreat" in Spain.

A second Government statement denied rumours that Queen Juliana might abdicate because of differences with the Cabinet over Irene's romance.

The Dutch Cabinet met again last night. Later Prime Minister Victor Marijnen, asked to comment on the "engagement" statement in Madrid, said: "We will know more when the Princess is back here."

5,000 scream 'welcome' to the Beatles

From BARRIE HARDING New York, Friday

FIVE thousand screaming, chanting teenagers—most of them playing truant from school—gave the Beatles a fantastic welcome here today.

More than 100 extra police were on duty to control the crowd as the group's jet landed at the John F. Kennedy Airport.

'Mad'

Pandemonium broke out among the stamping, banner-waving fans as the Beatles—John Lennon, Paul McCartney, George Harrison and Ringo Starr—stepped from the plane.

One policeman who has worked at the airport for ten years said: "I think the world has gone mad." And a veteran airport employee said: "I see it—but I don't believe it."

As the Beatles waved and clowned, teenagers at the front of the crowd on the airport roof struggled to keep from falling to the tarmac, 20ft. below.

Then, when the group had left the plane, thousands of their screaming fans rushed to the balcony above the Customs Hall to watch them pass through.

Girls between fourteen and twenty-two pressed their noses against the big windows, waiting for the Beatles to pass by.

There were screams and shouts as their guitars appeared on a luggage trolley.

There were fresh squeals as the Beatles finally appeared, surrounded by a "bodyguard" of New York policemen.

Fans waved huge posters. There was a huge banner which proclaimed "Welcome to Beatlesville, U.S.A."

One of the fans had travelled 1,500 miles from Arkansas to see the group arrive—and many more had travelled up to 300 miles.

Airport officials said the crowd rivalled anything since General MacArthur returned from Korea.

The airport Press conference which followed the Beatles' arrival was chaos.

Hundreds of reporters and photographers, plus seven T V cameras, had the room bursting at its seams.

Money

Part of the question-and-answer session between reporters and the Beatles went like this :

"Will you sing something?"
John Lennon : "No!"
"Can you sing?"
"Not without money."
"How much money do you expect to make in the USA?"
George Harrison: "About half a crown."
"Are you going to get haircuts?"
Lennon: "We had one yesterday."

They were also asked what they thought of an anti-Beatle campaign in

Continued on Back Page

Left *John, Paul, George and Ringo rehearse with Laurence Olivier for their act in The Night of a Thousand Stars at the London Palladium on 22 July 1964*

Top centre *Distinguishing mark of the Beatles was their haircut – 'Beatle Wigs' sold briskly in New York two days before the group's first American tour in February 1964*

Top right *Police come to the rescue of a girl who fainted from exhaustion after queuing for two days for tickets to a Beatles concert in London*

Centre right *Feigned fear by Paul McCartney as the Beatles, on a visit to Miami on 22 February 1964, lie down in front of Cassius Clay who was training for the world heavyweight title (afterwards calling himself Mahomet Ali)*

Left *The boys from Merseyside wave to fans at London Airport on returning from tour of Australia, 2 July 1964*

The beat which John Lennon, George Harrison, Paul McCartney and Ringo Starr invited Britain to respond to in the 1960s was refreshingly different from the 'dance music' played in the ballrooms of London, Brighton and Newcastle for 40 years non-stop in foxtrot, one-step, tango and waltz time by the big bands of Bert Ambrose, Roy Fox, Henry Hall and the rest. The English, and then everyone else, took to it – and the Boys from Liverpool – with manic fervour. And since they could only afford to buy their clothes from army surplus stores, their fans copied their blue jean fashion and made the drab material the with-it uniform of all who did not want to be thought 'square'.

Beatlemania, wafted on a wave of million record sales for each new composition, swept the world. Pandemonium broke out in every town they appeared. Extra police had to be called in wherever they gave a concert of the bewitching New Sound. 'I think the world has gone mad' said the cop at John F Kennedy Airport when 5,000 screaming, chanting teenagers besieged the mop-haired quartet. Yeah! Yeah! it certainly had. And Top of the Pops to you!

Right *Beatlemania was international – Dutch teenagers with a Beatles beach towel sold to promote their Amsterdam concert of 6 June 1964*

1965

Sir Winston Churchill arrives back home on 14 May 1963 after a 35-minute appearance in the House of Commons, his first since an accident in June 1962

When Sir Winston Churchill MP died on 24 January 1965 at the age of 90 he had been a member of the British House of Commons for 65 years. He was given a state funeral on 30 January. His fame rested on his period of leadership in the dark days of World War 2, but his political career extended both up to and after those four years when his name was never out of the front pages. He headed his first peacetime Conservative government in October 1951, and surviving a heart attack in 1953 celebrated his 80th birthday the following year. With his resignation as prime minister in April 1955 came the end of his active political life in which his first big government office was as First Lord of the Admiralty from 1911 to 1915. No one more deserved the acclamation of 'national hero', and a forceful statue of him in bronze, emphasising his bull-dog determination, was soon erected in Parliament Square facing the House of Commons which he had dominated for so long.

The portrait which the painter-politician disliked and his wife destroyed. Winston Churchill at the Westminster Hall ceremony when Graham Sutherland's picture was formally presented to him in November 1954

Far right *Four faces of Churchill – stamps issued on 9 October 1974 to mark the centenary of his birth*

Above *Winston Churchill, artist, wearing his famous 'siren suit' and a sombrero, with his oil painting* The Blue Sitting Room, Trent Park. **Above right** *The dead premier's coffin is carried aboard the Port of London launch* Havengore *at Tower Bridge from where it was taken to Festival Pier, and then by train from*

Waterloo Station to Bladon. **Below** *Londoners line the street to pay a last tribute to the great war leader whose resolution in Britain's darkest hour saved them from Nazi conquest and Nazi ideology. The funeral followed a lying in state at Westminster Hall*

Evening Standard

WEST END FINAL CLOSING PRICES

UDI—Smith goes it alone

BRITAIN SLAMS TOUGH SANCTIONS ON THE 'REBELS'

No more tobacco buying

'REASON HAD FLED THE SCENE . . .'

Evening Standard Parliamentary Reporter

The British Government is embarking immediately on drastic and comprehensive sanctions — almost everything short of military force — to bring the now rebellious, illegal and outlawed regime of Mr. Ian Smith in Rhodesia to its knees.

In a grim and determined statement to a packed and tense House of Commons this afternoon Mr. Wilson announced emergency action aimed at restoring the rule of law, legal Government, and, as he put it, freedom in Rhodesia.

Mr. Wilson then announced "All British aid will cease".

ARMS exports will be banned. Rhodesia has been removed from the STERLING area and special exchange control restrictions will be applied. Exports of UK capital to Rhodesia will not be allowed.

CENSORSHIP FOLLOWS THE BREAKAWAY

SALISBURY, Thursday.— Mr. Ian Smith, in a voice trembling at times with emotion, today defied Britain and seized independence for Rhodesia in the first rebellion of its kind since America broke away as a colony in 1776.

His unilateral declaration of independence came in a drama-charged broadcast to the nation of 217,000 Whites and 4,000,000 Africans.

Mr. Smith said the "end of the road had been reached" in negotiations. But his action did not mean that the principles enshrining in the present constitution would be torn up. The Union Jack would continue to fly in Rhodesia and the National Anthem would continue to be played, he said.

He proclaimed unswerving loyalty to the Crown. "God save the Queen," he said.

Then shortly after the broadcast the Government announced the imposition of censorship. The announcement said no one shall print or publish any publication without prior authority of the Director of Information.

A fuller report—PAGE SIXTEEN

CENSORSHIP DETAILS
PAGE SEVENTEEN

Smith's proclamation
PAGE EIGHTEEN

THE CITY TAKES IT CALMLY

QUEEN SUSPENDS SMITH

—and his Ministers

SALISBURY, Thursday.—Mr. Smith and all his ministers are now suspended from office —on the Queen's instructions.

It's here now, the new WOLSELEY 4/00

Still talking. Ian Smith shakes hands with Harold Wilson on leaving 10 Downing Street after another fruitless session

When in 1964 Northern Rhodesia in Africa, which had only become a British colony in 1924, became an independent member of the Commonwealth as Zambia with Kenneth Kaunda as president, it was natural that Southern Rhodesia, with its population of three million of whom 220,000 were European, would also seek independence, having seceded from the ten-year Federation of Nyasaland, North and South Rhodesia (1953–63) along with the others.

Harold Wilson, Britain's Labour prime minister, was prepared to make Southern Rhodesia independent so long as whatever government took over promised unimpeded progress towards majority rule and a policy of ending racial discrimination. Southern Rhodesia's prime minister, Ian Smith, a farmer and a fighter pilot in World War II, found these terms unacceptable, and in September 1964 he declared his aim was 'independence by Christmas'. Britain pointed out that such a step, if taken unilaterally, would be illegal. The colony could only become independent by an Act of the British Parliament. In spite of all warnings, in November 1965 Ian Smith made a unilateral declaration of independence (UDI) and cut off Southern Rhodesia from all her ties with Britain, who declared his government unconstitutional and imposed economic sanctions.

Deadlock. Ian Smith, prime minister of Southern Rhodesia, meets the press in London on 9 October 1965 after his independence negotiations with British prime minister Harold Wilson break down

RAND
Daily ✠ Mail

JOHANNESBURG, WEDNESDAY, SEPTEMBER 7, 1966.

A NATION MOURNS DR. VERWOERD

DAILY RAND MAIL

A heinous crime

IT is with a sense of the most profound shock and horror that the people of South Africa are today still trying to grasp the overwhelming fact of Dr. Verwoerd's violent death at the hand of an assassin. The circumstances are enough to make the mind reel.

● Here was a man, a Prime Minister, a world figure, struck down, not by a sniper's bullet or a desperado's bomb as he rode through crowded streets or stood exposed on a public platform, but by the knife of a petty official within the inner sanctum of Parliament.

● Here was a man who had already survived, miraculously, a previous attempt on his life when he was shot in the head at point-blank range, and who recovered from his wounds to grow to the fullest stature of a national leader.

● Here was a man who had built up the military strength and internal security of his country to an unprecedented level only to be cut down, unsuspecting and without resistance, at the very cockpit of power, the Prime Minister's front bench itself.

● Here was a man who had just concluded an historic meeting between White and Black Prime Ministers in the Union Buildings, Pretoria, opening a potential new era of friendly co-operation between South Africa and the emerging states of Southern Africa.

● Here was a Prime Minister about to make his first major speech in Parliament since his return to power, a speech on foreign policy, just at the moment when international hostility is about to be focused once again on South Africa at this week's Commonwealth conference in London and at the United Nations General Assembly later this month.

Extraordinary

Could there have been a more extraordinary conjunction of events in the setting for this outrageous crime? It is no wonder that it has been felt with stunning force throughout the country.

Chief architect

Uncertainty

—The Editor-in-Chief

— PASSING OF A PRIME MINISTER —

The body of Dr. Verwoerd is carried down the steps of the Houses of Parliament after his assassination in the Assembly.

Tsafendas described as man of mystery

From GEORGE OLIVER

Dagger to the heart kills him at his Assembly bench

From GEORGE OLIVER
CAPE TOWN.

DR. VERWOERD died at his bench in the Chamber of the House of Assembly yesterday afternoon after he had been stabbed four times by a Parliamentary messenger, Dimitrio Tsafendas.

Donges appeals: Stay calm

CAPE TOWN.

School as usual today

Dr Voerwoerd, South African prime minister, who was assassinated in the parliament chamber by a white man for no particular political motive in September 1966, was the prime mover of the republic's apartheid policy. Keeping the black and white races apart became the policy of the National-st Party in 1947 in the belief that with two-thirds of South Africa's population being Afri-can, a black and white equal, one-man one-vote at the polls would result in Black rule and put an end to the power of the white minority. From 1950 a series of laws were passed by a government in the election of which the blacks played no part, to maintain Apartheid. Marriage between black and white was forbidden; each race had separate schools; native reserves were established – Bantustans.

With the violent death of Voerwoerd, his successor Balthazar Vorster pursued the same policy of Apartheid for the whole of the 12 years he was in power.

Dr Voerwoerd, prime minister of the Republic of South Africa

THE SUNDAY TIMES

No. 7531 ☆ ☆ ☆ 1 October 1967 Tenpence

Inside the Vatican in full colour in today's MAGAZINE

Philby: I spied for Russia from 1933

INSIGHT reveals that top Russian spy was being groomed to head Britain's Secret Service

In Red Square – the biggest spy in British history

THIS IS THE FIRST picture to be taken of the British master-spy "Kim" Philby since he vanished from Beirut in January, 1963. Philby, relaxed and looking less than his 55 years, is standing in Red Square, Moscow. The dark mass on the right of the picture is the wall of the Kremlin.

The picture, taken from an INSIGHT investigation which has demonstrated that "Kim" Philby was, by a shatteringly wide margin, the most important Soviet agent ever to penetrate the Western intelligence system. He was groomed as head of Britain's intelligence system, and as link man with the American Central Intelligence Agency had almost total knowledge of all Western intelligence operations against Russia.

This picture was taken by Philby's eldest son, John, a British photo-journalist, who made a trip to Moscow two weeks ago. Philby explained to his son that his real allegiance had been to the Soviet Union most of his adult life. He made several fascinating disclosures:

Philby said that he was recruited into the Soviet intelligence organisation after working as a courier in Germany. This was only a few months after he left Cambridge in the autumn of 1933.

He said that the next year, 1956, when he went to Beirut as correspondent for The Observer and the Economist, he was still on the British secret payroll. This assertion was the last piece of evidence needed to substantiate the fact that

14 Britons die in bus crash

By Geoffrey Sumner

FOURTEEN British university students were killed and 13 injured yesterday when the bus in which they were coming home after a 14,000-mile good-will expedition to India was in collision with a crane travelling on a lorry 36 miles from Zagreb, Jugoslavia. Six students were unhurt.

The crane ripped open the left side and top of the double-decker bus. Accounts of the cause of the accident varied.

Miss Susan Kettyle, 20, who was sitting beside the driver and was slightly injured, said: "It was a clear road and we were not travelling fast. Then all of a sudden this crane pulled out in front of us for no apparent reason.

"It was so unexpected that our driver could do nothing to avoid it. He swerved to the right, but it was too late. The crane caught the side of the bus and tipped it over. We ended upside down."

Miss Kathleen Gibson said: "Another vehicle was coming in the opposite direction. We swerved and the next thing I remember was being thrown out."

First reports from local police said the bus was passing a car and as it did so, it hit the lorry-borne crane, coming the other way.

The crash occurred at 9.31 a.m. near the village of Popovaca, at a slight bend in a flat stretch of the main road. Around the bus were scattered cameras, bags, umbrellas, and other belongings. Minutes later a local bus came and the passengers scrambled out to help, but they could do nothing. Twisted metal and shattered glass emerged the dead and injured.

The crane was used to lift the wreckage. The injured were pulled out and two passing doctors gave first aid.

Many of the students, aged 18 to 25, are from Durham University. One of them, David Richardson, 21, of Rudyard Avenue, Sunderland, who was injured in the left eye, was reported last night to be seriously ill. The British Consulate in Zagreb said the dead would be identified this morning.

Mr Zeljko Barac, investigating judge for the district, announced last night that most of the injured should be able to leave Zagreb hospital today.

Pictures of crash—page 3

Smith triumphs

By Ronald Legge

Salisbury, Saturday

MR IAN SMITH has once again emerged from "trial by Party congress" as the dominant figure on the Rhodesian political scene and the country's undisputed leader.

The challenge from the Right wing of the Rhodesian Front to his moderate policy, on the introduction of a republic and apartheid measures, collapsed dismally at today's session of the Government Party's annual congress.

Not only did Captain Louis Boshoff—the South African-born contender for the Party chairmanship nominated by those who want a Republic now—withdraw when he saw the way the tide was flowing, but two controversial resolutions debated in secret session were hastily retracted after Mr Smith had attacked them.

He was particularly scathing about the calling for complete rejection of the proposals made at his meeting with Mr Wilson aboard H.M.S Tiger. Nobody would vote for it, he said, "except a monkey or a nut-case."

This was a plain indication that he is determined to continue efforts to reach a settlement with Britain right up to the last possible moment.

China joins sanctions busters—page 2

HARRODS
THE AMERICAN ROOM

Right *Guy Burgess, spy for Soviet Russia*

Far right *Donald MacLean, spy for Soviet Russia*

Harold 'Kim' Philby spied for the USSR undetected for 30 years. For two years during the war (from 1944 to 1946) he ran, as a member of the Secret Intelligence Service, the British anti-Russian counter-intelligence system. After the war in which Soviet Russia had been Britain's ally, Philby worked closely between 1949 and 1951 with the American Central Intelligence Agency in Washington, and managed yet again to escape detection in keeping his Moscow masters informed of all the West were doing to infiltrate the Russian espionage system. The first time his loyalty to Britain came under suspicion was in 1951 when the Foreign Office had reason to believe he may have helped Donald Maclean and Guy Burgess to escape to Moscow. It was alleged that he had warned them that they were being investigated and

'Me a spy? Don't be ridiculous!' Harold Philby invites the press to the home of his mother in Drayton Gardens, London, to disclaim all suggestions of disloyalty on 8 November 1955

advised them to leave before they were arrested. Surviving lengthy interrogation which failed to break his cover, he was asked to leave the Foreign Office, without however any charge being brought. Four years later he was rehabilitated with his reputation apparently untarnished.

It was the best sustained bluff in the history of espionage. And it was only revealed as such when one day in Beirut in 1963 he admitted to an ex-Foreign Office colleague, who had been sent to wheedle the truth out of him, that all the allegations made against him had been true. He was then allowed (?) to leave Lebanon for Russia where he was immediately granted Soviet citizenship. The spy's defection at so late an hour and in such mysterious circumstances came almost as an anti-climax, and the Press had few adjectives left to describe the revelation of so traitorous a deception which had begun the day he was recruited by Soviet agents as a Cambridge undergraduate in 1933. And even then the whole story did not come out until the *Sunday Times* investigation in 1967.

The Evening News
and STAR

TEL AVIV: 'We acted to stop blitzkrieg' **CAIRO: 'Our holy duty to repel enemy'**

WAR SWEEPING MIDDLE EAST

The Middle East is in flames tonight. Israel and the Arabs have been at war since 7 a.m. London time.

JERUSALEM under fire

AND IN LONDON AN ARAB CLAIMS: 'THE HOLY CITY HAS FALLEN'

WILSON IN 'HOT LINE' HUSTLE

BRITON KILLED IN ADEN

'Tanker tries to block Suez'

Petrol rationing 'in weeks'

Top *Israeli forces advance in the vicinity of Suez*

Above *Flanked by high ranking officers, King Hussein of Jordan watches troops massing near his country's border with Israel, 30 May 1967*

M any army commanders have dreamt of a quick 'knock-out blow' as the answer to all their problems, but not many have risked one and had it meet with the success achieved by Israel's General Dayan during the Six Days of 5 to 10 June 1967.

The Egyptian leader Colonel Nasser's plans for uniting the Arab states of the Middle East were based on his persuading them that their common enemy was the upstart state of Israel. He showed the way on 22 May 1967 by seizing the fortified post of Sharm El Sheik at the mouth of the Strait of Tiran, closing it to Israeli shipping, which Israel had told him would always be regarded as an act of war. Israel decided that an immediate 'pre-emptive strike' was the only way to stop further aggression.

At 7 o'clock on Tuesday morning 5 June Israeli planes flew to Egypt's airfields and by lunchtime had destroyed 400 of their aircraft, two-thirds of Nasser's airforce, on the ground. That same morning the Israeli land and air forces advanced across the Sinai Peninsular, and by Thursday afternoon had killed or captured the entire Egyptian army, which of course now had no air cover. Israeli paratroopers had spent Wednesday securing Sharm El Sheik and another Israeli contingent had freed Old Jerusalem of the army of Jordan which had signed a defence agreement with Egypt on 30 May. On the sixth day the Israelis completed their occupation of the

Right *Women fight alongside their male comrades in the war to protect Israel's frontiers from her Arab enemies*

Centre right *General Hussney, Egyptian Military Governor of the Gaza Strip, is taken prisoner by the Israelis, 10 June 1967*

Far right *Day Three of the Six Day War, 7 June 1967 – excited troops raise the Israeli flag at a captured air base*

west bank of the river Jordan and dug in on the Golan Heights overlooking Syria. The Six Day War brought a major realignment of Middle East frontiers – and a lot of red faces in the Egyptian and Jordanian high commands.

1967

RAND

Daily Mail

JOHANNESBURG, TUESDAY, DECEMBER 5, 1967.

Stuttafords

HEART MAN SPEAKS

'I am much better' his first words

OWN CORRESPONDENT

CAPE TOWN.
"I AM much better. What kind of operation did I have? You promised me a new heart." These were the first words spoken by Mr. Louis Washkansky in Groote Schuur Hospital yesterday morning.

Mr. Washkansky spoke only 24 hours after being wheeled out of the operating theatre with the world's first transplanted human heart.

He was addressing Professor Chris Barnard, leader of the team which carried out the transplant, seconds after the respirator tubes had been removed from Mr. Washkansky at 8.39 a.m.

Operation was a medical 4-minute mile'

Professor Barnard's reply was "You have got a new heart."

The Medical Superintendent of Groote Schuur Hospital, Dr J. G. Burger, was continuously answering telephone calls yesterday. He received more than 130 calls, many of them from radio, television and newspaper journalists in the United States, Britain and Australia.

Meanwhile an up-to-the-minute of tests and analyses was quietly being followed in Room 271.

The entire corridor leading to the sterilised room where Mr. Washkansky is lying, has been sealed off from the public.

But the high-pitched 'bleepbleep' of the electro-cardio

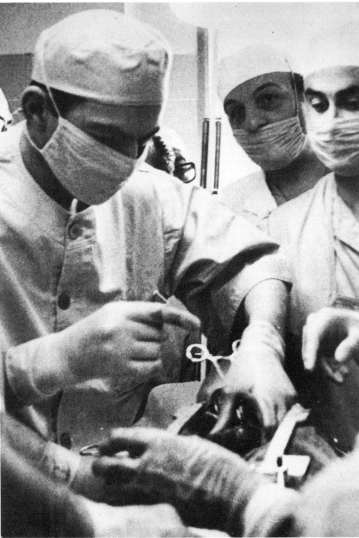

Until 1967 the idea of removing the heart of a dying man and replacing it with that of another who had just died, belonged to the realm of science fiction. And the heart which the team headed by South African surgeon Dr Chris Barnard gave Louis Washansky in Groote Schuur hospital in Capetown on 4 December 1967 was a young girl's. The donor who saved his life had been knocked down and killed by a motor car while crossing the road with her mother, watched by her father, clothing salesman Edward Davall, only a few hours before the operation.

The world's first successful human heart transplant was the culmination of ten years intensive research. It was certainly no fiction, but it must have seemed akin to a miracle for Louis Washansky to hear Professor Barnard telling him, on pulling out of the anaesthetic, 'You have got a new heart.'

The sensational operation of the heart transplant – Dr Barnard demonstrates his method in 1968.
Below *Dr Chris Barnard, heart transplant surgeon*

LATE LONDON EDITION
FRIDAY MAY 31 1968
NO. 57,265 SIXPENCE

THE TIMES

STUDENTS IN REVOLT:
WHAT THE PUBLIC
THINK—PAGE 9

French Army reported to be surrounding Paris

DE GAULLE STOPS FLOW OF GOLD AND MONEY

Troops were reported to be ringing Paris early today, ready to support General de Gaulle after his broadcast yesterday in which he made it clear that he will stay on as President. Officials would make no comment on reports that reinforcements from the 55,000-man French Army were standing by to cross the Rhine if called on and that tanks were being brought into the Paris area.

At midnight, exchange controls were imposed on the flow of currency and gold in and out of France. M. Pompidou, who remains Prime Minister, began forming a new Cabinet and signed a decree raising the wage minimum by 35 per cent.

In his broadcast, General de Gaulle said he would call a general election within 40 days. M. Mitterrand, leader of the Federation of the Left, described the broadcast as "an appeal for civil war" but an enormous demonstration of 250,000 Gaullists in Paris showed that the de Gaulle medicine had begun to work again.

When journalists call any group of young people between 12 and 30 'students' they are always likely to be doing their readers a disservice. More often than not the 'students', who take part for instance in violent street fighting, are not the schoolchildren and undergraduates taking the time off from their studies which the word implies. A civil power which acts to protect the rest of the population from the effects of their violent behaviour is naively seen by many reporters as 'over-reacting' to a spontaneous display of youthful high spirits. And that could not suit the organisers of such rioting as occurred in Paris in 1968 better.

The President of the French Republic, General de Gaulle, certainly believed the 'student' riots of that year had been organised, and told his listeners so when he broadcast to the nation on 30 May. Students were being prevented from studying, he said, and workers from working, by intimidation, intoxication and tyranny organised by well-trained groups within, and by a party which was an extension of a totalitarian enterprise. He promised to hold an election within 40 days when the *whole* French people could make their voice heard – unless they were prevented from doing so by those very same elements.

It was a situation of force – revolutionary pressure, as *The Times* Paris correspondent wrote, to overthrow the Government and the regime from the streets and factories. People were trying to compel France to resign to a power which, said de Gaulle, would impose itself in the midst of national despair – the power of a conqueror, of totalitarian communism.

Over-reaction? On the night of 12 May 30,000 people had done battle with 8,000 police in the Latin Quarter, using whatever cars they found parked there as barricades and burning 100 of them. Demonstration and protest Oui; force Non. Louis XVI under-reacted and lost his head. President de Gaulle was determined not to have another French Revolution on his hands.

General Charles de Gaulle

Top centre *An injured demonstrator is helped to his feet by sympathisers in the Latin Quarter of Paris, 25 May 1968*

Right *In one of the hottest springs Paris had had for years, 'students' throw paving stones at the police in the riots of May 1968*

'Good-bye Charles!' A poster in a Paris street reflects the feeling of many French people – that it was time for General de Gaulle to go

The Globe and Mail

125th YEAR No. 37,035   METRO EDITION   TORONTO WEDNESDAY AUGUST 21, 1968   38 PAGES   TEN CENTS

Johnson meets U.S. security council

RUSSIANS, WARSAW PACT ALLIES CROSS CZECHOSLOVAKIA BORDER

Transit strike deadline postponed for 24 hours

People told not to resist

When Alexander Dubcek tried his hand at introducing Socialism with A Human Face to Czechoslovakia in 1968 and got it firmly sat on for his courage, no western power thought it worth the risk to come to his aid. To be the Stalinist dictator of a communist satellite state meant ruling with a rod of steel, and that is how Novotny acted when he became the country's president in 1957. But for all the strict adherence to idealogy, clumsy planning and dishonest administration brought an acute housing shortage, a failing economy, chaos in public transport and a breed of discontented intellectuals who ridiculed his attempt to stifle criticism of his

The unbelievable happens – Soviet tanks in the streets of their capital tell the Czechs the Prague Spring is over

ineptitude. The replacement of Novotny in January 1968 by Svoboda, Dubcek, Cernik and a group of 'progressives', ushered in the 'Prague Spring' during which they planned to make the National Assembly a democratic body with real power. Censorship was abolished and the grip of the security police relaxed. They had no intention of leaving the Warsaw Pact, only reinvigorating the economy and liberalising society. Marshal Tito of Yugoslavia and President Ceausescu of Rumania visited Dubcek and gave him their support.

But to the Kremlin such behaviour was intolerable, and after sending a warning Warsaw Letter to 'suppress anti-socialist forces', on 21 August 1968 200,000 Russian troops supported by 200 planes crossed the Czech

Brave Czechs protest at the presence of Russian troops in Prague, but demonstration cannot stop armed invasion

Right *Smoke still pours from a building on 26 August as helpless crowds watch the Russian dispay of force in the ancient Czech city.* **Inset** *Houses still burning after the fierce fighting in front of the broadcasting station in Prague, 26 August 1968*

border to 'save' it from what to Soviet communists was a heretical sliding towards western decadence. Dubcek and Cernik were arrested, taken to Moscow and forced to accept the Russian ultimatum to drop all further liberalisation, or else. Czechoslovakia was from then on occupied by the Russian Army, Dubcek was replaced and in time all those who had had anything to do with the brief Prague Spring were duly purged.

1969

'You might as well ask me to go to the moon' was for centuries a phrase which people used in declining to undertake a job which they considered beyond them. From 1969 however they had to think of some other way of expressing their reluctance. For in that year someone *did* go to the moon – and, moreover, proved it was not made of green cheese, by landing on it and walking on it, and then coming down to earth to tell the story to an astonished world who would have had difficulty in believing it if they had not watched the whole operation as it happened on their television screens.

On 20 July American Neil Armstrong descended from the 'lunar module' which had been shot into space by the monster Apollo II booster rocket from a site in Florida on the 16th, and became the first man to set foot on the earth's lifeless satellite. He and Edwin Aldrin who followed him down the ladder, both dressed in weird space suits to enable them to breathe and communicate, and to keep their balance in a state of weightlessness, then explored the bleak surface of the moon and collected valuable information and rock samples to bring back for the world's scientists to examine. With Michael Collins, pilot of the command module, they splashed down in the Pacific Ocean 900 miles south of Hawaii on 24 July. The National Aeronautics and Space Administration (NASA) who had spent millions of dollars and many years planning the eight-day mission, were well satisfied with the functioning of technology of a kind which hitherto had been associated only with the more colourful flights of imagination of sci-fi writers. The minds of the lay public still boggled at the accomplishment of what they had always considered a Mission Impossible. Others like J M Roberts were better able to put it in perspective: 'Landing on the moon was the most complete and dazzling affirmation to that date of the belief that Man lives in a universe he can manage' (*The Hutchinson History of the World*).

Right *American Neil Armstrong, the first man on the moon*

Below *Three years later American astronauts took a vehicle with them to traverse the gaunt lunar wastes*

Daily Mirror

The date: July 21, AD 1969

5d. Monday, July 21, 1969   No. 20,393

MAN WALKS ON THE MOON

The landing site

THIS is where they touched down, the two Space heroes in the lunar module Eagle. They landed perfectly in the Sea of Tranquillity. It shows up on this Moon map as just a dark patch. But to the neighbours it showed up as rock fields — "very rough" — and Armstrong and Aldrin had to pilot their craft manually to a smooth landing site.

Man has walked on the Moon. Astronaut Neil Armstrong launched a new era for mankind when he stepped from the lunar module today. America, a land of frontiersmen, had opened a new frontier.

FULL STORY—BACK PAGE: THE FIRST WORDS—PAGE 2: THE PATHFINDERS—CENTRE PAGES

Below *Edwin Aldrin lugs passive seismic and laser gear across the pitted surface of the moon*

Above *Neil Armstrong places the United States flag on the moon*

Below *Apollo II's team: Neil Armstrong, Michael Collins, Edwin Aldrin*

In England remembering the gunpowder plot to blow up the House of Lords way back in 1605 as a protest against the treatment of Catholics, takes the form of jokey parties to watch the lighting of bonfires and the setting off of fireworks, characterised by good-hearted bonhomie and a considerable amount of laughter and beer-drinking. In Northern Ireland however, unlike Guy Fawkes Night, the humourless celebration of the relief of Londonderry by King James's Catholic troops in 1689 by an 'Apprentice Boys Parade' is more likely to end in violence, as it did in August 1969.

On that occasion troops fired rubber bullets and water cannon to disperse demonstrators and rioting youths whom they sprayed with coloured dye as they broke away from the main body of marchers hurling bottles and stones. The trouble had started at Craigavon bridge which led to the Irish Republican Army (IRA) 'No Go Areas' of the Bogside and Creggan. Only five Ulster Defence Association senior officials were allowed to approach the barbed wire. Earlier, as the march began in the predominantly 'Protestant' Waterside area, British troops mounted a major security operation after Mr William Whitelaw, Ulster Secretary in the British Government, had banned the crossing of the bridge.

An elderly couple who were married in the afternoon posed with masked armed men of the IRA who stood guard during the wedding service. Others went on with their shopping as well as they could. IRA supporters opened a IRA Community Co-operative Stores and sold household goods at wholesale prices; the check points were manned by IRA masked gunmen. On every entry and exits into the No Go Areas IRA members stopped traffic and inspected people just as the the British troops did; and the IRA were armed with SLR rifles of the same make as those used by the young men of the regular British infantry regiments carrying out the duties required of them on yet another Northern Ireland posting.

Above left *Disciplined British troops play it cool in the face of laughing Irish youngsters out on a spree*

Left *Londonderry boys spend an afternoon baiting weary Ulster police officers – but fail to provoke them*

Above right *The entrance to the 'Catholic' Bogside area of Londonderry*

Right *A police water cannon douses burning barricades*

Daily Mirror

5d. Friday, August 15, 1969 • No 20,415

Man shot dead .. five people wounded

ULSTER GUN BATTLES

The tough job

THE decision to put British troops on to the riot-torn streets of Ulster is the right one. Vastly regrettable, but regrettably unavoidable.

The government of Major James Chichester-Clark in Northern Ireland has had its chance to bring peace to the region. And it has failed.

The first task for the troops is to help restore order. An unenviable job. As the men in the middle, their presence will be resented by extremists on both sides.

It is right, as Mr. Callaghan emphasised last night, that the troops are under the command of the G.O.C. who is responsible to Whitehall.

Under no circumstances could their control have been put into the hands of the Ulster Government, which in the eyes of many people is discredited.

● It would be totally wrong to let British troops function as another arm of a police force which is, rightly or wrongly, suspected of being partisan.

● It is essential that everyone in Ulster, whether Catholics or Pro-

Continued on Page Two

Guns at the ready. British troops face the Bogside rioters across a barbed-wire barricade

Cheers in Bogside as the British troops arrive

By MIRROR REPORTERS

A MAN was shot dead in new, savage street fighting in Ulster last night.

The death—the first in the wave of violence which has swept Ulster—came as police, civil rights marchers and militant Protestants battled in Armagh.

The dead man was 24-year-old John Gallagher, father of three. Two other men were wounded by the gunfire.

The First Jumbo Jet

It was the heavy, ungainly shape of the American Boeing 747 jet airliner which gave it the name 'Jumbo Jet'. One had flown over the north pole non-stop from Seattle on the west coast of America to Le Bourget airport in June 1969 for the Paris Air Show, and was immediately the centre of attraction. With seats for 400, it was the largest passenger airliner which had ever flown.

The first Jumbo Jet to be seen in Britain belonged to Pan American Airways, and flew in to London's Heathrow Airport on 12 January 1970 bringing 300 employees of the airline and members of the US Federal Aviation Administration in preparation for the opening of a fare-paying passenger service on 21 January. In May the British

The first Boeing 747 'Jumbo' jet to be seen in Europe arrives at Le Bourget for the Paris Air Show

Overseas Airways Corporation took delivery of their first Boeing 747 at Heathrow.

The coming of the Jumbo Jet Era was not all beneficial; those who lived under the flight paths approaching airports were soon complaining of atmospheric pollution, noise and vibration. The later, Anglo-French supersonic *Concorde* was at first refused a landing licence at New York.

British Overseas Airways Corporation takes delivery of its first elephantine passenger airliner at Heathrow

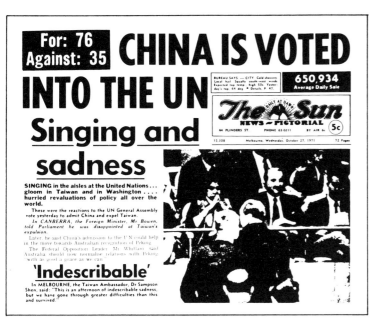

CHINA IS VOTED INTO THE UN

Singing and sadness

The Sun
NEWS-PICTORIAL

650,934
Average Daily Sale

64 FLINDERS ST.   PHONE 63-0211   BY AIR 6c   5c

15,308   Melbourne, Wednesday, October 27, 1971   72 Pages

SINGING in the aisles at the United Nations... gloom in Taiwan and in Washington.... hurried revaluations of policy all over the world.

These were the reactions to the UN General Assembly vote yesterday to admit China and expel Taiwan.

In CANBERRA, the Foreign Minister, Mr Bowen, told Parliament he was disappointed at Taiwan's expulsion.

Later, he said China's admission to the UN could help in the move towards Australian recognition of Peking.

The Federal Opposition Leader, Mr Whitlam, said Australia should now normalise relations with Peking with as good a grace as we can.

'Indescribable'

In MELBOURNE, the Taiwan Ambassador, Dr Sampson Shen, said: "This is an afternoon of indescribable sadness, but we have gone through greater difficulties than this and survived."

There had been no United Nations involvement in the Vietnam War because neither North Vietnam nor the People's Republic of China with nearly a quarter of the world's population were members. After the communists had driven Chiang Kai-shek's Nationalist government from China in 1949 and forced it to take refuge in Formosa (Taiwan), the USSR proposed that the People's Republic should now represent China on the Security Council. When the proposal was defeated and China continued to be represented by its government-in-exile outside the mainland, Russia boycotted the Security Council and all other UN organisations – but returned in 1950, when the UN had voted, in her absence, to send help to South Korea. It was not until 1971 that Taiwan was expelled from the Security Council and its place taken as the representative of China by the People's Republic.

Right *Chiao Kuan-hua, Chinese vice-chairman of foreign affairs, addresses the United Nations Assembly*

Below *U Thant congratulates Kurt Waldheim, who has succeeded him as Secretary-General of the United Nations*

1972

Daily Mirror

BRITAIN'S BIGGEST DAILY SALE

3p Monday, January 31, 1972 No. 21,167

ULSTER'S BLOODY SUNDAY

From JOE GORROD in Londonderry

THIRTEEN men were killed yesterday as Army paratroopers broke up a banned Civil Rights march in Londonderry.

13 die.. Army accused of 'massacre'

Another twelve people—including two women and a child—were wounded by bullets when the Paras stormed into the Catholic Bogside Area.

The soldiers claimed last night that they opened fire when they came under sniper attack. They said they were arresting about fifty demonstrators who had been hurling stones at troops behind barricades.

Five soldiers were hurt in the fierce battle—three of them hit in stabs and two burned by acid bombs.

March

Eighteen demonstrators were taken to hospital with injuries that were not caused by bullets.

The marchers who died were aged between sixteen and forty.

Last night shocked Civil Rights leaders were calling the incident a massacre. Bernadette Devlin, the Mid-Ulster M.P. who took part in the anti-internment march said: 'It was murder by the Army.'

'This was our Sharpe-

ville, and we shall never forget it.'

Miss Devlin was referring to the killing of sixty-seven Africans by South African police in 1960.

She claimed: 'It was a peaceful meeting. Then they let loose with bloodthirsty guns at anything that strayed into their sights.'

'Let nobody say that they fired in retaliation.'

Mr. John Hume, Londonderry's M.P. at Biermont, declared: 'It was cold-blooded mass murder—another bloody Sunday.'

And Mr. Ivan Cooper, M.P. for Mid-Derry, said: 'The soldiers showed no mercy. I was shot at while waving a white flag. People

were falling all over the street.

There were immediate threats of revenge from the official I.R.A. in Dublin, and the Provisional I.R.A. in Londonderry.

A spokesman for the provisionals claimed 'At no time did any of our units open a fire on the Army prior to the Army opening fire.'

The shooting broke out as 15,000 demonstrators who had marched through the Bogside tried to pass barricades put up to stop them getting into the city centre.

Some of the marchers fought a forty-five-minute battle with troops before men of the 1st Battalion of the Parachute Regiment burst through the barricades and charged into the crowd to make arrests.

Bodies

Minutes afterwards the first shots rang out.

The bodies of two men claimed by the Army to have been firing at them were recovered by troops.

A public inquiry into the shooting was demanded last night by Cardinal William Conway, Primate of All Ireland.

He said: 'I have received a first-hand account from a priest who was present at the scene and what I have heard is really shocking.'

An impartial and independent public inquiry is immediately called for and I have telegraphed the British Prime Minister to this effect.

'SOLDIERS DIDN'T FIRE FIRST SHOT'

THE Army's Ulster chief claimed last night that his men did not 'go in shooting' against yesterday's marchers in Londonderry.

'They did not fire until they were fired upon,' said Major General Robert Ford, commander of land forces in the province.

He claimed that the dead 'might not have been killed by our soldiers'.

BBC TV interview that the paratroops' guns 'went arrived backwards who had been attacking them' as the soldiers went in, acid bombs were dropped from a block of flats and two of three were injured — two seriously.

At the same time gas-

Continued on Page Two

THE LAST RITES Kneeling in the road, a priest gives the last rites to a dying demonstrator... Picture by Stanley Matchett. More of his dramatic pictures—See Centre Pages

Left *A policeman gets ready to fire his tear smoke pistol at Bogside rioters.* **Below** *A 120lb bomb explodes in the street, and a young girl is helped away suffering from cuts and shock*

Though the counties which constituted 'Northern Ireland' were part of the United Kingdom and not the Irish Republic, with their own MPs in London, they also had their own Parliament at Stormont in Belfast. Inside Northern Ireland however there were people who made it their business continually to foment unrest in order to provoke whatever administration was in power at Westminster to wash its hands of troublesome Ulster and, for better or worse, make the solving of its troubles the responsibility of the politicians in Dublin. Their violent demonstrations to call attention to their cause inevitably gave rise to counter-demonstrations by those who wished Ulster to remain as it was, and in 1968 and 1969 these reached such a peak that British troops were called in to prevent a complete breakdown of law and order.

In 1972, in an attempt to reduce the violence, Brian Faulkner, prime minister in the Northern Ireland government, introduced internment without trial of anyone *suspected* of having committed acts of violence. Several hundred were rounded up and interrogated by 'security forces'; there were allegations of ill-treatment, and instead of falling, the violence increased alarmingly. The worst incident took place one Sunday in January 1972 when British troops fired on protest marchers in Londonderry and killed 13 of them. 'Bloody Sunday' was followed by the burning down of the British Embassy in Dublin; and in March 1972 the Stormont Parliament was suspended. From then on Northern Ireland was administered by direct rule from London. Brian Faulkner resigned.

Outrages do not become less outrageous by their multiplication, or by newspapers calling their perpetrators 'commandos', 'terrorists', 'extremists', 'guerrillas' or 'anarchists' which gives them an air of romance they rarely deserve. Murder does not become less horrific or a more civilised way of effecting change when murderers claim to be acting for a Cause or seek to dignify their always sensational (and so newsworthy) but ineffective action by giving themselves fancy names such as 'Red Army Faction' (Germans) or 'Black September' (Palestinian Arabs). Bored and emotionally charged individuals calling themselves both these were particularly active in 1972 and 1973.

In May 1972 Japanese young men joined forces with Palestinians to kill 26 people and wound 70 in an indiscriminate attack on Lod Airport in Israel – though what common cause other than the pursuit of excitement, the subjects of the Emperor Hirohito had with the Middle East adventurers is anyone's guess. Young Palestinian arabs from families living in the refugee camps to which they had been confined since the creation of the Israeli state in 1948, with no work and nothing to lose but their lives, acting under the orders of *Al Fatah*, the largest of the groups within the fragmentated 'Palestine Liberation Organisation', murdered Wasfi Tell the Jordanian prime minister in Cairo; attempted to murder the Jordanian ambassador in London; had a go at high-jacking a Belgian airliner in Tel Aviv, and made an abortive attack on the Israeli embassy in Bangkok. In March 1973 eight of them forced their way into the Saudi Arabian embassy in Khartoum during a reception, seized George Moore, counsellor at the US Embassy (when they discovered the Ethiopian Emperor, their real target, had not turned up), beat him, kicked him in the face and shot him dead. They also killed the American ambassador and the Belgian chargé d'affaires. Seventeen of them were caught in Amman before kidnapping the Jordanian prime minister and holding him hostage with other Cabinet ministers. 'Our troops and people have lived through a hell of division and destruction' said King Hussein of Jordan, 'and have suffered tragedies at the hands of those calling themselves the "Palestine Resistance".'

The most sensational and pointless adventure planned by Salah Khalef, second-ranking leader of *Al Fatah* for a 'Black September' team, was in September 1972 when they seized 11 of the Israeli athletic team taking part in the Olympic Games in Munich. In a fight with the West German police all of the Israeli hostages were killed and five of the Palestinians.

Above right *Police ring the Olympic Village in Munich after the Arab atrocity*

Right *The scene at Furstfeldbruck airbase minutes after a grenade had been lobbed into the helicopter on the left killing nine Israeli athletes*

Evening News

Arabs shoot two Israelis dead, seize athletes

ASSASSINATION AT THE OLYMPICS

Then hour-by-hour drama of hostages

From IAIN MACDONALD and News Agencies
MUNICH, Tuesday.

ARAB terrorists armed with machine-guns broke into the Olympic village early today, killed two Israeli team members and held 26 other Israeli athletes and officials hostage.

Then, according to reports broadcast from Israel, they threatened to shoot one Israeli every two hours if Israel did not agree to free more than 200 guerilla prisoners.

The Arabs set a noon deadline. Tension mounted. But noon came and went . . . and then the ultimatum was extended, first to 1 p.m. and then to 3 p.m.

As negotiations went on, and a "hot line" was opened between Munich and Jerusalem, one of the dead men was named as 32-year-old Moshe Weinberg, the Israeli squad's wrestling trainer and a former leading wrestling champion. He was married and the father of a two-month-old boy.

Four of the hostages were named as Andre Spitzer, fencing trainer; Kehat Short, shooting; Yosef Gottfreund, wrestling; and Amitsur Shapiri, athletics.

An Israeli journalist said Weinberg was shot in bed after the Arabs, who climbed a fence, broke into the Olympic Village. Their faces were blacked and one of them was said to be a woman. Sources put the number of terrorists at between five and nine.

EX-CHAMPION WHO DIED . . AND THE MEN WHO FACE 'WE WILL KILL ONE EVERY TWO HOURS' THREAT

The Daily Telegraph

Egypt and Syria chose 6 October 1973 to launch their attack on Israel, planned to be the knock-out blow to revenge their defeat of 1967, because that was the holiest day of the Jewish year when nearly all Israelis would be in their synagogues, the Day of Atonement, in Hebrew 'Yom Kippur'. The simultaneous offensives of the two Arab powers did in fact take the Israelis by surprise, and it looked bad for them when units from Jordan, Iraq, Morocco and Saudi Arabia joined their enemies.

The Egyptians swept unopposed across the Suez Canal and had soon recaptured some 450 square miles of the Sinai Desert before a savage counter-attack by the Israelis secured them a bridgehead on the west bank of the canal from which they advanced into the interior of Egypt some 20 miles. Similarly the Syrian army's attack won them the Golan Heights they had lost in the Six Days War, from which they advanced into Galilee. An Israeli counter-offensive drove them back.

In response to a UN Security Council resolution, Egypt and Israel agreed to a cease-fire on 22 October. By then the Egyptian Third Army of 20,000 was trapped between the main Israeli forces in Sinai and those west of the Suez Canal who were in control of 500 square miles of Egypt proper. The Syrians had lost all their initial gains and been forced back into their own territory, with Israeli forces in control of 300 square miles of Syria and within 20 miles of Damascus. The Egyptians had lost 850 tanks and 210 aircraft.

On 9 October the Organisation of Arab Petroleum Exporting Countries (responsible for 30 per cent of world production) decided to reduce petrol production progressively by five per cent until Israel withdrew their forces. In addition some Arab countries imposed a

Right *A road junction on the Golan Heights*

Below *It was not quite so hilarious after they had debussed*

Below *For her, life will never be the same . . .*

total embargo on shipments of oil to the USA, and to the Netherlands, which was alleged to be pro-Israel. On 16 October the Gulf States announced a 70 per cent increase in the posted price of crude oil. Cut-backs and price increases caused a major energy crisis, particularly in the USA where President Nixon announced a series of measures to reduce oil

Below *Egyptian soldiers ferry food supplies for the Third Army across the canal from Suez.* **Below right** *A taxi driver in Calcutta, protesting at the new taxes on petrol, takes his fare on his head*

Above *Petrol savers in Milan travel by Muscle Bus – the 'driver' merely steers.* **Top right** *Signs of the times in New York.* **Right** *Sunday is 'No Motor Day' in Holland – so in Amsterdam they take to the saddle*

consumption. In Britain motorists were urged to observe a 50 mph speed limit, reduce Sunday driving and save fuel wherever possible. The sale of petrol in cans was prohibited. On 13 November the government introduced a state of emergency giving it wide powers to cope with a crisis which heralded an international recession.

1974

The front page of The Morning News / The Call newspaper:

WEATHER
Partly sunny today.
High about 80.
Tonight fair, cool.
Saturday fair.
High about 80.

The Morning News
THE CALL

HOME EDITION

Stocks Pages 10, 11
Racing Page 16

New Jersey's *Only All Day Newspaper*

84TH YEAR—VOL. 198   PATERSON, N.J., FRIDAY, AUGUST 9, 1974   36 PAGES   PRICE 15¢

NIXON QUITS

First U.S. President to Resign; Ford Taking Oath at Noon Today

Nation to Get 38th Highest Executive

His Congressional Support Dropped

THE PRESIDENT tells nation of resignation Thursday night.

Officials Relieved

Senators Line Up 13 VP Candidates

Nixon Career Is Spotlighted

The News today contains feature background stories and highlights of Richard Milhous Nixon's career prior to his resignation as President of the United States.

Top left *President Nixon holds his last cabinet meeting in the White House, 7 August*

Top right *Richard Nixon has resigned and, surrounded by his family, bids farewell to his staff, 13 August*

Right *Thumbs up? with son-in-law David Eisenhower beside him, the ex-president puts a (fairly) brave face on it as he bows himself out of office one jump ahead of impeachment*

The 'Watergate Scandal' which brought about the first ever resignation of a President of the United States arose from the arrest of five men on 17 June 1972 inside the building known as 'Watergate' which housed the offices of the Democratic Party National Committee. It was five months before President Nixon would have to stand as Republican candidate in the 1972 presidential election. The men were charged with breaking into the offices, planting electronic surveillance devices in them and photographing Democratic Party documents. That autumn articles appeared in the *Washington Post* accusing senior White House officials and members of the Committee for the Re-election of the President of being implicated in the raid, in order to secure information on the tactics of the opposition in the forthcoming campaign, if not having actually organised it. President Nixon repudiated any suggestion he or his staff had had any hand in 'this kind of reprehensible activity'. But on 30 April 1973 he had to accept the resignations of three of his closest aides, and in a broadcast admitted receiving information that persuaded him there was 'a real possibility that some of these charges were true'. But he refused to be examined by the Senate Select Committee appointed to investigate the affair, or to comply with a sub-poena to release the White House tape recordings. In August 1974 he admitted withholding information on the affair, and in a broadcast on the 8th he announced his resignation. The following day Gerald Ford, vice-president, was sworn in to take his place.

162

Obsessed with the evil of Communism, the United States government's military presence in South East Asia was designed to stop South Vietnam from falling under 'communist' control. They believed that if South Vietnam was occupied by the forces of Ho Chi Minh's Vietminh (now renamed Vietcong) the other states of South East Asia would fall into their hands, and the embrace of Communism, 'like a row of dominoes'. In fact 'Communism' was not the unifying element which America believed it was, and there were as many tribal rivalries inside 'communist' states as any other. Many believed the whole exercise, so costly in terms of death, destruction and social devastation, was based on an emotional fear which had little basis in fact. Perhaps, it dawned on some Americans, the South Vietnamese would *prefer* to be 'communist' – whatever that meant.

American involvement in this frantic war, which began with President Kennedy sending 4000 'advisers' to help South Vietnam in 1962, was now reduced. In December 1970 there had been 350,000 troops in the area, but by 1972 they were less than 40,000. In March 1972 the whole North Vietnamese army attacked across the 17th Parallel. The American airforce prevented the South Vietnamese from being overrun, and by September the offensive was ended. In January 1973 the US, North Vietnam, South Vietnam and the Vietcong signed a cease-fire agreement. By this the neutrality of Laos and Cambodia was to be respected, all US troops were to withdraw within 60 days, all Vietnam was eventually to be reunited. The non-communist government for which America had fought for 18 years was installed in South Vietnam, but was hopelessly corrupt and inefficient, its army dangerously weak. Fighting in fact continued, and in April 1975 'communist' forces were in South Vietnam's capital Saigon. The war which had begun in 1946 was over – and 50,000 Americans had been killed.

Above right *An American official dislodges a refugee from the doorway of an already overloaded plane during the frantic flight from Saigon during the last days of the war*

Right *Government troops wait inside Pnom Penh, Cambodian capital threatened by the Khymer Rhouge*

Centre right *White resistance patrols of Sereika advance through waterlogged country towards the Thai border*

Far right *Who said Cease Fire? A Khymer Rhouge fighter on the Cambodia-Thai frontier*

War continues in Cambodia

While Prince Sihanouk, ruler of Cambodia, was trying to keep his country from becoming involved in the fighting in neighbouring Laos and South Vietnam, he was helped in this endeavour by the United States and China. But by 1967 he had broken with both of them, and his attempt to remain neutral in the Vietnam War was thwarted by his inability to prevent North Vietnamese and Vietcong troops using uninhabited areas in the north east of his country as supply bases. By 1969 Vietnamese 'communists' controlled much of Cambodia, and the ruthless Cambodians who called themselves Khymer Rouge were stirring up trouble in other parts; so the United States willingly resumed their aid to keep Cambodia independent. In March 1970 however a General Lon Lol, who considered the prince too 'left-wing', ousted Sihanouk, who fled to Peking.

For the next five years Cambodia was in a state of chaos, a battlefield for warring factions, Buddhist versus Christian, intellectual versus peasant, 'communist' versus 'non-communist'. Military operations largely concentrated on blocking the roads into the capital, Phnom Penh. American military operations in Indo-China ended on 15 August 1973 when congress voted to cease bombing Cambodia.

In July it was revealed that US aircraft had repeatedly bombed Cambodia between March 1969 and May 1970 at a time when the administration officially claimed to be respecting Cambodian neutrality, and that official records had been falsified to conceal this from Congress.

Phnom Penh was taken from General Lon Lol in April 1975, a fortnight before the fall of Saigon, which led to the brutal regime of Pol Pot during which more than four million died of starvation or were murdered. During 1979 Vietnamese invaded Cambodia and occupied almost all of it.

Evening Standard

WEATHER:
Clear spells.
Lighting-up time:
4.36 p.m. to 6.56 a.m.
Details—Back Page.

London: Thursday November 20 1975

CITY PRICES

6p

After 36 years the old dictator dies
EXIT FRANCO —ENTER CARLOS

GENERAL FRANCO

The paper with pull

THESE are testing times for Fleet Street. But there is good news today about this newspaper from the very latest National Readership Survey.* For the Evening Standard has a far stronger grip on the London evening newspaper market than ever before.

Here are the facts
1 The Evening Standard has increased its readership in the all-important category of ABC1 readers —the decision makers— from 832,000 during the six months January-June 1974 to

891,000

during the same period this year.

Standard Reporter

MADRID, Thursday.

GENERAL FRANCISCO FRANCO, the man who held Spain in his iron grip for 36 years, is dead.

The old soldier's last battle ended at 3.40 this morning at the La Paz Hospital in Madrid. It was the 35th day of his illness.

For weeks he clung grimly to life. Since being taken ill after a heart attack on October 17 he survived the kidneys, phlebitis and severe internal bleeding which led to massive surgery.

But a few days ago after many crises it became clear that the General was finally losing his fight for life. His condition became critical. And the last medical bulletin, issued only a few hours before his death, made it clear that the end was near.

Daughter at bedside

Franco's only daughter, Carmen, was with him when he died together with four of his grandchildren and the Duke of Cadiz, husband of his favourite granddaughter. Franco's wife of 52 years, Dona Carmen Polo de Franco, was not at the hospital. She visited him late yesterday and then returned to the Pardo, their home for 46 years, to wait for his death. As she left the hospital she said: All we can do is pray.

Today it was revealed that Franco left a crudely typed last testament which referred to the threat of Communism and called on the people to show loyalty to his chosen successor Prince Juan Carlos.

Spain's Premier, Carlos Navarro, wept as he told the Spanish nation on television that Franco had forgiven his enemies on his deathbed and asked them to forgive him.

Franco had warned the Spanish people to be watch-

After ruling Spain for 36 years, General Franco (the *Caudillo*) died in November 1975 at the age of 82. For years he had been reviewing the pros and cons of the various forms of government by which the country might be ruled after his death, and in 1947 had settled for monarchy. Just who would be King of Spain on his demise was decided in 1969 when he named Prince Juan Carlos, grandson of the last King, Alfonso III, as the future head of state.

King Juan Carlos kept Arias Navarro, Franco's prime minister, for the first six months, and then in July 1976 exercised his constitutional right of appointing a young lawyer of his choice, Alvaro Suarez, in his place. In 18 months king and prime minister, with a politically neutral army, guided Spain from dictatorship to free parliamentary elections with the minimum of opposition. Under an amnesty political prisoners were released; political parties, including a Communist party, were legalised; and in June 1977 a general election was held with universal suffrage in which Suarez's Democratic Centre Union won 47 per cent of the vote in a legislature which included Socialists, neo-Francoists and Communists.

*Below left The new monarch takes a constitutional oath. **Below** A king and queen preside at the opening of Parliament in Madrid. **Right** General Franco attends the christening in 1963 of the daughter of his protegé, the grandson of the last king of Spain, to whom he has chosen to hand over power. **Bottom right** The future of Spain is in their elegant hands – King Juan Carlos and Queen Sophia*

1976

Self appointed Life President of Uganda, 'Dr' Idi Amin Dada who gave himself a British VC and DSO, and the title Conqueror of the British Empire

When in 1962 Uganda, the mainly agri-cultural state in the centre of Africa, received self-government within the Commonwealth, with the Kabaka of Buganda as president and Dr Milton Obote as prime minister, it seemed that this beautiful country had attained a semblance of stability. In the national assembly Dr Obote's Uganda People's Congress had 68 of its 91 seats, and there were welcome signs of cohesion. But in fact for eight years from 1969 the country suffered the most grotesque period of its entire history under the domination of a one-time army sergeant-major of huge proportions, Idi Amin, who became a laughing stock to every-one but the Ugandans, some 350,000 of whom he shamelessly killed in cold blood as 'political opponents'. He never tired of humiliating Europeans. But before he was finally removed and chased out of Uganda into exile in 1977, one of his most notorious actions was thwarted when, the year before, a commando group of Israelis landed at Entebbe airport unopposed and rescued the passengers of a hi-jacked air liner whom he was holding hos-tage.

Above *Amin with Sarah, one of his six wives, and one of his 20 children.* Below *An army sergeant convicted of murder is publicly shot by firing squad during 'Field Marshal' Amin's regime*

Above *A soldier of the Ugandan army is captured by Tanzanian troops at Jinja during the fight for a Nile dam in 1979.* Below *By 1979 Amin's crude dictatorship is almost over – Tanzanian guns annihilate what few troops remain loyal to their brutal President*

1977

President Sadat with Mr Begin, prime minister of Israel (wearing glasses) on arrival at Ben Gurion Airport

It was evident, from the non-functioning of her armed forces in the Six Day War and the Yom Kippur War, that Egypt was never going to get her way with Israel by force of arms. The problems created by Britain's withdrawal from Palestine and the Jews setting up their own state surrounded by hostile Arabs, had remained unsolved for 30 years, and so long as Israel existed they were unlikely ever to go away.

As the strongest and largest Arab nation, Egypt felt it was incumbent on her to present the Arab case to the intruders, and try to reach an accord on a man-to-man basis on such matters as the 'rights' of the Palestinian arabs, the need to give Jews, Christians and Moslems access to Jerusalem and the need for Israel (if she was staying and no one looked capable of dislodging her) to have secure frontiers.

So in November 1977 the President of Egypt, Anwar Sadat, boldly took the unprecedented step of making a personal visit to Jerusalem, meeting Menachem Begin the prime minister and speaking to the Israeli Parliament. Begin made a return visit to Cairo in December. In September 1978 Arab and Jewish leaders again met, this time in America under the auspices of President Carter at his country retreat at Camp David. Here they agreed on the terms of an Egyptian-Israeli Peace Treaty, and a Framework for Peace in the Middle East. It did nothing to solve the Palestinian Question or the Jerusalem Question, but insofar as it relieved the tension between Israel and Egypt it proved Winston Churchill's contention that jaw-jaw is better than war-war. Each of them were awarded the Nobel Peace Prize.

The Egyptian leader visits the Memorial of Jewish Martyrs in Jerusalem

By 1977 most of the world's airlines were flying oversize Jumbo Jets – with the risk that any accident involving one or more of them would be equally oversized. It happened on Sunday 27 March 1977 – on the ground. A Boeing 747 of the Dutch national airline KLM and another of Pan American Airways were both taxi-ing for take-off on the fog-bound landing strip of Santa Cruz airport at Tenerife in the Canary Islands. It was about six o'clock in the evening. Each was full of holiday-makers returning home; and the fuel tanks of the KLM plane had just been fully topped up.

'The two planes seemed to be jogging each other on the runway,' said an eye-witness. 'Then one shot in front of the other. They seemed to get tangled up – and then there was a big explosion.'

The ground collision caused both aircraft to burst into flames. All 263 aboard the Dutch jumbo were killed; some 300 on the American Boeing – with 60 survivors. The total of 563 dead made it, in 1977, the 'worst ever air disaster'.

The wreckage of one of the jumbo jets on the runway of Santa Cruz airport

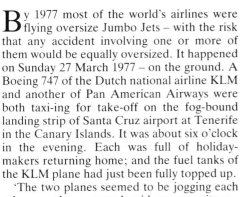

DAILY Mirror

BRITAIN'S BIGGEST DAILY SALE   6p

Monday, March 28, 1977

WORST AIR DISASTER

A jumbo in the livery of Pan-Am, America's leading airline

Jumbo jets in collision on holiday isle

A Boeing 747 of K L M, the Dutch national airline

AT LEAST 563 people were killed yesterday in the world's worst air disaster.

It happened when two jumbo jets loaded with holiday-makers collided at a fog-shrouded island airport.

One of them, a Boeing 747 of KLM, the Dutch national airline, was fully laden with fuel.

Babies

It exploded into flames after the high-speed ground collision with a Pan-American 747 at Los Rodeos airport on Tenerife in the Canary Islands.

Official figures issued last night put the death toll at 563. All 263 on board the

563 DEAD

By PETER STEPHENS, ALASTAIR McQUEEN and JOHN PEACOCK

Dutch airliner were killed.

The dead included twenty-five young children and six babies.

More than sixty passengers from the American plane were reported to have got out alive. But many of them were badly hurt.

Both airliners were taxi-ing for take-off at 6 p.m. local time when the tragedy happened.

One witness, 38-year-old businessman Jose Manuel from Barcelona, said: 'The two planes seemed to be jogging each other on the runway. Then one shot in

front of the other. They seemed to get tangled up – and then there was a big explosion.'

An airport employee said: 'The shock as they hit was enormous.

'I thought several bombs had exploded next by all at the same time.'

Then the small airport was lit up by a terrible glare as both planes caught fire. And a dense pall of choking black smoke drifted over the

Continued on Back Page

VICTIM: Stewardess A. Bouvy from KLM.

VICTIM: M. Tom, KLM hostess.

I WAS BLOWN TO SAFETY!

...E ma...ho lived ...rough ...locust ...ship...m

bed: 'I was struggling to get my wife Elsie out with me, but she is in the emergency room here now and is hurt very badly.

The plane went up completely in flames

'I was in the first-class compartment and after the impact people started just tumbling down from the lounge

above on top of me.' He said his main aim was to try to save his wife, and he went back once to try to rescue her.

'But we got separated and then I saw a body falling out of the plane.' he said. 'It was my wife.'

Seventeen survivors, all Americans, were early today making 'satisfactory progress' at

Tenerife's biggest hospital, the Hospital Civil.

And their escape from the disaster was described as 'a miracle' by the hospital priest, Bill Moxon.

He said: 'They managed to get out from the crashed planes by clambering on the wings

'It is incredible that anyone could survive what happened.'

CRASH THAT HAD TO COME · PAGE 2

1978

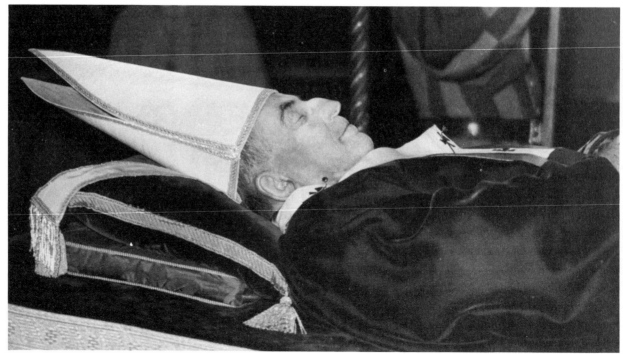

Above *Pope John Paul I, who died 33 days after becoming pope, lying in state in St Peters, Rome*

Top right *Sixty five year old Cardinal Albino Luciano, Patriarch of Venice, during his installation ceremony as Pope John Paul I on 3 September 1978*

In 1978, the Catholic Church, in desperate need of a new leader for the latter stages of the Twentieth Century, found two. Pope Paul VI died on 6 August. He was 80, a remote leader despite his world tours, who had split the Church by his refusal to consider change on contraception and on the priesthood while modernising traditional services. His successor, elected by 111 cardinals meeting in secret conclave, was a surprise choice: Cardinal Albino Luciani, 65, Patriarch of Venice and almost unknown outside Italy. He took the names of his predecessors, John and Paul, was informal, dispensed with much of the pomp of the Vatican but died after just 33 days as Pope. The cardinals next chose a younger, fitter man from outside Italy: Cardinal Karol Wojtyla, 58, Archbishop of Krakow in Poland. He took the name John Paul II and shared his predecessor's common touch and dislike of grandeur. He stuck to the traditional teachings of the Church yet his courage, personality, plans to travel wide and willingness to speak out against social and political ills proved to the world's 700 million Catholics that they had a worthy leader.

Right *The Polish archbishop who became Pope John Paul II, the first non-Italian pontiff for five centuries*

Far right *Instead of being carried on a papal throne for his first outdoor audience in St Peter's Square, Pope John Paul II broke with tradition by riding in an open car*

The Recorder

Monday, Aug. 7, 1978   Amsterdam, New York   Fifteen Cents

Pope Paul VI Dead

Bishop Reacts To Death

ALBANY — Bishop Howard Hubbard of the Diocese of Albany, the youngest bishop in the nation, Sunday night issued the following statement in reaction to the death of Pope Paul VI.

"Pope Paul was a magnificent spiritual leader who guided the Roman Catholic Church during a challenging and difficult period of change and renewal engendered by the Second Vatican Council.

"His was the arduous task of preserving the ancient verities upon which our church is founded and apply them to the present needs of knowledge and our cultural situation.

"This he did with un-common zeal, vision, courage, strength and patience.

1897-1978

Cardinals Begin Process Of Selecting Successor

By JACK R. PAYTON

VATICAN CITY (UPI) — Pope Paul VI, who led the world's 700 million Roman Catholics for 15 turbulent years of controversy and reform, died at his summer palace Sunday night. He was 80.

As the faithful knelt in prayer for Paul's soul today, intense speculation immediately arose over who will succeed him on the Throne of St. Peter. Observers said the reign of the next pope could be a fateful time for the church.

Efforts for religious unity and world peace were the twin themes of Paul's papacy. The first pope to leave Italy in nearly 200 years, he tirelessly pursued his goals in pilgrimages to six continents.

The church came dangerously close to schism during Paul's years, however, and his attempts to end hostilities in the Holy Land and other world trouble spots met with scant success.

Cardinals Gather

As preparations began for Paul's burial in a crypt under St. Peter's Basilica, members of the College of Cardinals — the most varied group of cardinals ever, because of reforms effected by the late pope — gathered to elect his successor. Vatican sources said the new pontiff is almost certain to be Italian, like all of his predecessors for the past 450 years.

The pope's death came at 9:40 p.m. (3:40 p.m. EDT) Sunday, three hours and 10 minutes after he suffered a heart attack while listening to a mass in the private chambers of his Castel Gandolfo summer palace, in the mountains 15 miles south of Rome.

Doctors were administering oxygen to the pontiff in a futile attempt to keep him breathing when he died, Vatican officials said.

Thousands Crowd Square

As news of the Paul's death flashed across Italy, thousands crowded into St. Peter's Square and into churches throughout the country to attend requiem masses.

Cardinals around the world headed for Rome to take part in the conclave to elect a new pontiff. Vatican officials said the meeting would open between Aug. 21 and 26.

Vatican sources said the pope was conscious and lucid until his last moments. A church official at Castel Gandolfo said the pope's last words before dying were "The death of a pope is like that of other men, but it can always teach others something."

The death came one day after his personal physicians ordered the pontiff to take several days of bed rest because of what was officially described as a flareup of the arthritic condition that had for years made it difficult for him to walk.

Paul's death was announced by a sobbing Rev. Pierfranco Pastore, deputy chief of the Vatican press office.

Chicago Tribune

Green Streak
Latest markets

Tuesday, November 21, 1978

4 Sections · 15¢

400 in sect lined up to die

San Francisco Examiner reporter Tim Reiterman photographed the Port Kaituma ambush scene with Gregory Robinson's camera after Robinson was slain. More photos on Back Page. Sec 3.

Guyana poison rite described

From Tribune Wire Services

GEORGETOWN, Guyana—More than 400 men, women and children reportedly lined up for doses of poison brewed in a tub in a mass suicide after members of a California sect ambushed and killed five Americans, including U.S. Rep. Leo J. Ryan (D-Cal.), Saturday night.

American lawyer Mark Lane, who was at the People's Temple camp just before the mass deaths occurred, said Monday that suicide was discussed at a community meeting and two sect members later told him. "We are all going to die now.

"They were smiling . . . they looked genuinely happy." Lane said

"I got out as the killing was taking place," Lane said after he arrived in this capital city, 150 miles southeast of the camp.

sect leader denies—and then admits—presence of guns. Americans know Guyana as a good place to avoid. Stories on Page 2.

Lane and a lawyer colleague, Charles Garry, fled into the bush near the commune settlement after the massacre.

LANE SAID he counted 80 bursts of semiautomatic weapons fire when the Peoples Temple sect gathered at an open-air auditorium at the commune, presumably for a mass suicide rite.

The American lawyer said he had heard that the commune's doctor and nurse had carried a tub of poison to the auditorium before the mass suicide.

It was not clear if Ryan's group had already been ambushed before the meeting or if the camp residents were debating going ahead with the ambush.

MEANWHILE, THE Guyanese information minister, Shirley Field-Ridley, confirmed the deaths and said the whereabouts of the remaining 500 to 700 'Americans at the camp was not known, but they apparently had fled into the surrounding jungle in the northwest cor-

Rep. Diggs draws 3-year jail term

WASHINGTON (AP)—Rep. Charles Diggs (D., Mich.) was sentenced Monday to a maximum of three years in prison for his conviction on charges of mail fraud and making false statements.

U.S. District Judge Oliver Gasch ordered Diggs imprisoned for up to three years on each of the 29 counts on which he was convicted but the sentences are to run concurrently.

In appealing for leniency, Diggs told the judge his conviction "has been a very devastating experience. I know that the conviction has been a very painful experience for me personally and professionally.

The congressman stood impassively as the judge stated his sentence and then avoided reporters when he left the courtroom.

THE PROSECUTION had demanded that Diggs be given some form of incarceration for his offense. Attorney John Kotelly argued that Diggs' conduct "does not call for leniency, does not call for a period of probation, but calls for a period of incarceration."

He described Diggs' crimes as "stealing money from the citizens of the United States.

But Diggs' attorneys maintained that his reelection to Congress from his Detroit district earlier this month was reason enough to grant him a suspended sentence or probation.

The 12-term Michigan congressman had said previously that he will appeal his conviction in the $66,000 scheme.

DIGGS WAS FOUND guilty Oct. 7 of inflating the salaries of several staff

Continued on page 5, col. 2

Rep. Charles C. Diggs Jr.

Fear cult horror in San Francisco

By Michael Coakley and Ronald Yates
Chicago Tribune Press Service

SAN FRANCISCO—Fearing still further horrors, this beautiful city once again is confronting the spectre of cult-like fanaticism, this time apparently the work of a man who was one of the highest municipal officials up until a year ago.

Concerned that San Francisco-area followers of the Rev. Jim Jones may react to the apparent mass suicide in Guyana by taking their own lives, the FBI and local police are attempting to locate and piece together the remnants of the shattered People's Temple empire here.

The warning of possibly more suicides to come—this time by Jones' sympathizers who did not follow their leader to his South American hideaway—was relayed to the FBI Sunday by former Temple members.

THIS OMINOUS REPORT was only the latest in a string of grim developments.

Relatives and friends of the religious cultists reacted with stunned disbelief that possibly more than 400 of Jones' disciples have taken part in a mass suicide pact at their jungle commune.

Shortly after the first reports Saturday of the murder of a California congressman and three newsmen who had gone

Continued on page 16, col. 4

Continued on page 16, col. 1

One of the most bizarre yet horrifying events in recent times was the enforced mass suicide in November 1978 of an American religious cult in Guyana. In all 913 members of the 'Peoples' Temple' died including its leader, the megolomaniacal 'Reverend' Jim Jones. After moving his followers from San Francisco he had set himelf up as a God in the jungle cut off from the rest of the world.

Reports of abuses soon began to provoke others to investigate the cult. Congressman Leo Ryan and 3 newsmen got too close to the truth of this petty tyranny and were shot dead. Events soon took a further turn for the worse with Jones realising that his days were numbered. He chose to order his followers to take their own lives by means of poison. Those who refused were shot. Jones himself died after shooting himself.

The Jonestown Mass Suicide showed how precarious the line could be between normal behaviour and savagery even after centuries of progress.

Some of the 400 deranged followers of crazed Jim Jones strew the grounds of the 'People's Temple' after they had been persuaded to shoot and poison themselves in the hope of attaining who knows what

Above *These two followers died in each other's arms.*
Below *The ecstacy is over – rigor mortis sets in beneath Jim Jones's throne*

Right *Jim Jones, leader of the Peoples Temple.*
Below right *Bodies lay strewn about a vat containing a drink laced with cyanide*

THOSE WHO DO NOT REMEMBER THE PAST ARE CONDEMNED TO REPEAT IT.

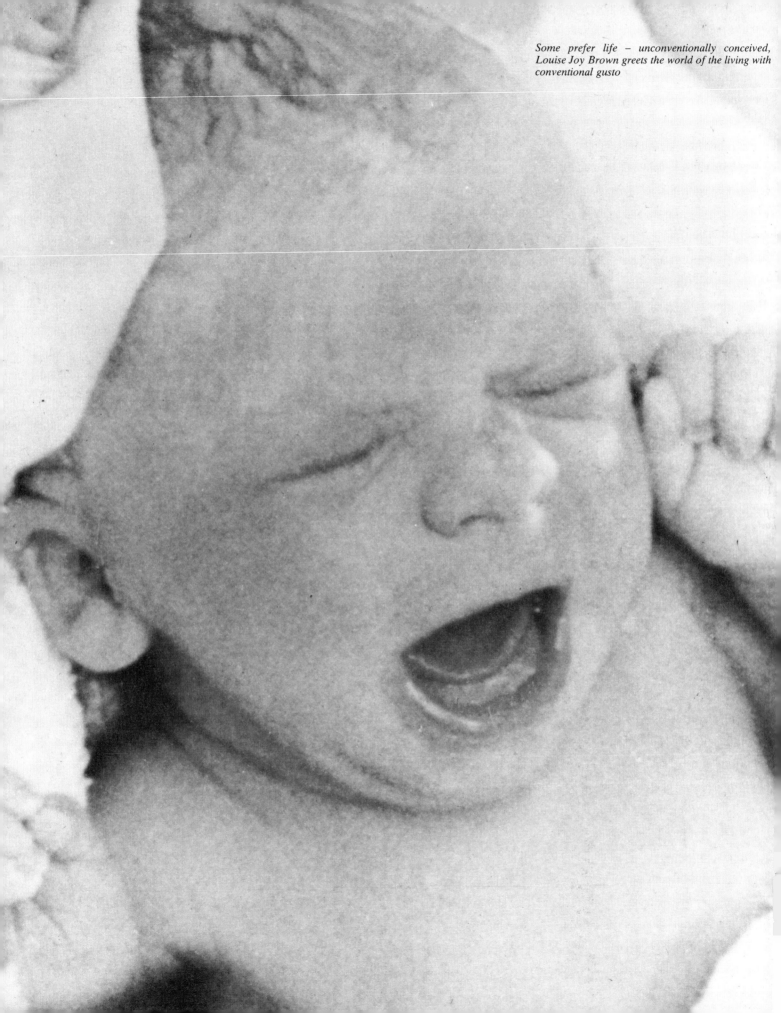

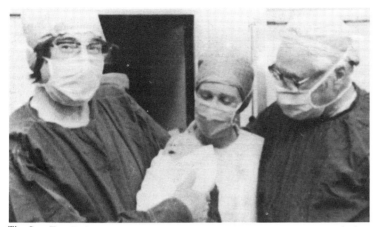

The first Test Tube Baby is shown to disbelieving newsmen – 'see, it works!'

The first baby conceived outside its mother's body – in a test tube – was born in Oldham General Hospital outside Manchester on 25 July 1978 to 31 year old Lesley Brown of Bristol who, like other infertile wives, had been told she could never have a child. The first 'Test Tube Baby' was a healthy, normal girl of 5 lb 12 oz. She owed her entry into the world – by Caesarian section – to the dedicated research of Oldham gynaecologist Patrick Steptoe and Cambridge physiologists Dr Robert Edwards and Dr Barry Bavister. Together these three perfected a technique by which an egg taken from a wife's ovary was fertilised with the sperm of her husband in a test tube, and then placed back in her womb for maturing naturally over the usual number of months.

News of the experiments at Cambridge in 'creating human life in a laboratory' broke in February 1969. The first proof that after nine years they had found all the answers – the birth of Louise Joy Brown of Bristol – brought hope to childless women everywhere.

Patrick Steptoe and Dr Robert Edwards tell television viewers the story of their achievement

DAILY EXPRESS
THE VOICE OF BRITAIN

PLAY TIME EXPRESS See P. of 20

No. 24,281   Wednesday July 26 1978   Weather: Rainy at first   8p   ★★★★

Born safe—the world's first test-tube baby weighs in at 5lb 12oz and mother's delighted

By Harry Pugh

IT'S A GIRL

Steptoe's obsession

IT'S A GIRL! THE WORLD'S FIRST TEST-TUBE BABY WAS BORN LATE LAST NIGHT. SHE CAME INTO THE WORLD NEAR MIDNIGHT. BOTH MOTHER AND BABY ARE WELL.

There were no hitches, the mother, 32-year-old Mrs Lesley Brown, is "doing well" and the baby is perfectly formed. A living miracle weighing in at 5lb 12ozs.

The birth will bring world acclaim for Britain's medical profession, after 12 years of research.

The two men who have created life in a test tube, gynaecologist Mr Patrick Steptoe and scientist Dr Robert Edwards, were said to be "enthralled."

They had taken an egg from driver's wife Mrs Brown, fertilised it with her husband's sperm, then replanted the foetus in her womb.

Mrs Brown, childless after nine years of marriage because a fault in her fallopian tubes had her baby in a 45-minute Caesarean operation

MAGIC MOMENT

There was time later for a cuddle—as her husband John, 38, a divorcee who has a teenage daughter by his first marriage watched close to tears.

It was the magic moment everyone had waited for.

EXTENSIVE CHECKS

'...doing well' John Brown: watched in tears

FALL OF SHAH OF IRAN

The Shah of Persia showed himself extremely astute in the attention he gave to his country's economic, agricultural and industrial problems, but nowhere nearly astute enough in his attitude to religion. His handling of the country's oil resources which brought it enormous wealth and his redistribution of land, both of which helped raise the standard of living very considerably between 1953 and 1978, could not be faulted. Under his rule, health services and education were greatly improved; the army became the strongest in the Middle East; Persian women were emancipated. The 1971 celebration of the 2,500th anniversary of the Persian Monarchy seemed to be a symbol of stability, looking to another 2,500 years.

Aware that Iran, as it was now called, was not an arab country and had no reason to subscribe to the cause of Arab Nationalism, he was equally alive to the fact that his subjects were moslems. He was not convinced however that strict adherence to the law of the Koran was consistent with bringing the country into the centre of the modern world, only with keeping it on the edge of it. In that he was probably right, but he had not calculated that so many would listen to the mullahs (Islamic religious leaders) who wanted Iran to stay where it was.

In January 1978 there were religious demonstrations in the holy city of Qom urging the re-assertion of traditional Islamic values. The Shah made quick concessions – but too late. The benefits he had brought the country were forgotten in a wave of personal hostility stirred to white heat by the 76-year-old Ayatollah Khomeni who returned from his exile in France to a tumultuous, emotional reception in Teheran, demanding the replacement of the government of the Shah, and all alien Western culture, with a total Islamic republic. There is no reasoning with a religious fanatic, or with the people he has hypnotised, and in January 1979 the Shah of Iran left his palace for good.

Right *The Ayatollah Khomeini at the end of his 15 year exile in Paris*

Centre right *The Shah of Iran with his children*

Far right *Members of the Iranian Islamic Republic Army demonstrate their support of the new regime in the streets of Teheran*

The Daily Telegraph

FINAL

WIPAC
HAIR RAISER
Halogen driving lamps

No 38746 LONDON, THURSDAY, JANUARY 3, 1980   Printed in LONDON and MANCHESTER   **10p**

Carter decides on firm response to invasion of Afghanistan

U.S. RECALLS ENVOY

Russian tanks and planes slaughter hundreds

By STEPHEN BARBER in Washington

PRESIDENT CARTER recalled America's Ambassador to Moscow, Mr Thomas Watson, yesterday for consultations on the Russian invasion of Afghanistan, the White House announced last night. He is due back in Washington today.

Guerrilla casualties heavy'

By BRUCE LOUDON in New Delhi

The move was decided on at a special session of the National Security Council at which a number of other decisions were taken in response to the Kremlin's actions Mr Jody Powell, the presidential Press secretary, said.

Mr Powell said the council meeting had considered other steps to be taken in response to the Russian "invasion" and that these would be made public after consultations with America's friends and allies.

One of the steps it is believed will be to seek

Other Afghan war news, and picture—P1; Editorial Comment—P12

Soviet 'Riot Act' for Khomeini

By AMIT ROY in Teheran

MR VLADIMIR VINOGRADOV, the Soviet Ambassador in Teheran, flew to the holy city of Qom yesterday and promptly read Khomeini the riot act, according to informed diplomatic sources.

CAMBODIA RELIEF HALTED

By Our General Correspondent

THE troubled international relief effort to help to feed Cambodia is being sharply curtailed.

Sinn Fein chief arrested

By COLIN BRADY in Belfast

GERRY ADAMS, vice-president of Sinn Fein, the legal political voice of the Provisional I.R.A. was

Unions seeking steel embargo

By ROBERT BEDLOW Industrial Staff

ALL iron and steel-making in the British Steel Corporation came to a halt yesterday as the first national steel strike since 1926 got under way.

As unions attempted to strengthen their stranglehold on the industry, the private steel makers became embroiled in the dispute.

The procedure was familiar. The Russian leader Leonid Brezhnev telephoned President Carter in Washington on 28 December 1979 to tell him his forces had been 'invited' to protect Afghanistan, with which the USSR had a border, 'from some outside third-nation threat'. By this, the official newspaper *Pravda* later explained, was meant 'counter-revolutionary groups', some 5,000 strong, trained in Pakistan by American, Chinese, Egyptian and British intelligence officers. The Chinese saw the invasion of Afghanistan as a stepping stone to Russian control of all South East Asia and a threat to China's security. Brezhnev had no reason to telephone the British prime minister Mrs Margaret Thatcher, but it was learnt that she had told him that she was 'profoundly disturbed' by what had happened.

This was that Soviet troop carriers had begun landing at Kabul airport on Christmas Eve, and 200 military transports with 5,000 troops on Boxing Day. On 27 December the Russians assassinated President Hafizollah Amin who, as head of one of the two warring communist factions, had formed the country's first Marxist dictatorship only three months before, after destroying his own People's Democratic Party and waging unsuccessful war against tribal insurgents. Reinforcements by air and land across the Oxus river frontier soon built up the Russian army to 40,000 who at once garrisoned the main towns. On 1 January 1980 they installed their own head man, Babrak Karmal of the Parcham faction, who spoke to the nation that night on television.

But the supporters of the dethroned Amin were not going to give in as easily as that, and they carried on guerilla harrassment of the invaders which in 1984 was still keeping the Russian forces on their toes and still deployed in force in that rugged, inhospitable country.

The Economist has been proved right when, in January 1980, it wrote: 'Like other invading armies before them, the Russians may find that it is not the getting in that is hard but the getting out.'

Right *Harrassment of the enemies of the Mojahadin involves arduous treks across bleak hillsides such as this*

Top right *Afghan rebels position a 75 mm Chinese gun in Paktia close to the Pakistan border*

Below *An Afghan Muslim rebel – one of the Mojahadin who are putting up strong resistance in a holy war against both Afghan and Russian armies*

A determined young member of the Hazbi Islami group of rebels commanded by mullah Jalladin

1980

Communism perhaps – if it works; totalitarian communism not at any price. Police intimidation and arbitrary arrest apart, in Poland the alien ideology of communism was patently not working; the economy was sinking rapidly, food and fuel were always short. But the free trade union Solidarity, in spite of its ten millon members, had no alternative but to pledge themselves not to challenge the 'leading role' of the Polish Communist party of Stanislaw Kania. It was a pledge made under the threat of force, but in December 1980 it looked as if Poland might follow the fate of East Berlin in 1953, Hungary in 1956, and Czechoslovakia in 1968 and see the threat replaced by reality. It would then be unable to offer co-operation in stabilising Poland; it would be forced to do what the army of occupation told it to do.

Lech Walesa who became leader of the strike in Gdansk shipyard in August 1980 and elected leader of Solidarity for the next two years in October, saw the priority as preventing armed intervention by Soviet and other Warsaw Pact forces, and the need to cool the more hot-headed of his lieutenants and convince them that the pursuit of reconciliation and national peace was no betrayal of their cause. Within a year however relations between government and union had worsened. In December 1981 the new Moscow-approved prime minister General Jaruzelski had declared martial law and set up a Military Council of National Salvation. He had lost patience with Solidarity, he said; the country had been not days but hours from total collapse. A curfew was imposed; riot troops dispersed meetings with water cannon. Lech Walesa was not arrested but called to Warsaw for negotiations. The totalitarian communism, which only a handful of Poles would have *chosen* for their form of government and ten million of them had openly rejected, had brought the country to the brink of civil war. It definitely was *not* working.

Right *Lech Walesa chairs a session of the National Coordinating Commission of 'Solidarity', the free Polish trade union, in Gdansk*

Lech Walesa talks to chemical workers at Oswiecim

Daily Mail
MONDAY, DECEMBER 14, 1981   15p

Civil war near as Solidarity urges general strike

MARTIAL LAW DECLARED IN POLAND

By DAVID FLOYD, Communist Affairs Correspondent

POLAND is on the brink of civil war after the declaration of martial law and the arrest of most leading members of the trade union Solidarity.

About 1,000 people were reported to have been interned in a swift overnight operation ending in the proclamation by Prime Minister General Jaruzelski that he had set up a 'Military Council of National Salvation.'

He said he had lost all patience with Solidarity, and declared that the country was 'not days but hours' from total collapse.

Blizzard swings off course

Pope prays for peace — Page 14
Balance of power — Page 15
The greatest gamble — Centre pages

Fished out . . . a lone walker braves the blizzard on the A46 near Bath yesterday

Terrorist fears as bomb kills two in London

Full report : Page NINE

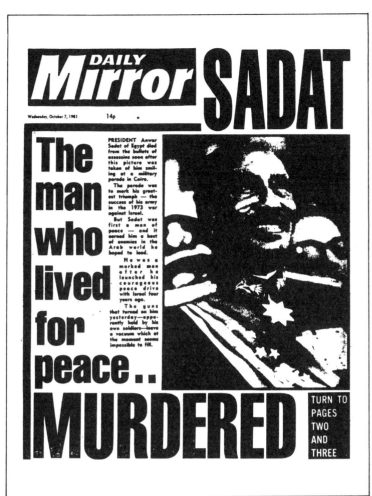

DAILY Mirror SADAT

Wednesday, October 7, 1981   14p

The man who lived for peace.. MURDERED

PRESIDENT Anwar Sadat of Egypt died from the bullets of assassins soon after this picture was taken of him smiling at a military parade in Cairo.

The parade was to mark his greatest triumph — the success of his army in the 1973 war against Israel.

But Sadat was first a man of peace — and it earned him a host of enemies in the Arab world he hoped to lead.

He was a marked man after he launched his courageous peace drive with Israel four years ago.

The guns that turned on him yesterday—apparently held by his own soldiers—leave a vacuum which at the moment seems impossible to fill.

TURN TO PAGES TWO AND THREE

1981

The plan devised by the enemies of President Anwar Sadat of Egypt to end his rule and his life was unbelievable – which was why it succeeded. The soldiers of his own army whom he was reviewing in a triumphant parade to mark their successes in the war of 1973, stopping in mid-procession, jumping from their vehicles and rushing the platform where he sat to gun him down in full view of all beside him and all who watched. A scriptwriter who suggested such a scene for an adventure film would have been laughed out of the front office. Yet it happened in Cairo on 6 October 1981. Six others were killed with him.

The mode of his assassination was as breathtaking in its originality as Sadat's seeking out the Israeli prime minister in Jerusalem and offering to make, of all things, peace – the act for which the extremists who killed him were never able to forgive him. What price Arab-Israeli unity? What price Arab unity? What price unity within one Arab nation?

Soldiers in a troop carrier point their guns at Sadat's reviewing stand during the fated military parade

Pandemonium after Sadat's assassination. A victim's body is covered (left) while soldiers grapple with a photographer (bottom right)

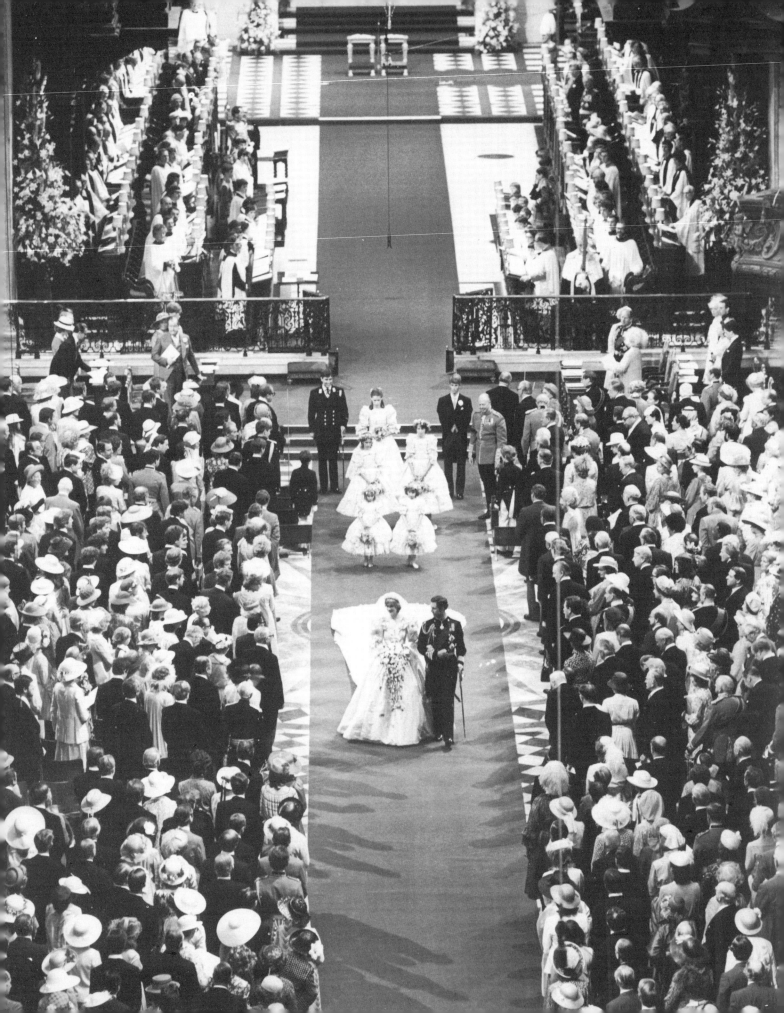

The Daily Telegraph

World audience sees Palace kiss set the seal on day of pageantry and joy

FAIRY TALE WEDDING

Millions share happiness of sparkling couple

BY TONY ALLEN-MILLS

The Prince and Princess of Wales appear on the balcony of Buckingham Palace as man and wife. **Below** *In the open carriage on their way to Waterloo Station for the start of their honeymoon at Broadlands*

Few royal occasions have captivated the world as the wedding of Prince Charles, heir to the British throne, and Lady Diana Spencer, scion of an ancient noble family, in London's St Paul's Cathedral in July 1981. Heads of State, presidents, prime ministers, ambassadors, admirals, generals and representatives of every section of the community attended the service in the huge church, which was followed by millions all over the world on their television screens. Thousands lined the streets from Buckingham Palace to Ludgate Hill to watch the glittering procession of carriages and their mounted escorts carrying the whole royal family on that fine sunny day, and cheer the romantically beautiful young bride in her 'fairytale' wedding dress, Britain's future Queen, as she rode wreathed in smiles to the colourful ceremony.

Just married – the Prince of Wales with his Princess on his arm walks down the aisle after the marriage ceremony in St Paul's. **Below** *'Everything under control?' – a relaxed moment in the cathedral*

1982

DAILY EXPRESS
THE VOICE OF BRITAIN
Wednesday June 16 1982 ● 17p ● Weather: Sunny intervals

The Falklands are once more under the Government desired by their inhabitants
GOD SAVE THE QUEEN
GENERAL MOORE'S DRAMATIC SIGNAL FROM PORT STANLEY

V-F DAY

THE FALKLANDS VICTORY, SPECIAL EDITION: PLEASE SEE INSIDE

On 31 March 1982 the Foreign Office believed that an attempt by the Argentinian navy to capture the islands they called the Malvinas, and regarded as theirs, was by no means imminent. Two days later (2 April) they did just that however, and Lord Carrington, Foreign Secretary, resigned for this failure in intelligence. The 79 Royal Marines stationed in the islands' capital, Port Stanley, were quickly overwhelmed, and the British Governor sent packing. Crowds in Buenos Aires cheered the three-man military junta who had grabbed power for themselves with the promise of coping with the 130 per cent inflation, and General Galtieri preened himself for the effectiveness of plans which had apparently taken the British by surprise. There was no hesitation on the part of HM government in taking action to expel the invaders, and orders were given to HM Navy to mobilise and put to sea as soon as they could, which was Friday 5 April. Government and Opposition praised Mrs Thatcher for her resolution.

The crisis which had developed so rapidly now slowed as the 150-ship Task Force sailed

Gurkhas are piped aboard the liner Queen Elizabeth 2 *to join the Falklands Task Force, 12 May 1982*

Centre right *A* Sea King *helicopter of the Royal Navy lands on the flight deck hastily fitted to the liner-turned-troop carrier*

Bottom right *A bomb narrowly misses two Royal Fleet Auxiliaries in San Carlos Bay, East Falkland*

first to Ascension Island and then on to the Falkland Islands. The US Secretary of State, General Haig, failed in his shuttle diplomacy to persuade the two erstwhile friendly countries to discuss their differences round the table. The outlying South Georgia was seized, and a total exclusion zone by air and sea announced, which Argentina was dared to breach at its peril. All talking ended in the first week of May, and gave way to a fierce exchange of gunfire. On 2 May a British nuclear-powered submarine torpedoed Argentina's 13,600 ton cruiser *General Belgrano*, and two days later an Argentinian fighter-bomber fired a French-made 'Exocet' missile which knocked out the British destroyer HMS *Sheffield*. The naval skirmish then gave way to a full-dress military operation, and the Battle for the Falklands had begun.

By 16 June it was all over and the islands were once again in British possession.

Right *Union Jack and White Ensign are raised on South Georgia.* **Far right** *Children from the settlement of Port San Carlos help Royal Marines dig in on East Falkland*

For three days in succession, 16, 17 and 18 September 1982, what were described as ill-disciplined, armed 'Christian militiamen' ('Phalangists'? Major Haddad's South Lebanese army?) ran amok with machine guns and knives in the densely populated Sabra-Chatila area of West Beirut. This consisted of the lean-to shacks and tents, underground shelters and earthworks thrown up in 1948 for refugees, mainly from north Palestine, but now housing a mixed community of 20,000 of whom some 5,000 were registered Palestinians. Of the latter less than 2,000 were 'fighters', but the place was certainly a Palestinian stronghold. The operation was apparently intended to flush out such Palestinian guerillas. But the Israelis who had surrounded Sabra-Chatila with tanks after the breakdown of law and order in the Moslem sector of Beirut after the murder of the Lebanese president-elect Bechir Gemayel, were accused of letting it continue long after it became obvious that a massacre of civilians was taking place, an orgy of uncontrolled, wild slaughter.

It was a thoroughly bestial operation of savage brutality in which its perpetrators seemed to have exulted – taking time to carve crosses on their victims' chests, slitting their throats, slicing their breasts, killing doctors and bedridden patients in hospitals, chaining men together and dragging them behind jeeps.

Above right *A Palestinian woman weeps over the bodies of her relatives in the refugee camp of Sabra, while in the background a red cross volunteer sprays disinfectant*

Inset *Some of the hundreds of men, women and children massacred by fanatical volunteer soldiers, the so-called 'Christian Militia', in Sabra*

Right *Evidence of indiscriminate machine-gunning by the extremists whose aggressive instincts got out of hand when faced with defenceless civilians*

1983

A storm of international protest met the news that 269 passengers and crew had been killed in September 1983 when the pilot of a Soviet fighter plane, acting on orders from the ground, shot a missile at, and destroyed, a Korean Airlines Boeing 747 Jumbo Jet airliner on flight 007, which had strayed into Russian air space on a journey from Anchorage in Alaska to Seoul in South Korea. It exploded in mid-air, and what was left of it and its occupants fell into the Sea of Japan. The victims included 61 American citizens, including a congressman, 110 Koreans and 28 Japanese. The Russians claimed the plane showed no lights, and was mistaken for an American RC-135 intelligence aircraft; and that their pilot had fired warning tracer bullets along the route of the Boeing – which the Americans later confirmed to be the case. It seemed to be a genuine, though tragic, mistake, but the Soviet leaders saw no reason to admit it and apologise. How the Korean pilot came to be off course and whether he saw the warning

DAILY ◉ NEWS
NEW YORK'S PICTURE NEWSPAPER

SOVIETS SHOOT DOWN JETLINER
30 Yanks among 269 victims;

shots remained a mystery, but the airliner was certainly not on a spying mission.

The International Federation of Air Line Pilots Associations recommended a 60-day ban on all flights to the USSR; and President Reagan demanded Soviet guarantees that such an incident should never recur and compensation for the American dead. South Korea moved closer to Japan as a result of the accident which, said the former's Defence Minister, showed the importance of security cooperation in the region.

Top Relatives waiting at Kimpo International airport breakdown on hearing that the South Korean jet is believed to have been shot down

Below Bereaved families of passengers in the Korean Airlines plane throw flowers and pray over the spot off Sakhalin Island where the bodies fell into the sea

Below *A Korean Airline official confirms that a metal object painted with the letters 'HL' is a fragment of the shot down Jumbo Jet*

In 1983 the clamour of the anti-nuclear campaigners gathered momentum all over Europe as normally docile men-in-the-street and their wives became worried about the extent to which the governments of the two Super Powers were becoming so obsessed with their ideological differences that they looked like becoming blind to the consequences of insisting that only the 'right' ideology prevailed – their own – and that the other should be forcibly extinguished. In 1983 'peaceful co-existence' had become a dirty word. Thus in Holland arose The International Peace Coordinating Centre; in West Germany the anti-nuclear Green Party and the Burgerinitiativen of Jo Leinen, the federation of local anti-nuclear groups, 1000 delegates of which met in Cologne in February 1984 to plan its future; in France the Humanitas International of which singer Joan Baez is president; on the continent in general 'European Nuclear Disarmament'. In Britain the Women For Peace picketed and encircled the Greenham Common air base where Cruise missiles were housed (but failed to stop their arrival). The Campaign for Nuclear Disarmament (CND) claimed 230,000 took part in the demonstration they organised in London on 6 June 1982, and, when Cruise missiles were successfully brought to England and West Germany, they met in Sheffield in December 1983 to plan new strategy. The Roman Catho-

lic pacifist priest Monsignor Bruce Kent, who is general secretary of CND, intends to oppose the British Government's plan for Trident missile-carrying submarines. In 1983 he claimed a membership of 85,000 – double the number of 1982 – with some 250,000 supporters in local groups. In 1984 new members were being enrolled at 300 a week. Neil Kinnock the new Leader of the Labour Opposition has pledged to withdraw and dismantle Britain's Polaris submarines after an electoral victory by the Labour Party which has opted for unilateral disarmament without leaving NATO (though Shadow Foreign Secretary Denis Healey disagrees). The Super Powers the USA and the USSR produce ideas for containing the effect of nuclear war – the latest from America applies the 'deep-strike' principle using Emerging Technology (ET) – but none for removing the mistrust which makes each think a stockpile of nuclear weapons is essential for 'effective deterrence'. Fear of the stab in the back has always existed – whether from a hand-held dagger or a rocket-launched bomb. As in primeval times war is no longer declared.

Right *CND's general secretary, Monsignor Bruce Kent (left) puts the case against nuclear armament.*

Below *In London men and women of all ages take part in a Campaign for Nuclear Disarmament protest march, 22 November 1983*

'Fair and beautiful' is how the Prince of Wales described his son to reporters on leaving St Mary's Hospital, London, on 21 June 1982 after witnessing the child's delivery at nine o'clock that evening after his wife's 16 hour confinement. A notice announcing the birth of the second in line to the British throne was posted outside Buckingham Palace, and the news soon spread to all corners of the United Kingdom and Commonwealth. The baby weighed seven pounds and one and a half ounces. The Home Secretary is no longer required personally to attend a royal birth – King George VI discontinued the 'archaic custom' in 1948 – but he was informed by telephone. Princess Diana's mother Mrs Shand-Kydd and her father Earl Spencer were early visitors, and an excited mother-in-law came at once to see her third grandchild. Many members of the public journeyed to Paddington to offer good wishes and make presents of flowers. Less than 24 hours after the event the Princess of Wales returned home to Kensington Palace.

On 28 June the baby's names were given as William Arthur Philip Louis – to be known however as Prince William of Wales. Three days later the Princess celebrated her 21st birthday – 11 months after her wedding. The new prince was christened on 4 August. If her son ever becomes King William V it is unlikely to be much before the year 2032, by which time the British monarchy will have had a very healthy 966 year innings since William I opened the batting in 1066. The birth of Prince William augured well for a continuation of that political stability which Britain has enjoyed – and been envied for – under her constitutional monarchy for so long.

Prince William of Wales faces press cameramen from all over the world at Kensington Palace, London on 14 December 1983

'Look! – no supporting hands!' Prince William gives public proof of his ability to walk unaided

1984 – and the footsteps lead to the future. . . .